FOUNTAIN
SAFARI

ORO Editions
Publishers of Architecture, Art, and Design
Gordon Goff: Publisher

www.oroeditions.com
info@oroeditions.com

Published by ORO Editions

Graphic Design and Drawings: Fluidity Design Consultants
Editor: Yelpson Bifindi, Assistant Editor: Boringo Florinti
ORO Managing Editor: Kirby Anderson

Typeset in TT Commons

10 9 8 7 6 5 4 3 2 1 First Edition

Library of Congress data available upon request. World Rights: Available

ISBN: 978-1-961856-19-6

Color Separations and Printing: ORO Editions, Inc.
Printed in China.

International Distribution: www.oroeditions.com/distribution

ORO Editions makes a continuous effort to minimize the overall carbon footprint of its publications. As part of this goal, ORO Editions, in association with Global ReLeaf, arranges to plant trees to replace those used in the manufacturing of the paper produced for its books. Global ReLeaf is an international campaign run by American Forests, one of the world's oldest nonprofit conservation organizations. Global ReLeaf is American Forests' education and action program that helps individuals, organizations, agencies, and corporations improve the local and global environment by planting and caring for trees.

FOUNTAIN SAFARI

JAMES GARLAND

ORO

Soundings

"Let them build many cities.
Let them lay the bricks of the cities in pure places.
And I, Enki, god of fresh waters, will establish well-being there."
—Sumerian Flood Story

"...But there went up a mist from the earth, and watered the whole face of the ground."
—Genesis

"...And a river went out of Eden to water the garden; and from thence it was parted,
and became into four headwaters."
—Genesis

"Look within. Within is the fountain of good, and it will ever bubble up, if thou wilt ever dig."
—Marcus Aurelius

"Water is deemed perfect which makes good bread, and in which greens are quickly boiled;
and which, being boiled, does not leave any fur or sediment at the bottom of the vessel."
—Vitruvius

"In times of war he was as invincible as a lion;
in times of peace he was as generous as water over the dry earth."
—Ibn Nasr

"This is a palace of transparent crystal;
those who look at it imagine it to be a boundless ocean."
—Ibn Zamrak

"Blessed be He who gave to the Imam Muhammad, noble ideas with which to grace his mansions. For are there not marvels in this garden, Which Allah has made incomparable in beauty, And a sculpture of pearls of transparent clarity whose edges are trimmed with dewdrops? Melted silver runs between the pearls, One as the other in beauty, white and pure.
Water and marble seem as one, So we know not which of the two flows. Do you not see how water spills over the basin,
But is hidden forthwith in the channels? It is a lover whose eyelids brim with tears; tears which then hide in fear of betrayal. Is it not, in reality, but a white mist emptying its waters on the lions.
—Ibn Zamrak

"The sea is the universal mirror and unique resting place of the wandering waters of the rivers."
— Leonardo da Vinci

"When a drop of water falls into a calm sea,
the surface of the sea must imperceptibly increase its level."
— Leonardo da Vinci

"The center of the gravity of the water and of the earth might be concentric with the center of the world if the earth were perfectly spherical. The center of the world would then be the center of the sphere of the earth, as of the sphere of the water. But it would not produce land animals."
—Leonardo da Vinci

"Like as the waves towards the pebbled shore,
So do our minutes hasten to their end;
Each changing place with that which goes before,
In sequent toil all forwards do contend."
—William Shakespeare

"Bright streams of water must run through the garden,
and above all must start up unexpectedly, their source a grotto."
—Leon Battista Alberti

"I am in Circle Three. And rain falls there, endlessly, chill, accursed and heavy, its rate and composition never new. Snow, massive hailstones, black, tainted water pour down in sheets through tenebrae of air. The earth absorbs it all and stinks, revoltingly."
—Dante Alighieri

"The crystal water welled up against the clean granite, or the unblemished moss, with a sharpness of outline
that delighted while it bewildered the eye."
—Edgar Allen Poe

"The edge of the whirl was represented by a broad belt of gleaming spray; but no particle of this slipped into the mouth of the terrific funnel, whose interior, as far as the eye could fathom it, was a smooth, shining, and jet-black wall of water, inclined to the horizon at an angle of some forty-five degrees, speeding dizzily round and round with a swaying and sweltering motion, and sending forth to the winds an appalling voice, half shriek, half roar, such as not even the mighty cataract of Niagara ever lifts up in its agony to Heaven."
— Edgar Allen Poe

"The Renaissance palaces of Venice are not more picturesque in themselves than the club-houses of Pall Mall; but they become delightful by the contrast of their severity and refinement with the rich and rude confusion of the sea-life beneath them, and of their white and solid masonry with the green waves."
—John Ruskin

"Here lies One Whose Name was writ in Water."
—John Keats

"But look! Here come more crowds, pacing straight for the water, and seemingly bound for a dive. Strange! Nothing will content them but the extremest limit of the land; loitering under the shaded lee of yonder warehouses will not suffice. No. They must get just as nigh the water as they possibly can without falling in. And there they stand—miles of them—leagues."
—Herman Melville

"Yea, foolish mortals, Noah's flood is not yet subsided; two thirds of the fair world it yet covers."
—Herman Melville

"Consider the subtleness of the sea; how its most dreaded creatures glide under water, unapparent for the most part, and treacherously hidden beneath the loveliest tints of azure."
—Herman Melville

"And how nobly it raises our conceit of the mighty, misty monster,
to behold him solemnly sailing through a calm tropical sea:
his vast, mild head overhung by a canopy of vapor, engendered
by his incommunicable contemplations, and that vapor—
as you will sometimes see it—glorified by a rainbow,
as if Heaven itself had put its seal upon his thoughts."
—Herman Melville

"Yes, as everyone knows, meditation and water are wedded for ever."
—Herman Melville

"The eyes of fire, the nostrils of air, the mouth of water, the beard of earth."
—William Blake

"Such is the force of water
that it will with gentle pressure
shape itself to every vessel
and yet pierce the very rock."
—Emperor Meiji

"A bit of water here,
there, between the trees—
the sea!"
—Sen No Rikyu

"As this storm passed over the forests which surround the Corcovado, the sound produced by the drops pattering on the countless multitude of leaves was very remarkable, it could be heard at the distance of a quarter of a mile, and was like the rushing of a great body of water."
—Charles Darwin

"Wave after wave, each mightier than the last
'Til last, a ninth one, gathering half the deep
And full of voices, slowly rose and plunged
Roaring, and all the wave was in a flame."
—Alfred Tennyson

"That which the fountain sends forth returns again to the fountain."
—Henry Wadsworth Longfellow

"The conscious mind may be compared to a fountain playing in the sun and falling back into the great subterranean pool of subconscious from which it rises."
—Sigmund Freud

"At that time, the idea became firmly established in me that I must live by a lake. Without water, so I thought, one could not exist at all."
—Carl Jung

"They greeted each other briefly, drank tea, and sat listening in the matutinal stillness to the sound of the small jet of water from the fountain, a melody of eternity."
—Hermann Hesse

"Often, after the rest of the family had retired for the night, I took the boat, and passed many hours upon the water. Sometimes, with my sails set, I was carried by the wind; and sometimes, after rowing into the middle of the lake, I left the boat to pursue its own course, and gave way to my own reflections."
—Mary Shelley

"On Earth, too, the deities were exceedingly and humanly attractive. In the form of lovely youths and maidens they peopled the woodland, the forest, the rivers, the sea, in harmony with the fair earth and the bright waters."
—Edith Hamilton

"I have been dragging the Serpentine."
"For heaven's sake, what for?"
"In search of the body of Lady St. Simon."
Sherlock Holmes leaned back in his chair and laughed heartily.
"Have you dragged the basin of the Trafalgar-Square fountain?" he asked.
"Why, what do you mean?"
"Because you have just as good a chance of finding this lady in the one as in the other."
—Sir Arthur Conan Doyle

"...and how fine the fountains were at the Place de L'Observatoire (water sheen rippling on the bronze of the horses' manes, bronze breasts and shoulders, green under the thin-flowing water)..."
—Ernest Hemingway

"They were seated in the boat, Nick in the stern, his father rowing. The sun was coming up over the hills. A bass jumped, making a circle in the water. Nick trailed his hand in the water. It felt warm in the sharp chill of the morning."
—Ernest Hemingway

"I was observing the motion of a boat
which was rapidly drawn along a narrow channel
by a pair of horses, when the boat suddenly stopped
– not so the mass of water in the channel
which it had put in motion;
it accumulated round the prow of the vessel in a state of
violent agitation, then suddenly leaving it behind,
rolled forward with great velocity, assuming the form of a
solitary elevation, a rounded, smooth and well-defined heap of
water, which continued its course along the channel
apparently without change of form or diminution of speed.
I followed it on horseback, and overtook it still rolling on
a at a rate of some eight or nine miles an hour,
preserving its original figure some thirty feet long
and a foot to a foot and a half in height.
Its height gradually diminished, and after a chase of one or two
miles, I lost it in the windings of the channel.
Such, in the month of August 1834, was my first chance interview
with that singular and beautiful phenomenon
which I have called the Wave of Translation."
—John Scott Russell

"If I had fifty-three minutes to spend as I like,'
the little prince said to himself,
'I'd walk very slowly towards a water fountain . . .'"
—Antoine De Saint-Exupéry

"Water's my will, and my way,
And the spirit runs, intermittently,
in and out of the small waves."
—Theordore Roethke

"Fountains and wells, ever since the scriptural days,
have been noted gossiping-places in hot climates;
and at the well in question there is a kind of perpetual club
kept up during the livelong day, by the invalids, old women,
and other curious do-nothing folk of the fortress,
who sit here on the stone benches, under an awning
spread over the well to shelter the toll-gatherer from the sun,
and dawdle over the gossip of the fortress,
and question every water-carrier that arrives
about the news of the city,
and make long comments on everything they hear and see."
—Washington Irving

"At San Vito I wanted to express the natural meaning of water and
the field, of water and the earth: water is the source of life."
—Carlo Scarpa

"Two open porticos flank the entrance court of terraces. In front
of each portico is a reflecting pool which drops its water in a
continuous sheet about 70 feet long into a basin two feet below.
The sound would be gentle.
The stepped entrance court passes between the porticos
and their pools with a fountain, around which one sits, on axis,
designed to be the source of the portico pools."
—Louis Kahn

"I have a long-standing enthusiasm for water,
for its particularly potent magical quality
to lead our thoughts from wherever they are
to all the water in the world."
—Charles W. Moore

"Every drop of water on the planet takes part in the water cycle.
The cycle guarantees that all water is connected in a
continuous global chain, so that water never remains an
isolated incident and never exclusively belongs to any specific
time or place. Even the tiniest drop of water shares a heritage
with the greatest ocean."
—Charles W. Moore

"It was the sweetest little room in the world, with a soft
comfortable bed that had sheets of green silk and a green velvet
counterpane. There was a tiny fountain the middle of the room,
that shot a spray of green perfume into the air, to fall back into
a beautifully carved green marble basin."
—L. Frank Baum

"The sea, the great unifier, is man's only hope.
Now, as never before, the old phrase has a literal meaning:
we are all in the same boat."
—Jacques Yves Cousteau

Park Guell Staircase Fountain, Barcelona, Antonio Gaudi.

"Paul fell asleep to dream of an Arrakeen cavern, silent people all around him moving in the dim light of glow-globes. It was solemn there and like a cathedral as he listened to a faint sound—the drip-drip-drip of water."
—Frank Hebert

"The rain was thinning away and the girl was walking in the center of the sidewalk with her head up and the few drops falling on her face . . . 'The rain feels good. I love to walk in it.' . . . She licked her lips. 'Rain even tastes good.'"
—Ray Bradbury

"My name is Water:
I have sped through strange dark ways untried before,
By pure desire of friendship led, Cochituate's Ambassador:
He sends four gifts by me,
Long life, health, peace, and purity."
—James Russel Lowell

"I've known rivers ancient as the world
and older than the flow of human blood in human veins.
My soul has grown deep like the rivers."
—Langston Hughes

"We had been traveling over a high, wooded plateau.
The brook where we had caught the trout had been joined by other streams and was now a big creek.
Below us, at a place we hadn't reached yet, it would plunge over high cliffs in a super-Yosemite fall.
But here, where we stopped to camp,
the water had cut a notch into the plateau,
forming cascades, before it took that dive."
—Robert Heinlein

"'Cascades' is a weak word.
Upstream, downstream, everywhere you looked,
you saw waterfalls—big ones thirty or fifty feet high, little ones a mouse could have jumped up, every size in between.
Terraces and staircases of them there were,
smooth water green from rich foliage overhead
And water white as whipped cream as it splashed into dense foam."
—Robert Heinlein

"...image of water, a brightness not gold, not silver,
rippling as if with laughter."
—Denise Levertov

Be like water making its way through cracks.
Do not be assertive, but adjust to the object,
and you shall find a way around or through it.
If nothing within you stays rigid,
outward things will disclose themselves.
Empty your mind, be formless. Shapeless, like water.
If you put water into a cup, it becomes the cup.
You put water into a bottle and it becomes the bottle.
You put it in a teapot, it becomes the teapot.
Now, water can flow or it can crash.
Be water, my friend.
—Bruce Lee

The scenic water town of Tongli, China.

"A fountain brings us peace, joy and restful sensuality and reaches the epitomy of its very essence when by its power to bewitch it will stir dreams of distant worlds."
—Louis Barragan

"The young man and his dog wander about in the forest and they go past a pond. Suddenly a hand reaches up from the water, grabs the dog, and pulls it down. The young man doesn't respond by becoming hysterical. He merely says, 'This must be the place.'

Fond as he is of his dog and reluctant as he is to abandon him, the hunter goes back to the pond to bucket out the water. Anyone who's ever tried it will quickly note that such bucketing is very slow work. In time, what they find, lying at the bottom of the pond, is a large man covered with hair from head to foot. The hair is reddish—it looks a little like rusty iron. They take the man back to the castle, and imprison him.

The King puts him in an iron cage in the courtyard, calls him 'Iron John,' and gives the key into the keeping of the Queen."
—Robert Bly

"A pool is, for many of us in the West, a symbol not of affluence but of order, of control over the uncontrollable. A pool is water, made available and useful, and is, as such, infinitely soothing to the western eye."
—Joan Didion

"...I heard that music of the water more and more
yet at the same time less; less
because it was no longer an intimate of mine;
the water was my blood, my life and I heard
that the music of my life and blood was the running water."
—Juan Ramón Jiménez

"Scientists estimate that it can take a single water molecule as long as 4000 years to complete one cycle."
—Joseph S. Levine

"Sunlight was in the sky above the crowns of the highest trees,
but the glad still held the chill grey of dawn.
Tenar sat with her hand on Alder's hand, her face bowed down.
She looked at the cold dew beading a grass blade,
how it hung in tiny, delicate drops along the blade,
each drop reflecting all the world."
—Ursula K. Le Guin

"When they began to take the books out of Galvamand,
the Oracle Fountain in the forecourt began to fail.
Little by little, as the books were taken out of the house,
the water ceased to run. When they were done, it dried up
entirely. It hasn't run for two hundred years..."
—Ursula K. Le Guin

"Such a case as this one," said Holmes as we passed along the edge of a ploughed field,"never fails to remind me of the old saying, that truth is like water: confine it how you may, it will find a way out."
—Denis O. Smith

"Once again I was a twelve-year-old boy staring for hours at the rain. Look at the rain long enough, with no thoughts in your head, and you gradually feel your body falling loose, shaking free of the world of reality. Rain has the power to hypnotize."
—Haruki Murakami

"The rain beat down on the car roof, lightning and thunder from time to time interrupting thoughts of the old namesake river that had once run through this town, long canalized and tapped dry, and crippled into a public and anonymous confession of the deadly sin of greed... He imagined it filling again, up to its concrete rim, and then over, all the water that had not been allowed to flow here for all these years now in an unrelenting return, soon beginning to occupy the arroyos and cover the flats, all the swimming pools in the backyards filling up and overflowing and flooding the lots and streets, all this karmic waterscape connecting together, as the rain went on falling and the land vanished, into a sizable inland sea that would presently become an extension of the Pacific."
—Thomas Pynchon

Contents

A typical canal in Venice.

1 Why

We could, perhaps with daring, make the claim that the greatest physical invention by humans yet on this Earth is the city, and not be so wildly wrong in doing so. What other invention serves so many, so constantly, and over such a long period of time? Is Damascus truly ten thousand years old, Rome's great-grand-father? Did Venice's Piazza San Marco really take a thousand years to refine? Have you climbed the hills in central Hanzhou and shouted out the demons with the elders? Are the canyons of Manhattan so very inferior to the natural sort? Is there anything grander than a Paris boulevard? Have high speed communi-cations, the Internet, jet travel, or electric lighting benefited humanity as much as the city? What about medicine, you say? The written word? The law? The wheel? Fire? Poetry? By these reckonings, is not the city pervasive and supreme? And do we not love our cities, finally?

Yes, there are many who seek the forests, streams, and mountains to recover from city life. But I take to the city in recovery of those excursions. Well, a little. Only a fool would deny Nature's due.

Further, isn't it sublime to witness that all cities are different—some very different, indeed, and that their differences are the stuff of exaltation? We visit the astonishing places—Medellin's perfect, leafy climate and intimate access to the Andes. Genoa and her bay on the Ligurian Sea. The canals of Amsterdam, Venice or Luzhi. The garden cities of Singapore, Kyoto or Canberra. The everything-containing carpet of Los Angeles. The happiness of Mumbai. Intricate San Francisco. London's wide parks. Chicago's unimpeachable stolidity. New Orleans, Munich, Buenos Aires—or Brazilia, for that matter. Capetown and her peaks. Wall-wrapped Lucca. Mexico City, Hong Kong, Prague, Tokyo, St. Petersburg, Barcelona, New York City. Lisbon's urbane slopes. Shanghai's tree-lined streets (and their bygone, softly clinking bicycles). Melbourne's Yarra. Edinburgh's smokie black rocks and Glasgow's St. George Square. The list rolls voluminously. There is no end to it, practically speaking. Mention any place and We Know. Point at the awkward and we will go and enjoy it. The good and the bad, the right and the wrong, the surprising and the plain. Do they not all have some wondrous spark, if not mighty jolts of human lightening?

And in all those cities, what is it, do you think, kind reader, that serves the glory of their places more supremely than their foun-tains? Are fountains not the exclamation point to the sentence of the city?

Are these questions actually rhetorical, so obvious are their answers as to gain in response little more than an eyebrow flutter? And located, as these fountains so often are, just where we want most to congregate, regarding each other and our aliveness, deepened by the engagement in great places.

May we have some examples of these wetly urban exclamation points, you ask, likely for the sake of asking, or to enjoy a little nap, dear friend?

So: here is the Anteros Fountain in Picadilly Square (about that love *returned*), where Londoners and guests cluster over those orbital steps in all but the coldest and wettest weather. And there we see Trevi, catching the sun in that odd space woven somehow into the fabric of Eternal Rome. Look at the pair in Paris, nicely bookending the ageless Egyptian obelisk at that proud, Place de la Concorde. See Seattle's Drumheller reflecting great Ranier. Rockefeller's Promethius, sunken but aloft, and the living, mossy fountains on Aix-en-Provence's Mirabeau, Chicago's hearty Buckingham, and the puckish, flaming fountains at Pat O'Brien's (yes, the powerful can be petite, even in that roguish town of New Orleans). Hemingway wrote of the L'Observatoire Fountain, plainly viewed from the Closerie des Lilas, and who are we to cut the man his views? Or Gaston his song? Wander north a way to the octagonal pool—the center of everything, where the little ones rent small boats with colorful sails, using those odd sticks to pary, while the cosmopolitans recline or cavort, taking their views from every possible angle on the wide, crushed granite sands, the very definition of urbanity, reflected on the wide waters, picture perfect. Wouldn't the Taj be lonely without its companion reflection? Would the Washington Monument have so much to say without the help from cousin Lincoln and his reflection pool? Here is Berlin's forceful Neptune Fountain, under attack from every way, and truly great in bronze, and there is Central Park's angelic Bethesda, John Wick's scenic pal, masterfully shaped by an American in Paris, cast to the northeast in Germany, then shipped six thousand kilometers, over the cold Atlantic, to New York City, to behold from there so far, for a hundred years.

"Is that it?," you say, "All this to-do about decorative flourishes?" Of course not, sweet spoiler, look to the neighborhoods of Viterbo for your answer, each with its piazza and fountain, Middle Age sources of water for drinking and washing, a spring for each community, and the foundation of their methodical existances, altogether building the system and the meaning of that fine city.

From each networked tapestry of cities arise, hopefully, a sufficiently watered land, and from the lands together unfold their countries and their continents. And as those great land masses wrap and spin to make our world, with water between, above and below, not happily, perhaps, not easily, certainly, but it is ours and the water, our shared necessity and our wealth, and with fountains as the conduits and celebratory talismans, our Oscars, our spectral urban keepsakes.

Fontaine l'Observatoire, Paris.

2 Seeing

Appreciation of the water arts is partly based in seeing water as accurately and fully as possible. Otherwise, we are left only with broad impressions. Broad impressions are valid enough, but they do not reach very far, aesthetically. Broad impressions are useful for building a swift picture in our minds of a complicated situation. But they are not very accurate, even when magnified by vivid feelings, and with accuracy comes the more fully founded poetry.

The connoisseur does not stop at the broad impression, but goes deeper, taking delight in the private truths delivered by sharp observation. Seeing water accurately takes just a little extra effort, and then a door opens, and we can perceive how a network of water actions are interacting wondrously with each other, with light, with people and objects nearby, and with the larger, spatial context. The fountain is alive.

With that level of observation, the close observer might then wonder why the water of a particular fountain was composed to perform in its specific way, and what that water statement means. With practice in seeing we can learn to discriminate "good" water expressions from those that are "not so good."

Our eyes are indeed marvelous tools, much more powerful than their everyday use might lead one to assume. With faith and practice, our eyes can judge the subtlest detail and help us unravel and solve complicated mysteries. To use our eyes to their maximum potential we need to understand something of their workings. A little knowledge helps us puzzle out the impressions we are receiving. This is not the place to lay out a detailed explanation into exactly how people see and how seeing can be better developed, nor is it necessary; an overview is sufficient.

When we see water in context, noticing, for instance, that on overcast days or in the shade, clear water (as opposed to foamy, white-water) is difficult to see. In full sun, the same clear water sparkles and becomes highly visible. Also, clear water over a pale-toned surface is harder to see than clear water over a darkly tinted surface. In both cases, in the presence of direct light or by the nature of the backdrop, seeing is based upon contrast; what artists call, "figure/ground", the contrast of the figure of reflective, sparkling highlights over a very different, darkly shaded ground. Contrast is fundamental to all seeing. Good water presentation configures water visibility (which is complex, due to water's ellusive properties) through techniques in basic, figure/ground contrasts.

White-water is more visible in most conditions than clear or "glassy" water, but it is visually flatter, and sometimes less compelling, having less dimension since we only see it's surface, and white-on-white detail is hard to make out, whereas with clear water we see through the water, three-dimensionally, and in greater complexity. The visual advantages of one or the other depends entirely on contextual conditions.

Here is a telling example: When a clear spray of water is observed, let's say, coming from a cream-colored stone sculpture, and the sun is behind us, we will see the sculpture very clearly with the sunlight washing over it, and we'll see the form of the spray lit by tiny reflections. But if we walk around the installation to where the sun is in front of us, what we see is very different—the sculpture is now silhouetted in shade, and presenting less detail, but the water is now vibrant in a great halo of large and bright sparkles. The sunlight refracting thorough the airborne droplets appears larger and brighter than that same sunlight's tiny reflections seen from the original side.

Close observers will notice water's scale, observing that when falling a short distance, such as half a meter, water appears and disappears so quickly that we do not get a clear picture of its shape. It's precise forms are a blur to us. But, when falling from a great height, and seen from a distance, water appears to move in slow motion, and we get quite a good, long look at its form and action. Of course, gravity is the same for both cases.

The rapid tempo of gravity is partly why some vertical or sloped water features are textured—to slow the water flow down. Slower movements are more observable. Slowing techniques are not always successful, but the principle of slowing water is a practical response to display problems.

We do not make naive statements about the rules of beauty. But we can, in a way, get around the problem by considering visual matters in associated ways. For instance, some water presentations might be classified as "significant" while others are not. Significant water actions are those with a special, identifiable visual charisma, to which we would mostly all agree. Many water expressions do not have that quality. A cup of the finest mineral spring water may not be particularly mesmerizing to look at, but that same water flowing from a turbulent pool over a dap-ple-edged weir, at an appropriate flow rate, to a measured fall height, with a contrasting backdrop, illuminated in a certain way, etc., might be unforgettably compelling. 'Significance' in water presentation might seem subjective, but it represents a quality one identifies with practice and generally finds agreement from others.

A common swimming pool, with its water level set below the pool's sides, will present on the pool's surface, in response to a swimmer's splashing, a chaotic scene of overlapping waves, impossible to follow. Alternatively, raise that pool's water level to overflow all around, where the water level is just slightly higher than the pool's side walls (in a condition sometimes referred to as a "zero-edge pool"), and the surface becomes much freer and the waves made by the swimmer are more observably singular, deliberate and comprehensible.

This is not to say that zero-edge pools are better than the more common, recessed pools. There are times when we want all that overlapping wave activity—such as at the lower pools at the two end fountains in Rome's Piazza Navona, which were composed by Borromini, to be made lively by their reflecting, overlapping wavelets and thereby engaging innumerable sparkles from the sun on their countless, small crests and shallows. In that case, the stilling character of an infinity-edge rim would have dulled the scene.

We observe and distinguish between "waterfalls" and "water-walls." Waterfalls fall freely in space, while the water of a water-wall mostly clings to the wall's surface, which is often textured to establish an intended water character.

When a fountain is equipped with an overflowing edge, that edge is called a "weir." There are many kinds of weirs and over-flow effects, too numerous to cover here. Most weirs fling water in some way or another and the variations can be delightful. Some weirs, alternatively, cause the flowing water to cling to the face below, as is the case with water-walls.

Overflow behavior does not result only from the weir, but also from the character of the water feeding it. Water overflowing a weir is animated and modified by the action in the pool feeding it. Weirs can be contrived to create clinging water at low flow rates and flinging water at higher flow rates. There is a weir at San Franscisco's Moscone Center that both clings and flings simultaneously by its special, tooled edge. At Trafalgar Square there is a remarkable weir that manages three simultaneous water action byproducts, generating aerial sprays, draping waterfalls and a smoothly clinging, entirely wet underside.

We might call some waterfalls especially beautiful. The ideal waterfall—the one in our minds—is simpler than the physical world's. When we stop to look closely at waterfalls, we can see that the flow begins as a rippling sheet, then breaks into clumps after falling a certain measure. The water might break again into finer droplets farther down. The perfectly fulfilling, unbroken "waterfall" sheet we see in our mind's eye is actually quite uncommon, and never very tall—always less than two meters. This is due to gravity and accelleration, air friction, and sometimes wind or other physical influences, any of which continually conspire to complicate flow.

A 'cascade' is a series of waterfalls, presenting in a visually beneficial repeating sequences, like a staircase. In nature, cascades are usually comprised of steps with quite a lot of variations in shape, fall, how the flows are distributed, and all their attendent variations in water expression.

Some cascades present in clear flows, while others generate foamy white-water action. At the Fountain of the Innocents in Paris, clear flows and white-water flows were carefully blended to stage white, lacy strands flowing through clear water panels, establishing an especially marvelous effect, and visually suc-

Villa Lante, near Viterbo.

cessful under many lighting conditions. (We use the past tense because those flows are not currently working properly. We see the original effect only from dated photographs.)

In the acounts above, I have used the terms, "weir," "wavelet" and "cascade" to make the content more specific, but this is not to suggest a specialist's infatuation with vocabulary. One might instead be concerned with the opposite. The common use of such terms can diminish the creative interpretation of what we are thinking or seeing. Words have their place, but it is important to keep in mind the wide flexibility of water presentation—or light presentation, for that matter—and not to let words do our seeing for us. The mind will conspire to suggest something is there that is not, especially if we label or "predefine" the thing upon which we gaze.

There is not a lot of evidence that words are very important in water appreciation. Seeing is important. Apprehending water's charismatic nuance and range is important. Developing a sense for water action quality is more valuable than knowing, for instance, the Italian word for the particular rustic rockwork used in grottos. There are books about fountains that define a collection of jets with terms, like "jet d'eu" or "geyser." Such terms might seem handy, but even here we are led by the word to see the form of a water expression in a certain way, as if a question is resolved from a catalog of diagrams, which is not the case. There are dozens of vertical jet variations.

Often words are misused. Almost every fountain part catalog shows a nozzle called a "cascade jet," even though there is nothing about it which cascades. And in casual conversation we often hear people use terms such as "waterfall" and "cascade" interchangeably, even though the words actually mean very different things. It's a good idea to be on guard with words, and place more trust in our eyes and minds.

The aesthetics of water sounds is also important. Admittedly, referencing "hearing," in a chapter about "seeing," may seem a stretch, but talking about sound is important, and the ideas are similar. We can learn to hear with extra discrimination, and we can build familiarity to help us distinguish "good" sounds from "bad," and to appreciate and enjoy those special cases when water performs with true sonic excellence.

Water sounds in nature are quite different from water sounds made by people or their machines. Natural water sounds are more complex, with a wider range of uneven frequencies, patterns and loudnesses. The sound of a shallow streambed with water flowing over tumbled rocks, such as in a trout stream in Spain or Colorado, or what we might find in the hills of the Lakes District to the north of England, is a special category of sound, entailing high-frequency "washing" sounds layered over medium and low-frequency "musical" sounds. There is something iconic in this sound.

The sounds of soft rainfall in Kyoto offers a certain kind of iconic character, which is very different from the much heavier rainfall we might hear in New Orleans. The water sounds of beach waves on a calm day can be mesmerizing, while the sounds of waves at the same beach after a storm are heavier, darker, and rougher.

Just as we can learn to differentiate visually significant water actions, we can also distinguish the sonically significant. We will judge good from not good, and hypothesize why we feel this way.

One might presume that all fountains sound good—as we are hearing the sound of moving water, after all—but some sounds do not bare up to critical listening. Many larger fountains create sounds mostly in a single, harsh pitch, which is very different from the colorful sonic ranges of nature. Sometimes water is too loud for a place, while at other times the water is too quiet.

There are fountains that make wonderful sounds. The single spout, two sprays, and several pours of the boat fountain at the Spanish Steps generates a rich sound that works well on both quiet and noisy days. The big jet bouquets in the garden fountains at Versailles sound wonderful, too, functioning as a product of their scale and the vast sonic chambers in which they reside. There is a cascade in Oklahoma City that is engineered to sound better some of the time, but look very good at other times, because it was discovered that the ideal flow rate for one was different than for the other, and so the flows are controlled to periodically fluctuate back and forth between the two intended effects.

New York's Bethesda fountain makes very gentle sounds while its tall, central sculpture is powerful and commanding. The famous, long runnel at Louis Kahn's Salk Institute makes no sound at all, beautiful as it is, though the small, triple-faced waterfall that feeds the flows does make a sound, modest and not bad, in a steady, middle frequency. You have to bend over to hear the water at the little stream in the garden at Ryoan-ji, but when you do you can hear a silvery tone, almost like birdsong. The play fountain at Grand Park, in Los Angeles, mixes the thunder of dozens of monumental jets up on its historic chalice with the much smaller sounds of the many knee-high streams down in the centimeter-deep, wading pool. The combination are part of the experience of its place.

For these examples, the character of sound is just as intentional as their visual presentations. And just like seeing, we can learn to hear with increased confidence and discrimination.

A fountain can be superbly engineered and badly designed. The pumps, filters, etc., can all work perfectly in a fountain that presents us with lackluster displays. Fountains have been turned into planters, a result of mechanical failure or by people simply giving up on their difficult maintenance. This can happen, too, to those fountains that function satisfactorily but have been judged to be not worth the trouble. All constructions require maintenance—and fountains are notorious for requiring more effort than most other kinds of assemblies. But societies will maintain the great fountains for hundreds of years because they are worth it. The great fountains are maintained because of their iconic identity, contribution to place, their beauty, their meaningfulness, their popularity, their history, and for all their other good qualities.

Seeing water well is the critical key to more fully knowing and enjoying the world's fountains. We can do this with just a little extra focus. The fountains stand ready to give us more, sometimes much more. All we need do to receive their extra gifts is to see.

NSW Parliament House, Sydney.

3 Fountain Safari

The original fountains have been lost to history. We can trace early examples easily back two millenia to ancient Rome, and then with some difficulty further back to Egypt and Mesopotamia. No one knows if the Hanging Gardens of Babylon truly existed, around 600 BC, though they were described with plantings fed by attractive watering systems. Most of the examples we visit today were built within the past thousand years, though a few of the water features still existing in Rome and those at Hadrian's Villa are about two thousand years old. The eldest of the celebrated fountains of the Alhambra are seven hundred years old, Paris' Fountain of the Innocents is five hundred years old, Trevi is in the neighborhood of two hundred and fifty years old, Central Park's Bethesda Fountain is one hundred years old, the Fountains of Bellagio are almost twenty-five years old. The idea of fountains and fountain building has been persistent through much of Western history. What is all this about?

Part of the answer exists too deeply in the labyrinthine structure of human consciousness for us to propertly treat, relating to that innate and gripping fascination we have for water, its fundamental basis in life, its musical sound, and its captivating dazzle in sunlight. But we can offer reasonable conjectures about the nature of fountains after surveying so many.

We build fountains—those vibrant symbols of life and physical embodiments of beauty—to mark and celebrate our favored places. This act is an honor to all, and like listening to music, it is understood on an intuitive level. If we visualize some great place we know with a fountain, and then imagine that place without it, we immediately understand what the fountain brings. Its bringing is its first purpose. And the realization of that bringing is its gift to place and visitor.

We also build fountains to commemorate life. Water is the basis for, and the symbol of, life. Many fountains are articulated to recognize some person, institution, or idea. Those particular recognitions are fused with water's deeper symbolism to convey everlastingness to the identities being celebrated. The representation of life additionally connotes ideas of creation, renewal, continuity, growth, creativity, etc. In addition to life symbolism, flowing water can also convey high value or time. Symbolism in the fountain unfolds continously with the flowing vivacity of its waters.

The brought idea of a specific fountain, of a form and in a place, comes from the people involved in its making. Their vision forms the fountain, its idea, placement, scale, organizing principle, water actions, aesthetic engagements, and all its crafted details.

All three dimensions noted above—place, symbol and vision, are inextricably interwoven in establishing the power of the work. In other words, the quality of the place, the quality of the symbol, and the quality of the vision, all contribute to the power of the fountain.

Lovejoy Fountain, Portland, Oregon.

At Place des Vogues, an ideal square is configured with elegantly proportioned symmetrical architecture on all four sides. It's central public space presents a highly controlled, calming retreat from the demands of the capital city. The square's four geometrically mirrored fountains form an elemental part of the fulfilment of the space, sanctifying its order with water's unequivocal charms.

The Princess Diana Memorial Fountain is uniquely formed and substantially built, with water actions of remarkable and varied characters. The fountain's installation at Hyde Park further contributes to its meaning and it's aura of poetic resonance.

Bernini's Fountain of the Four Rivers, Robert Woodward and Phill Taranto's El Alamein War Memorial, Peter Walker's Jamison Square Fountain, Ustad-Ahmad Lahori's reflection pool at the Taj Mahal, Mies van der Rhoe's pools at the Barcelona Pavilion, and Louis Baragan's Fuente de los Amantes, all show brilliantly developed ideas with exacting water expressions contributing to the value and experience of their places.

What makes these and other examples good? How can we look at fountains and see them more critically? What do we see when we look closer? How might water expression be the focus for art criticism?

"Fountain Safari" responds to these questions, placing on the shelf a sharply focused, comprehensive, useful and entertaining book aimed to provide a panoramic portrait of the fountain class of artistic endeavor. The work attends especially to the aesthetics of water expression, examining in detail numerous esteemed examples. In the process, the book also presents a sketch of the observable evolution of fountain development over some two millennia and across several cultures. Through the identification and review of superlative exemplars and the exploration of intrinsic topics, the the book attempts to deepen an understanding and appreciation of water features by identifying and clarifying their most essential aesthetic qualities.

The material is written for design professionals, architects, landscape architects, urban designers, planners, students of the arts or the built environment—and everyone else interested in this engaging, one-of-a-kind subject. The case studies presented are all important works, selected based on experience, written sources, advice from others, and legend.

The water features covered are organized by region and era, with older examples of a given area shown first, then moving forward in time, region by region, restarting with an earlier date upon each shift in territory. The purpose in this arrangement is to provide graspable continuity over the course of a worldwide, era-wide subject matter. The examples begin in Europe, then migrate to North America, then the Middle East, Asia, and Australia. An alternative sequence might work just as well, and better for some readers. The overriding idea has to do with organizing a simple format for the absorption and comprehension of numerous examples.

The chapters are conceived as stand-alone articles. A reader can start anywhere and review as little or as much as desired without much trouble. (Skipping this chapter would be a legitimate first step!) No one must read the work cover to cover for a useful experience.

Several very fine and important water features are missing, which was inevitable. The omission of certain examples or regions is not especially meaningful, since there are far too many cases to include. Moreover, the selections are not meant to suggest the last word in "best in class" or any kind of ranking beyond the good quality necessary for inclusion. Instead, a standard of excellence is advocated, and a range of types and characters are assembled to present as full a spectrum as possible of the subject's significance. From this perspective, the loss of this or that wonderful item is hopefully forgivable.

This text does not offer elaborate historic portraiture, as the intrigues of personality or momentous event would deflect attention from the art. Only sufficient historical information is provided in due respect to the participants and to contribute to the appreciation of the subject matter. Some of it is fairly colorful, admittedly.

In the same way, the engineering detail of flow rates, surface texture, cisterns, pipe diameters and their friction, valves, nozzle types and such are also mostly omitted as being slightly beside the point for our purposes, although interesting engineering information is occasionally provided. This book is not intended as a technical reference for design professionals. Rather, it attempts to offer a wide and worthy showcasing of the high fountain arts for more general purposes.

This book might be treated as a kind of survey or introduction to a subject, which would be fair enough. But we should never lose sight of the reality that looking at images and reading comments is no substitute for witnessing the masterworks in person, seeing their marvels, and making one's own thrilling discoveries. Maybe at its most innocent, the material will be used as a guidebook for travel planning, as it is helpful to consider how and where to start.

In my experience, premier water features all share three fundamental, qualitative tenets, together with numerous other wonderful qualities.

The best fountains in the world all offer Superlative Water Action. With practice we learn to discriminate between a good jet and a poor one, or a good waterfall, cascade, pool, spray, etc., and their less delightful alter egos. The finest water features achieve their station partly because the presented water character is far above even the norm for good. We see this in the cupola of the Fontain des Innocents in Paris (on the cover of this book), in the wavelets of the lower pools at the Piazza Navona, in many of the masterful fountains at Versailles, and in the frothy overflows at the Keller Fountain.

The best examples are Anchored Into Their Environments with such finesse and authority that those places would be far less convicing without them, and their fountains could not be rightly imagined quite anywhere else. We see this at Trevi, at the wall of the Hundred Fountains at the Villa d'Este, at Dallas' Fountain Place, at the Taj Mahal, and at the Salk Institute for Advanced Studies. The Anteros Fountain in Picadilly Circus has this quality to a large degree, and funnily enough, it used to be elsewhere, which was also the case for the Fountain of the Innocents. Sometimes the fountain has to find its home for its complete realization.

Finally, the best examples are Meaningful. By this I do not refer exclusively to symbolic content, although symbolic messages are regularly deployed in fountains. Rather, it connotes that the installation has a purpose and an idea, and that these are radiated in a way that can be understood, and that this understanding contributes to the power of its experience. This is the case for the Medici Fountain in Luxembourg Gardens (even though it, too, was moved and modified over time), for the pair of matching fountains at St. Peter's Square, for the water at Shalamar Bagh, and for Edwin Lutyen's twin fountains in at Trafalgar Square. These examples carry different kinds of meaning, and their meaningfulness is a central aspect of their power, whether we feel we fully understand them or not.

The great work resulting from artistic pursuit is enduring. Many of the ingredients that made older works avowed in the past are still pertinent today, though not necessarily in all their aspects (such as regards allegory, which has become less meaningful today than it was in the past).

Many of the cleverly wrought water presentations previously achieved, with their hand-made, lovingly delivered crafting are simply beyond the reach of most efforts today. It is a wonderful thing to appreciate the great accomplishments of the past, and this is doubly so when we can admit our near-inability to repeat them. I don't only refer to Bernini being dead and that nobody brought stone alive in quite the way he did, or his celebrated career in water; I refer to the water actions, such as those achieved by hand-tooled weirs at Versailles, or by the simple but effective custom jets at l'Observatoire.

Normally, visitors to fountains spend a short time apprehending the water and are charmed, to some extent or other. This charm provides a sense of satisfaction, which is taken in almost immediately. Charles Moore refered to water's "immediacy"; this is part of what he was getting at. That satisfaction (or felt sense of completion) opens and redirects our thoughts to reflect on whatever subject comes to mind—about which Baragan spoke so poeticaly. So, when we visit a fountain we stop thinking about it almost immediately. But if we apply the fountain's gift of a reflective disposition to the fountain itself, we can find ourselves pondering its meaning, or studying the lines of its sculpture, or even developing questions about its pumps. And in just this vague or dreamy way, we are lost—*again*. This elsewhereness is a virtue, but it poses a real challenge to sharp examination.

For this study, we must fortify our attention to stay focused on water's action, and then we can work to see that action as clearly, accurately, and sharply as possible.

The water arts will not lose their charms under close examination; just the opposite, our appreciation for them will be enhanced.

A friend in the film industry confided once that since his training he can't simply watch a film any longer; his mind is always thinking about camera angles, lighting techniques, what he knows is happening just off-camera, and how the actors are positioning themselves to deliver their studied crafts. A large measure of cinematic magic was gone for him. But we will have no such reaction as we learn more and more about fountains and water action. This is because water has the upper hand in complexity and physical beauty. As another friend mentioned to me quite recently, "I've been in this business for forty-five years and I am still surprised and making discoveries because of water's unpredictability." We have nothing to fear about close examination, magic-wise.

So, now there is one more book in that small collection on this subject. This one explores the nature of a cherished art form through the examination of numerous masterworks. Each of the water features presented plays a small role in a much larger story. No truly final answers are claimed, but we might expose some good questions.

While this view attempts to be panoramic, the subject ultimately regards that most essential aspect of the fountain, pertaining to water action and its presentation. Water action is about what the water is doing. Water presentation is about how it is made to be seen. Both are necessary for success.

Let us explore, then, with all this in mind, and let us see what we can of the wealth of this world's great examples, and let us absorb of them as much as we can, and ponder their life affirming poetries.

The Stork Fountain, Copenhagen.

The Other Connoiseurs

I had made my plans, assembled my kit and was ready. The early morning cab picked me up from the hotel and we drove with the breaking morning light to the exceptional garden with its famous fountains, dropping me off in the empty courtyard before the doors were open.

Or rather, the courtyard was nearly empty. Soon enough two other cabs showed up, each depositing a single occupant, each with packs much like my own. I will make very clear right now that I was there first.

We said nothing to each other and stood somewhat uncomfortably in a triangle, waiting something like Cary Grant in the prarie highway scene before the airplane comes in 'North by Northwest' or in the final scene of 'The Good, The Bad, and The Ugly'. The moment felt cinematic as we alternated between eyeing each other and pretending the others weren't there. Anyway, I had important work to do, not like those two poseurs.

The doors opened, and we all went in, spread out and went to work with our cameras and gear. It was a long but rewarding morning for me and finally as lunchtime neared I went first to the gift shop to pick up what books and maps they had. I always do this. Then I went to the cafe. Of course, the two chumps were there. We didn't even knod to each other and we sat at separate tables, even though there weren't many places. One of them had the gall to look pleased with himself. As soon as possible I fled, opening my camera for round two, and had a terrific afternoon, getting almost everything I was looking for, and the sunlight was most obliging.

It was nearing closing time at the end of a good day. The tourists had cleared out. Just we three were left. We jostled, just a little, for the honor to be last out.

4 Hadrian's Villa

Two thousand years old, a few kilometers from the Villa d'Este in Tivoli, less than an hour by car from Rome, are the remains of the Villa Adriana, or Hadrian's Villa, the very large country residence Imperial Rome's Emperor Hadrian.

Hadrian had built this vast estate for himself and his guests as a retreat from the complications of the Capital city, and as a reliquary of his military campaigns and architectural musings. The large property eventually incorporated over thirty buildings, together with courts, gardens, statues, and thirty-plus water features. Several of the buildings were architecturally inspired by places in the provinces controlled by Rome, which the Emperor observed during his wartime travels. The complex of buildings, deployed on the rolling landscape in angular interrelationships has proven so geometrically intriguing that the place has been fascinating to students of architecture for hundreds of years. The Villa's often published plan is dynamic, with many of the buildings' rotations generating complex relations to other structures, with appreciable results. Integrated with the design of the complex, were several pools, some of which remain today. Among them was once a physical manifestation of Egypt's Nile River, now lost.

The most romantically compelling of the remaining water features is referred to today as the, 'Maritime Theater'. Its purpose, like much of the villa, is lost to history, but the design of the Maritime Theater is not ambiguous. The structure is in comparatively good condition, with a cylindrical wall framing a round gallery with a colonade, ringed by a circular mote with bridges to a central island, which is lavished with columns, walls with arched openings, and complex sub-spaces. Its architecture would appear to be sufficiently delightful as to require no particuilarly critical function other than providing a good place within which to wander about and be inspired. One can feel that the architectural compositions once evoked specific meanings and narratives.

(Above and opposite page), the Maritime Theater. Unknown function, presumed for casual recreation. Elaborate architecture, solidly constructed and finely detailed. The canal is crossed at two bridge locations (upper right).

(Right), the Canopus. A long reflection pool with a stone collonade framing sculptures at one end and an apse construction at the other, presumably a bath house.

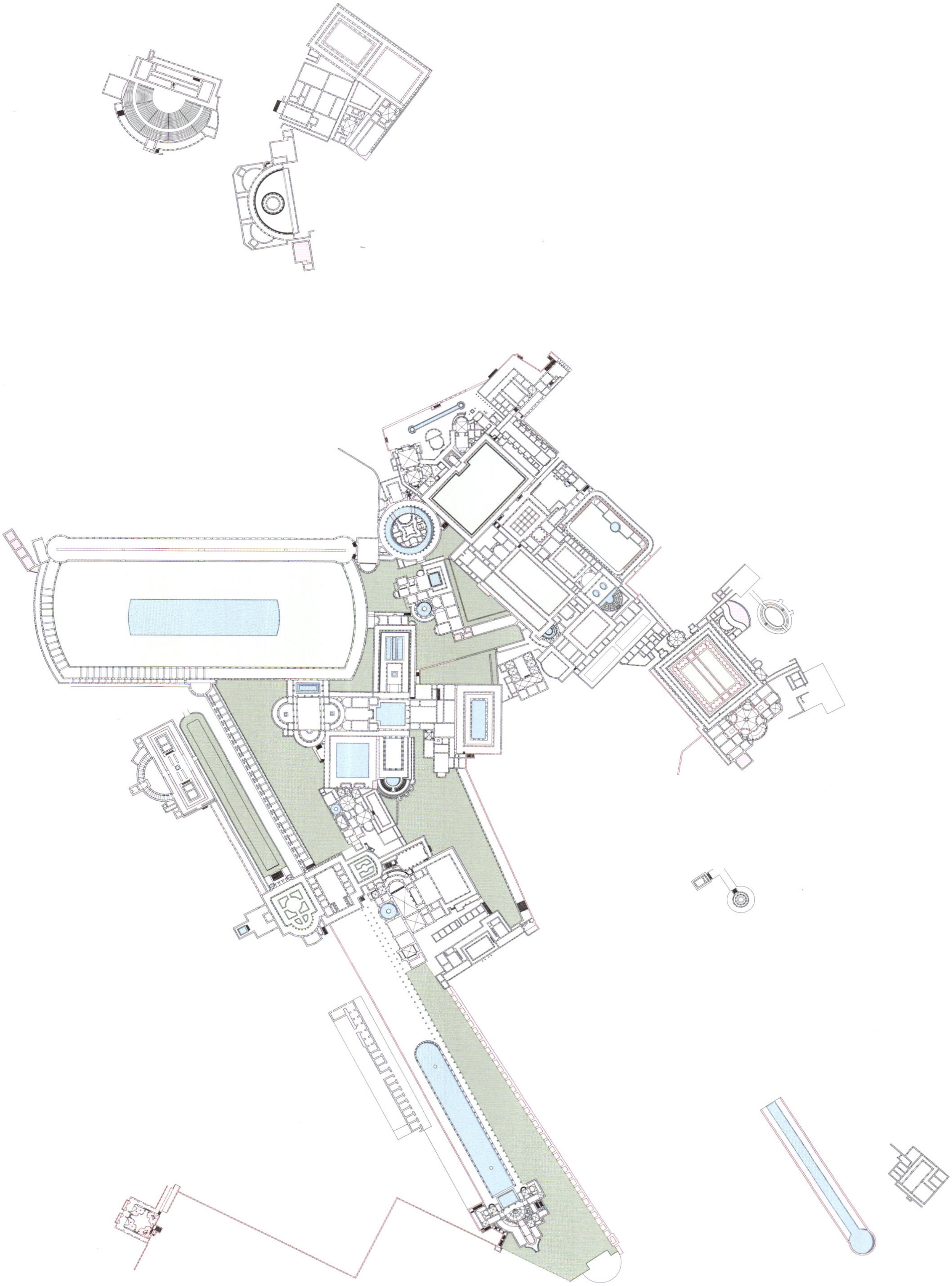

N

HADRIAN'S VILLA, ITALY

0 10 25 50 100M

(Left), Site Plan; (Right), the Canopus, (center, upper left), 37Peschiera, dry (upper right), the Pecile pond (lower).

(Top), The stretched panorama distorts the sizes of the island and mote. The space feels generous, with the mote about 4.5m wide and the island over twenty meters in diameter. The plan at right is a reproduction of a common conjecture; the actual original assembly is a guess, but the richness of the plan is based in archeology. The bi-axial symmetry, transparent layers, intricate complexity, and engagement with perimeter openings are all reliable aspects of the original construction.

(Left and above), The Canopus's colonade frames the reflection pool, directly, such that it's form is visible from a distance. At roughly 5m tall and slightly less than a half meter in diameter, the columns balance monumentalism with delicacy. The Canopus pool is roughly 120m long and a little less than 20m wide.

(Right), The Maritime Theater Plan.

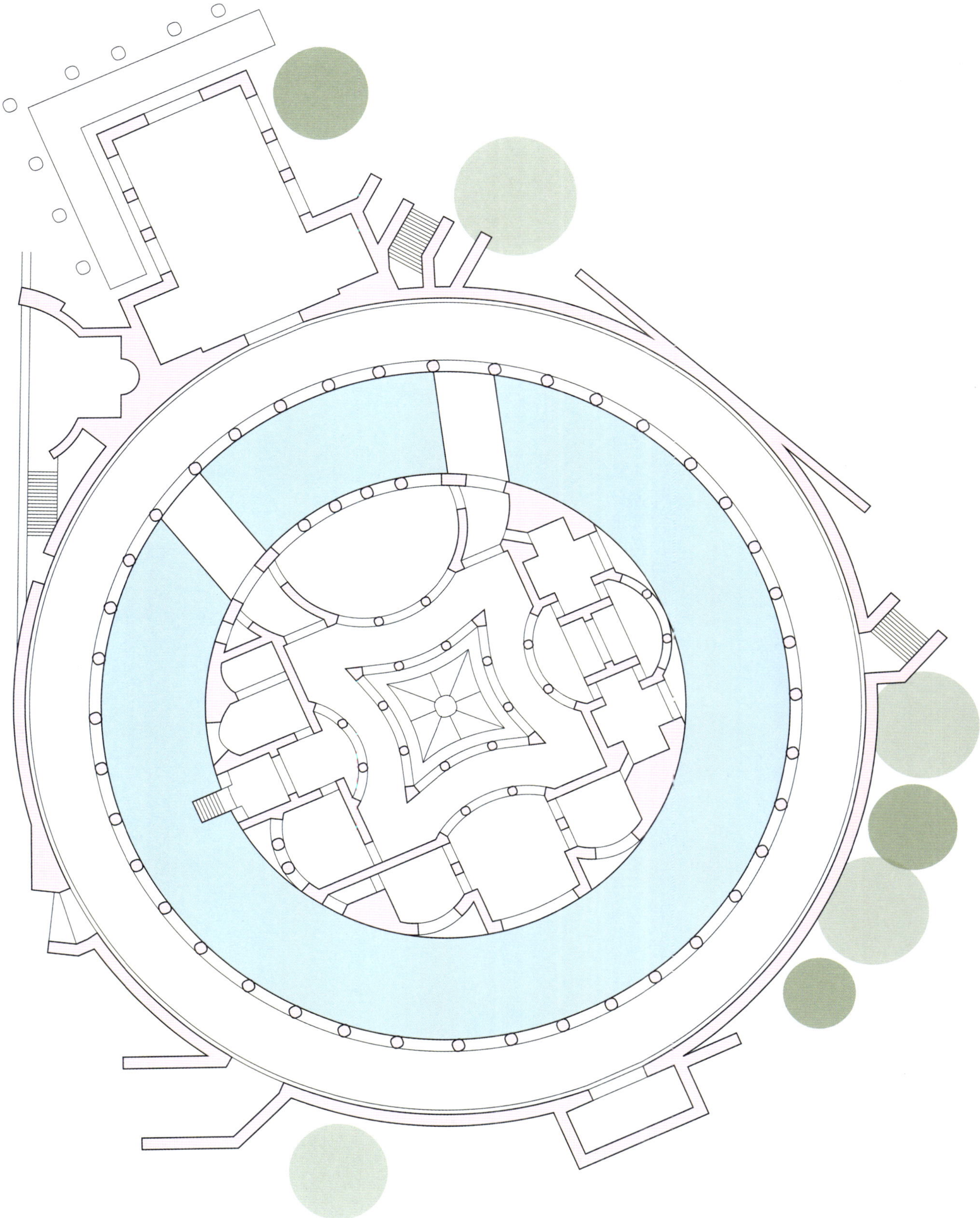

VILLA ADRIANA MARITIME THEATRE, TIVOLI

0 5 10 20M

5 Viterbo

Viterbo, a medieval walled town, rich in history and only two kilometers from the Villa Lante, remains unincurred by contemporary architecture within its protective walls. The town developed, over the years, neighborhood by neighborhood, building fountains along the way, each providing fresh drinking water for those immediate localities. The nieghborhood fountains of Viterbo share compositional traits, though each is differentated from the others by unique designs, motifs, and ellaborations. Viterbo's archaic fountains issue waters from a central pedestal, or "fuso," which is elaborated with sculptures, emblems and radial spouts that pour into basins raised above their surrounding urban spaces. Perimeter steps often monumentalize their aspect. The consistency among the fountains, their water offering purpose, and their visual prominance in the network of key open spaces contributes to Viterbo's unified aesthetic experience.

In a way, it is easy to underestimate the feeling or meaning of the fountains in Viterbo because they are so primal and they do not work so hard as to demand our attention. Some are less inspiring because they aren't working, such as the Fontana Grande, which was built in the year 1279, and has a terrific design, but the traffic pattern is very hard on it and it hasn't enjoyed flowing water in some time.

But if we stop for a moment and visualize a time, say, six hundred years ago, it's not hard to see the fountains as the lively centers that they once were, catalyzing their various social epicenters while providing fresh, cool, potable water from articulate, meaningful stone carvings. That fusion of relevant sculpture, social action, and freshwater provision was basic to the city of Viterbo, the essence of its experience.

(Left and opposite), the eighth century Fontana San Tommaso in the Piazza della Morte. Simple and well-proportioned, the Fuso stands about three meters above its surrounding paving with a basin lip set to a convenient rail height. Though not large, the fountain has a fine presence in a small, jumbled square amongst shade trees and good sun.

The fountain is approached from the north or south and presents well in both directions, with its form as its chief quality when viewed from the south and it's sun-lit spouted streams dominating attention when viewed from the north. The basin's waters are lively and colorful.

(Above), the Fontana Grande, with its cruciform plan and central Fuso, elaborated with lion heads and Gothic sub-pedestals on four sides supporting tilted flumes, each with five spouts; two cat masks on each flume side and a pig mask spout at the end. The pedestal is superimposed by quatrefoil crowns over a Corinthian capital. A Gothic spire rises over all.

(Right), the Fontana Pianoscarano; thirteenth century. Gothic arches present dimensionally carved lions and men trumpeting waters through slender iron pipes under a spire with an acorn peak. The ironwork supporting the colorful pendants is undated.

(Opposite), plan of Viterbo, indicating in blue the prinicple historic fountains in their neighborhoods.

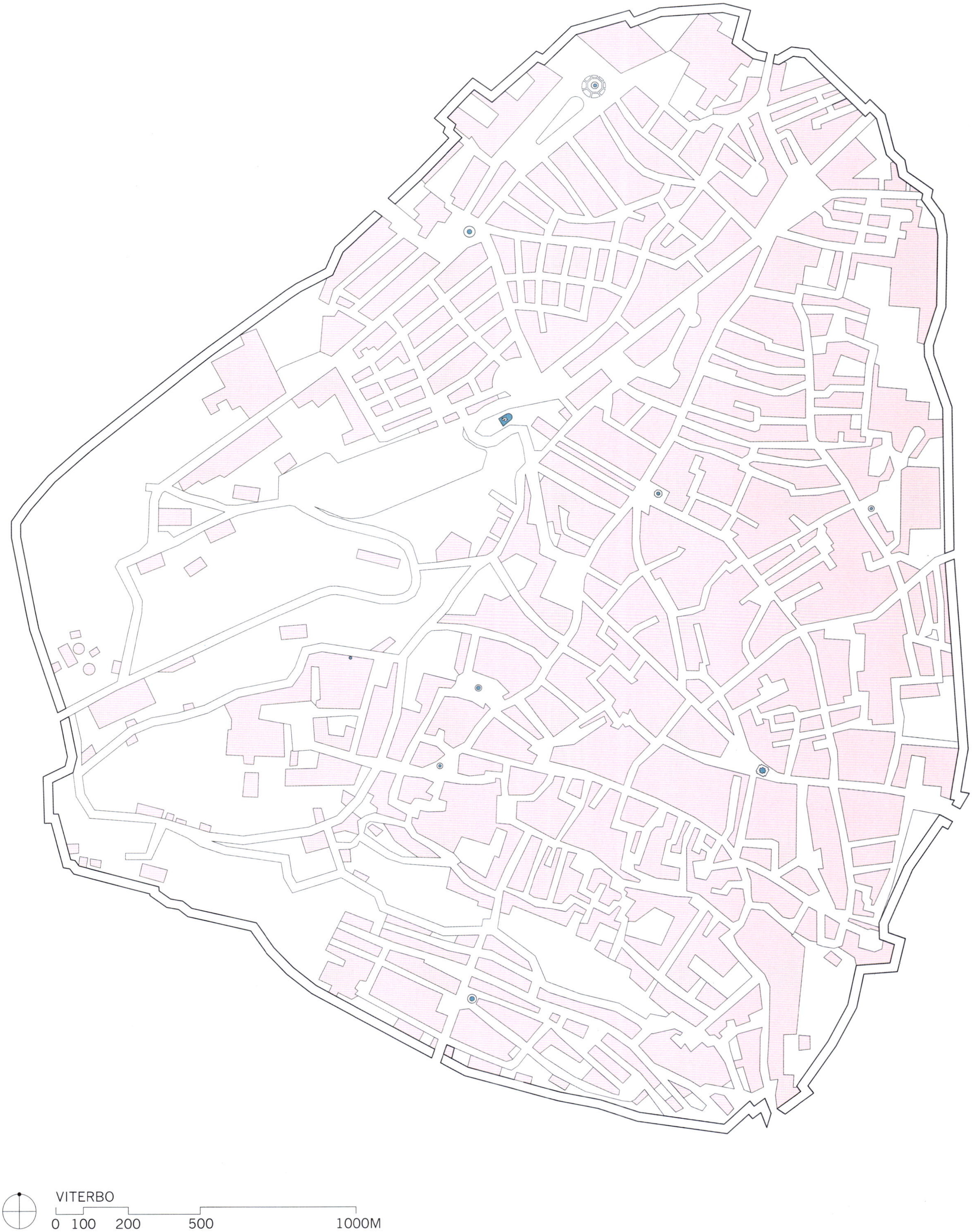
VITERBO
0 100 200 500 1000M

(Opposite left), the Fountain of Jesus; three sumperimposed basins with lions and Gothic ornament. A top spout gives to its basin in light rainfall to veil lions under a flaired stem. The subsequent basin uses lion masks spouting water to the final basin, which is raised on a single step plinth.

(Opposite right), the Fontana dei Lioni in the Piazza delle Erbe. A tiny spout is divided into four lateral sprays, reiterated below in quatrefoil basins, lion mask spouts and three-dimensional lions over brackets reiterated with god mask spouts. The fountain's monumental steps help it negotiate the piazza's sloped grade. A fountain (above), somewhat lost in its huge space, presents the characteristic superimposed basins, here with base steps ornamented with spouting masks and tiny pools.

6 The Villa Lante

The Villa Lante, located a few hours drive north of Rome, hosts an extraordinary fountain collection, the elements of which are rationally organized. The property is comprised of a matching pair of small villas, or "cassini," and an intricate garden populated by fountains following the site's sloped, major axis. The two houses were built a century apart from each other, and the gardens, too, were created in two waves of construction, with the upper section completed with the first cassini, and the rest following.

The project was initiated in 1566 by Cardinal Gianfrancesco Gambara, and believed designed by Vignola. The best known water features include the Fountain of the Deluge, presented in a grotto crowning a terraced sequence of linked fountains, the Fountain of the Dolphins—a dark, octagonal form of stepped, symmetrical terraces— the Catena d'Acqua—a water chain, twin ballustrades activated by tiny water elements— the Fountain of the River Gods, the Fountain of the Table, and the Fountain of Lights, a hemicircular stepped composition of jets and spouts. To the side of this axial garden design is the elliptical Fountain of Pegasus. Other fountains on the site exist, while some are now gone.

The second phase of the property's evolution was led by Cardinal Alessandro Peretti di Montalto, who built the twin cassini, almost exactly matching the first and placed symmetrically about the central axis, and the rest of the garden, including the Quadrato, with the Fountain of the Four Moors at its center. The gardens and fountains were heavily damaged during World War II and subsequently restored. Today, the grounds are in wonderful shape. We do not apprehend the wartime damage.

The water chain is among the best in the world, though it flows at minimal trickle. The tiny jets, spouts and little pools in the ballustrades are also the finest I have seen. The pond's twin gods are boldly scaled without being overwhelming. I touched the water in the Table, which once was employed to chill wine bottles, and it was indeed cool. The four-square fountain assembly to the north is visually impressive and the climax of any tour, but it is less developed than some of the others along the main way.

(Left) the Fountain of the River Gods culminate in a pair of bowls with tooled weirs which pleat the water into strands to capture sunlight. Boxwoods frame the square water partere (top right). The water chain leading down to the Fountain of the River Gods from the Fountain of the Dolphins (right) consistently manages the water action from top to bottom, allowing the waters to neither tire nor accellerate. The top bowl of the Fountain of the River Gods is fed skillfully by a crayfish, the emblem of the Cardinal Gambara, which also supplies water to the top of the Catena d'Acqua. Lost in monocular photography, the upper crayfish's spatial interplay with water, light, and shade is superb, even magical.

(Upper left) the Fountain of the Pegasus, tantalizingly presented at the entrance to the garden from the original cassini. The fountain centered in the water parterre, closed for maintenance during this visit. The bowls of the Fountain of the River Gods lead to a reflection pool, which spouts about a hemicycle to a perimeter trough. The slot of water in the Fountain of the Table was used for wine bottle chilling and food presentation on floating trays. The table spills (like that at Hellbrunn Palace's) to a lower level at the feet of its visitors.

(Bottom left) Fountain of Lights, similar in section to a cascade but uniquely developed with wall-topped slender jets in small overflowing bowls—suggestive of audience members seated in an amphitheater, and spouts expressing from the walls into the troughs between the walls. Diagrammatically, the jet-to-bowl/spout-to-trough composition weaves an elegant spatial figure of wet and dry elements. The visitor walking down to the lower platform is faced with the prospect of being watched (judged?) by the audience of water.

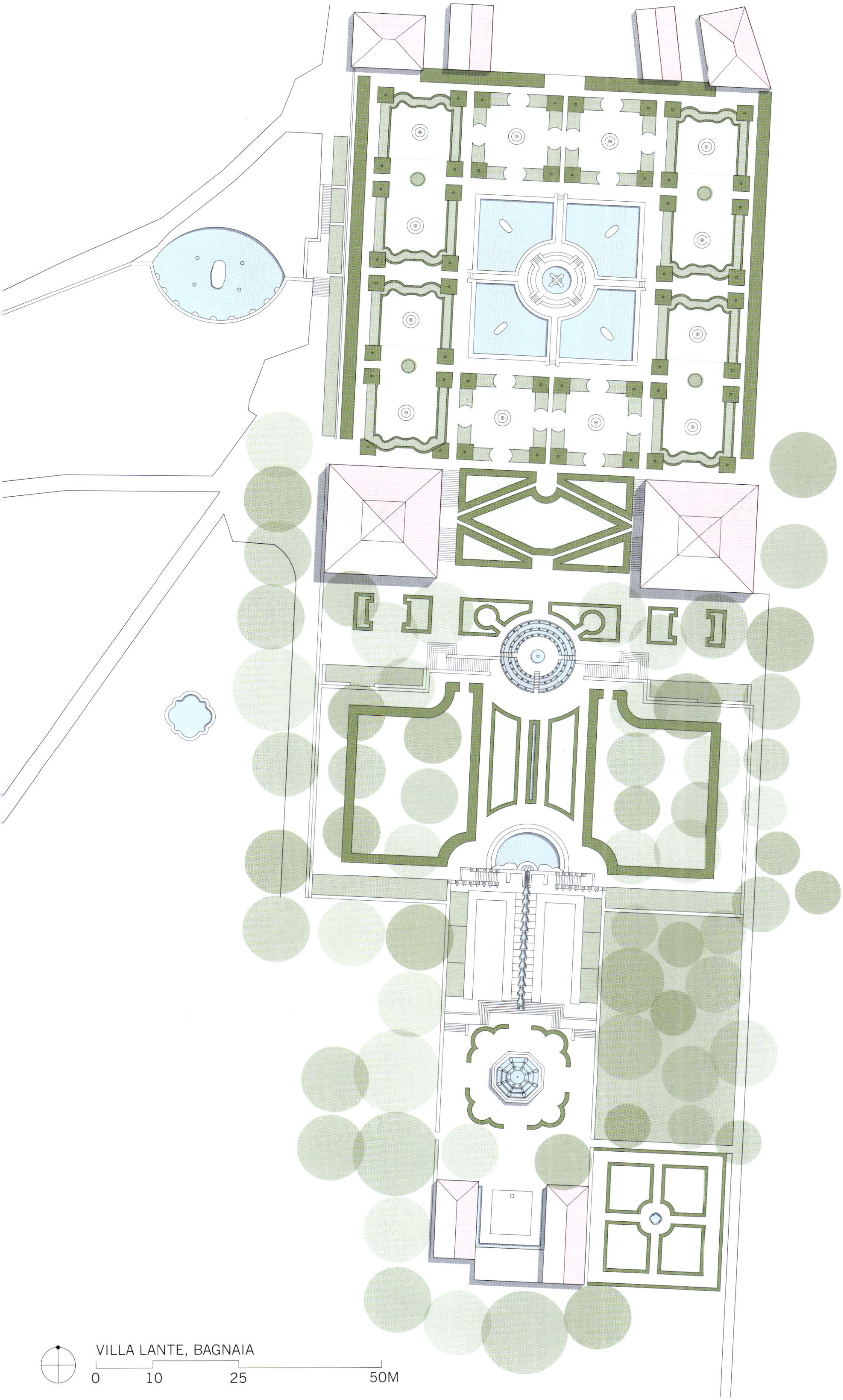
VILLA LANTE, BAGNAIA
0
10
25
50M

(Opposite) the the water of the Catena d'Aqua is kneeded by the evenly spaced double-step minor falls and side volutes, which work together to alternatively spread and compress the water chain flows. The streaming water's surface is characterized by standing waves (resulting mostly from finish texture) through which other wavelets move, which can be followed from top to bottom.

(Above) the staircases behind each of the River Gods and the ballustrade across the landing are inventively animated by tiny jets, bowls, spouts and pools. At the Villa Lante, once one enters the realm of water one is rarely left without it, as the intricacy of water's involvement in the staircases testifies. At this scale, splashes beyond the little basins is inevitable and casually tolerated.

Waters eminate from the Grotto's six niches (opposite top), festooned in rustic rockery, luxuriant plantings and sound-absorbtive mosses. The Fountain of the Dolphin's dark and compact, pyramidal silhouette incorporates complex sculpture, including spouting masks, crowned by a raised, overflowing bowl topped by a tall and thin, clear geyser (opposite lower). The bowl's overflow issues as fine rainfall, and we can guess that the worn age of the weir has resulted in most of the overflow's flawed inflection back towards its stem, though in places the water still projects slightly forward, as per the presumable intention (opposite center right and bottom right).

(Left) the Fountain of the River Gods' waterfalls capture the setting sun. The placid waters of the temporarily still and silent, Fountain of the Pegasus (center left). Adjacent Bagnaia, beyond the entrance to the Villa Lante, with a fountain monument in the late afternoon and its habitue congregants.

7 The Villa d'Este

What strikes the fountain seeker immediately upon entering the Villa d'Este's domain is that the environment is first and foremost a lush garden, and that its collection of very famous fountains serve to punctuate, animate, and emphasize the larger garden design with their varied characters.

The story of the creation of the Villa d'Este happened twice; here in Tivoli, and a hundred years earlier in Suzhou, China, at the Humble Administrator's Garden. In both cases, great men were denied their ambitions by loftier powers, to turn away and build magnificent gardens. (Admittedly, this is a gross simplification, if not a popular canard.) At the Villa d'Este, the man was the accomplished Cardinal Ippolito II d'Este, who's attempts to possess the Holy See were blocked no less than five times. Deflected, but honored, he was awarded the governorship of Tivoli, east of Rome. There, he built his palace and garden, starting in 1560.

Several of the fountains of the Villa d'Este are so excellent that they would certainly be praised if they stood anywhere else, though it cannot be denied that they are wonderfully integrated exactly where they are. These are the Wall of a Hundred Fountains, the Oval Fountain, the Neptune Fountain, the Water Organ, and the Mother Nature fountain (the Fountain of Diana of Ephesus). A second tier of fountains, which are also superb, include the Romanza group (or, at least the boat fountain part of it), the Dragon Fountain, the Fish Ponds, and (I would include) the Rustic Fountains. Other fountains are also of special merit, including the Pegasus Fountain, the tiny cascades at the southeastern staircase, and the some of the fountains that dominate various chambered spaces, like mystical, underground art engines (my term).

(left) The Neptune Fountain, one of the half-dozen or so finest of the many splendid fountains in the collection at the Villa d'Este, centers around a monumental seated sculpture of the Sea King (not visible though the waterfall in this photo) with a stone canopy over the Neptune figure and waterfalls to the front and sides. The falls employ a hand-tooled, rusticated weir to create their three fields of closely ribbed, naturalistic streamers, which capture sunlight to lush effect.

On either side of the waterfall-veiled Neptune are shallow, rustic cascades hosting multi-jet plumes. Their bundled nozzle strategy relies on the slightly tilted outward perimeter streams which are arranged around the principle geyser. Working altogether, with upward thrusting jets abraded by downward falling droplets, they create a plume which manifests in a sizzling core and a broad profile, laterally feathering at the sides with upward thrusts dominating the center, creating fireworks-like, charismatic sparkles dusted throughout. Behind, the upper level's rock-textured white-water flume, which is oriented approximately twenty-five degrees from the vertical, flows from a slender reservoir resting just below and beyond the railing of the Water Organ's terrace.

Behind the Neptunian ensemble, a hidden passageway leads by vaulted stone chambers occupied mysteriously by thick fan jets. A better researcher than this one might unearth explanations for these darkly beckoning subterranean issues. Above the construction, a Baroque architectural palazzo provides an apt den for the Water Organ, a musical automata, powered by water. The Neptune Fountain is axially reflected in the garden's three central Fish Ponds; stocked reflection pools from which rare fish were once obtained and served on special occasions to important guests.

(above) View from the palace's terrace, looking north along the garden's main axis, down over the Fountain of the Dragons (just seen by the crown of its tall geyser), and beyond, over the Fish Ponds, through the flat section of the garden, with various fountains, ultimately terminating at the main gate from which visitors used to enter the Villa d'Este.

Ippolito remained a very busy and successful man his entire life, and the work of the garden took place over the course of many years, though it was by no means a slow-going affair. The Villa d'Este was not finished in Ipplito's lifetime. Subsequent work continued in line with the original designs that he and his team established.

Very soon after receiving the title and property, Ippolito engaged the very qualified Pirro Ligorio to research the area, particularly the nearby Hardrian's Villa where he was to collect important artifacts. It was Ligorio who would work out the ideas for the new garden.

Self-taught painter, architect, cartographer, author, antiquarian and papal favorite, Ligorio served as the prinicipal designer of the Villa d'Este's gardens and fountains, while the palace was designed by Giovanni Alberto Galvani. Prior to his work in the gardens, Ligorio held the position of Architect of the Vatican for Pope Paul IV, and afterwards continued working under Pope Pius IV. Ligorio had successfully undertaken the restoration of the important Roman Acqua Vergine aqueduct—a five year project, which contributed to his suitability as conceptualist for the Villa d'Este's fountains. The project's hydraulic engineering was performed by Tommaso Chiruchi, who had previously engineered the universally respected water feature network at the Villa Lante. Claude Venard assisted in the garden's hydraulics work.

Ligorio and Ipplito planned the garden in accordance with allegorical narratives. The principal fountains participated in the narratives while specific pathways and sequences conveyed classical ideas.

The falls of the Neptune Fountain (left) are textured, catching sunlight at each of their closely spaced water strands. The weirs were achieved with hand-tooled weirs, rounded on top and heavily rusticated at the point of water departure. They function well even when veneered in a surface of algae.

The white-water flume froths quickly, accomplished by a jumbo, rolling weir, which accellerates the water to an activating tempo (top) before flowing over the monumental, textured panel.

Dark shadows from cypress trees play a role in the dance of sunlight on the fountain's moving waters and stone forms (images this page).

Ligorio's allegorical design involves three symbolic narratives, which are arranged along the garden's three most important axial pathways, as follows:

Narrative One is conceived as a reiteration of the verdant and noble Tiberian geography and its extension to Rome. This is literally represented in the connective line from the Fountain of Tivoli (The Oval Fountain) to the west along the ceremonial Hundred Fountains to the mytholigically presented Rometta (The Fountain of Rome).

Salutations towards the realm of waters, Narrative Two, are expressed in the parallel walk (but oriented to the east) extending from the Fish Ponds, up to the Fountain of the Sea (now, the Neptune Fountain), and the Water Organ (where the Fountain of Mother Nature used to be).

The intended entrance to the domain was originally from the garden's north gate, and the approach to the Cardinal's residence developed through the garden's central axis over, initially, level land. Visitors then moved up-slope to reach the terrace and the palace door. This sequence is perpendicular to, and therefore transects—or *encompasses*—the other two symbolic systems.

Narrative Three's line then begins at the gateway and moves south through the realm of waters to pause at the Fountain of the Dragon, which characterizes the celebrated d'Este family, their name and crest, and their symbolic ancestor, Hercules, a dragon slayer. Visitors then work around the astonishing Hundred Fountains to ascend to the residential entrance, viewing Bernini's Fountain of the Biccierone along the way. They are greeted at the apex by the modest but enchanting Tripod Fountain, with its grand overlook of the scenes experienced on the way up.

The Hundred Fountains, possibly the most famous of the garden's fountains, is fundamentally a quite practical retaining wall, firmly resisting the lateral thrust of steeply sloped meters of earthen topography. The waters and plantings wetly ornament its structural role. Perhaps more than the other fountains, it conveys the garden's main dual themes of art and nature.

The masks are of wild beasts, some of which are men (above). Partial view down from the Fountain of Pegasus (opposite lower left). The Fountains leads to (or from) the Oval Fountain to the east (opposite lower right). Water flow control valves are hidden under covers integrated into the mosaic paving (bottom left), allowing the maintenance staff to directly view the spray results of their tricky manipulations. The last mask intersects with a human face grotesque on the fountain's eastern side wall (bottom right). The view west is to Rome (below), as well as to the mythological Rometta.

The two spiraling handrail chains at the Dragon Fountain, left and right facing the center, fling delicate sprays from spaced seashells (upper left). In center position, the four dragons face outward (above) around a monumental geyser, the falls from which channel between the dragons to the pond. Water projecting horizontally compliments the verticalilty of the central jet. The sculpture's verdant mosses and the dark and cool, green pool make a strong, living impression in its contemporary guise.

The Rometta's boat (left), projects an aura of story, symbolism and viscereality. It's central stone architectural obelisk seems perfectly plausible in the stone boat, contributing to the composition's monumental statement. The Fish Ponds (below, left), rest in the garden's heart.

The sixteenth-century illustration below indicates how dramatically the garden has evolved over time, in comparison to its current plan (right). The Neptune Fountain did not exist, the Fountain of Diana was elsewhere. The north slopes are transformed, the labyrinths are lost, etc.

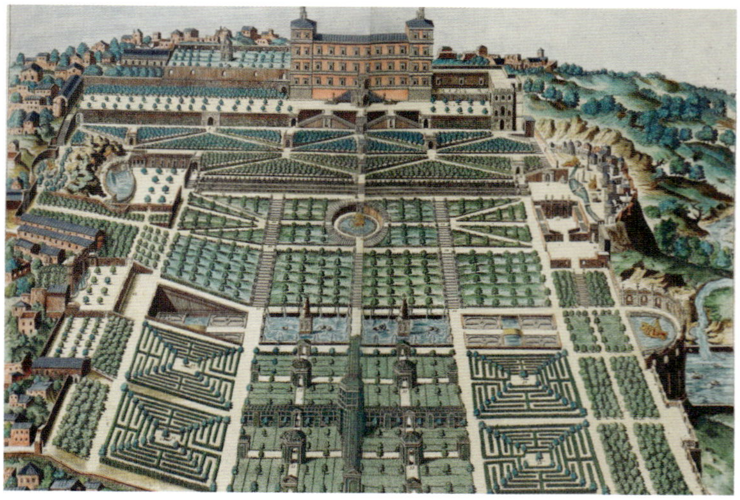

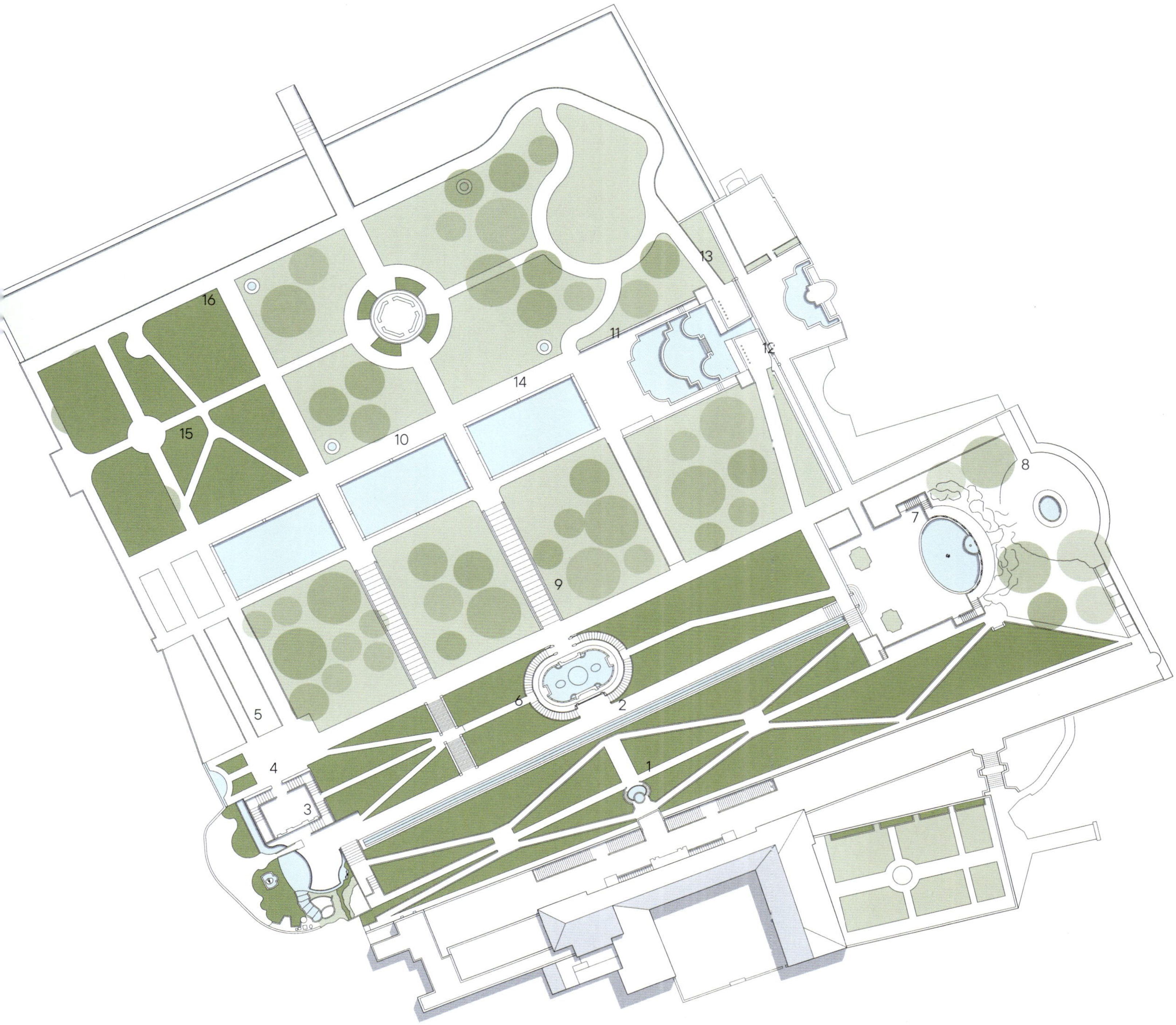

1—Tripod Fountain
2—Fountain of the Bicchierone
3—Fountain of Rometta
4—Fountain of Proserpine
5—Fountain of the Owl
6—The Hundred Fountains
7—The Oval Fountain
8—The Fountain of Pegasus
9—The Fountain the Dragons
10—The Fish Ponds
11—The Neptune Fountain
12—Fountain of the Organ
13—Fountain of Venus
14—Fountains of the Eagles
15—The Rustic Fountains
16—Fountain of Mother Nature

VILLA D'ESTE, TIVOLI

0 10 25 50M

The Villa d'Este's garden character transcends its superb fountain colletion, rather remarkably, given the fountains' quality. The verdency permeates, strengthens, and unifies all other aspects of the space design.

The Oval Fountain (above, below, opposite); original to the garden, presents a richly mannered waterfall, one of the finest in the world, issuing from a hand-tooled weir. The depth of the water over the weir is less than 15mm. The tiny sprays on the upper pool are only partly ornamental as their disturbance in the pool contributes to the waterfall's stability (opposite, middle left). The arcade is no longer open to the public; treated as a storage shed during this visit (opposite, right). Some years ago, visitors could loiter within the space immediately behind the waterfall.

Bernini's Bicchierone (lower left), shown before and after a restoration. The exposed form is curious, as is its rustic rock mosaic finish, imbued in ambiguous primal messages seemingly suitable to the garden.

While allegorical narratives may ellude most of today's visitors, one of the garden's planning ideas will resonate with anyone, the idea regarding the relationship between nature and art. In the Villa d'Este's garden we experience the refreshment of a visit to nature fused with the refreshment of a visit to art. This combined experience operates on us in obvious and stealthy ways. And the garden's vibrant fountains are the principle conveyors of this beguiling idea and feeling.

The nature and art concept can be directly witnessed at the Hundred Fountains, whose numerous water jets, carved masks and plantings are inextricably intermingled to unify in the formal statement of its long, garden wall. At the Rometta, a mythological, miniature Rome is composed with reduced scale, almost *bansai*-like hills, plantings and small scale flows. The Oval Fountain's plantings-encrusted arcade and heavily verdant upper terrace are essential to the design's aesthetic concept and primal allure—though the original construction was naked of the plantings, making a more pure, architectural statement. At the Fountain of the Dragons, the moss-soaked forms flow into, and unify with, a deep green, wavelet-activated reception pool. In all the fountains of the first generation, the water was generously exhuberant—and suffused in conceptually integrated, luxuriant greenery.

Notably, one of the Villa d'Este's largest and most famous fountains, the Neptune Fountain, does not merge plantings with the fountain arts the way the others do, but then it is not original. The Neptune Fountain was built in the 1930s, replacing an earlier cascade, which had been built by Bernini. Bernini's design was naturalistic, tumbling from the level of the Water Organ down to the Fish Ponds, wild with rocks, greenery and water. But it was long mechanically problematic and its replacement was welcomed, though very different in character. Marvelous as it is, viewed from this perspective we can see it is not aligned with the other water features.

The staircases on the garden's main slopes are variously ornamented in flowing waters (top and upper left). The Staircase of the Ballori (top).

The open garden immediately south of the Neptune Fountain offers a calm respite from the exceeding energies of the fountains, even here, softened by a small, delightful jet (left). The Water Organ (opposite top and left), an 'automata', whose doors are normally closed (see upper left), is shown here (opposite) open for a performance. The mechanisms use water to compress air for the pipes, while separately controlling tone play. Music has been especially written for the Water Organ.

The plumes of the Neptune Fountain echoing the garden's tall Italian cypress trees (opposite bottom right).

The rustic fountains (or, "Meta Sudans") on the northern quadrants are possibly the largest of their type in the world. The two fountains share the same height and rough silhouette, but they are different from each other. One has a base of thick legs with thin slots through in both directions whilie the other is formed into a lighter, more open, leggy structure with a largely carved away underside. Their rocky, textured forms are covered in plantings, mosses and algaes while the water is crystal clear. They were inspired by the monumental Meta Sudan fountain of Imperial Rome, built by Emperor Flavian and no longer standing.

The famous Fountain of Diana of Ephesus on the north wall, with its Pagen symbolism, towers monumentally over its visitors. The sprays from her many breasts are the chief display, but the streaming waters to her sides are more abundant. Sound is generated then from the sides, a dimensional sonic experience for the up-close visitor.

M·AGRIPPA·L·F·COS·TERTIVM·FECIT

8 Fontana del Pantheon

The category of grotesque sculpture is sufficiently unfamiliar to contemporary culture that we have difficulty grasping it. The charactures appear crude and graceless, even if skillfully carved, and the water actions are—at first glance, at least, unremarkable. The sculpture is well proportioned in its space, very well located, and it is not overwhelmed by the imposing and important, Pantheon.

Pressed into closer inspection, we discover that some of its jets are special and excellent. Regrettably, only the very sharp-eyed can see them, due to their high position and small scale. I saw them clearly for the first time only when looking through a telephoto lens.

The fountain we see today employs copies of the original sculptures, which were part of a refurbishment in 1711, when the obelisk and a new basin was installed. The original sculptures may well have been slightly different. The site's original fountain dates to 1575. When the delightful, tiny fan nozzles were incorporated into the pedestal of the obelisk is not clear. They may have been part of the original design, though if so they show a level of exquisiteness without equal during that early era.

Fan jets mounted on the four corners of the fountain's sculpture express from the open mouths of fish-styled sea monsters. The jets are unique with their very tiny side streams (with a throw of no more than 4cm), which relieve the fans of some of their water only to direct it back to their dappled sides. We might conjecture that the streams relieve trubulence, smoothing out the face of the fan, and by adding water to the sides of the flows help keep the fan wide, rather than contracting to a narrower form. Maybe they energize the edges of the flows. Tests would need to be performed to be sure. I am aware of no other nozzle like these four.

Past Masters

While on a business trip to deliver a paper in Rome where a conference on water was being held, I met a professional researcher, who, one night, walked another visitor and me around the city, pointing out the markers on certain walls, identifying the year of one or another disastrous flood, and how high the water had gotten. The city was at its most ancient under the black night sky and harsh, yellow street lights. Ten years later the same researcher published her book, which was most impressive and full of original scholarship. She connected dots I didn't know existed.

Around the time of that publication I was in a meeting in a real estate developer's office, high in a tall building with long views over a modern city. An architect in the meeting told me about when he was posted at the Academy and a famous, senior architect showed him fountains around Rome and how one could trace the past masters' skill with water, and how their abilities evolved, by seeing the fountains in sequence and knowing who was working on what, and when.

The researcher's book revealed something of the same. At the Piazza Navona, for instance, Giacomo della Porta, of the Mannerist era, designed the two elegant, well-proportioned and visually restrained fountains whose flourishes were reserved for water action, not expressive sculpture. A few years later Gian Lorenzo Bernini arrived with his characteristically gifted sculptural centeredness, adorning the basins with numerous sculptures. Last to the two end fountains was Francesco Borromini, who's incorporation of lower pools with slender streams achieved the most significant and delightful presentations with what might be seen as the slightest effort.

VACANZE ROMANE

9 Piazza Navona

The piazza's largest and most famous fountain—the central, Fountain of the Four Rivers, was the last of the three to be built, in 1651. The fountains to the north and south arrived nearly 75 years earlier, around 1577.

Those two original fountains, by Giacomo della Porta, which dressed up the slightly wild open space significantly, were then much simpler, carved in the restrained, Mannerist style. They were comprised of elegant reflection pools raised almost a meter from the ground, each topped by a comparatively small, stately pylon, or fuso, releasing water in low throws to the pools. Back in the late 1500s none of the many sculptures that now occupy the fountains were in place. They showed up later, accumulating over time into the populated assemblies we see today.

The southern fountain, now called, The Fountain of the Moor, is presided over by Bernini's Moor. The Neptune Fountain, to the north, is given its current identity by its sculpture of Neptune, by Antonio della Bitta. Borromini added the ground pools to both fountains. He also secured the aqueducts and piping to bring more water to the existing fountains and the not-yet-designed fountain planned for the center of the piazza—a commission he coveted.

Bernini's Fountain of the Four Rivers fully embodies the Baroque era with its emotionally charged, dynamic figures and flamboyant scenery. The travertine and white marble formation supports a tall Egyptian obelisk, salvaged from the Forum of the imperial era.

It was Borromini who developed the concept of a Fountain of the Four Rivers, representing Catholocism's reach into four continents, and Pope Innocent X approved. But Bernini, his rival, won the commission even though the competition took place while Bernini's reputation was at a career low, due to a slight mishap's cracking of St. Peter's facade. Ahem. The Pope's nephew, Prince Nicolo Ludovisi, commissioned Bernini's design after submissions by other artists were found wanting. His model of the four rivers concept (the Danube, Nile, Rio de la Plata, and Ganges) topped by the Egyptian-styled obelisk balanced over biaxial, cave-like voids, was sufficienty astounding that both the design and its creator were elevated to good graces, quoting the Pope, "The only way to resist executing his works is not to see them."

Reportedly, there was widespread disbelief in the sculpture's structural integrity, with its huge obelisk impossibly pressing down heavily over the void in the base. Theatrically, Bernini announced he would solve the problem, racing to the piazza by carriage. With the crowd held back, he and his assistants showily tied four slender silken to the obelisk, stabalizing the construction. The appreciative crowd applauded and disbursed, their worries relinquished.

Although the heroic sculptures far surpass their water's expressions in formal importance, the water is superbly wrought in all three fountains, with interestingly varied and intriguing spouts, streams and sprays.

In Bernini's fountain, the four rivers are symbolized by four groupings of several streams (not four rivers), some of which flow very nicely even today—three hundred and fifty years later, though the fish, dragon and lion around the base were not operational during my last visit.

The sculpture is in good condition, though the comparatively soft travertine is more worn away than the white marble of the articulate gods or the 2,000-year-old granite of the (Imperial Rome) obelisk. Notably, the figural stonework is assembled from separate blocks, which are impressively assembled with very tight, clean, consistently mortared joints, leading to its formal and structural integrity.

The glittering activity in the reception pools (Above, Fountain of the Moor; below, Neptune Fountain) are caused by streams splashing from above, causing wavelets to expland outwads and reflect and overlap in complex patterns. This effect is skilfully engendered by the perimeter coping's faceted geometry, courtesy of Borromini.

The plan of the Piazza Navona (Opposite page) shows the scale of the space, which is roughly three blocks long. The central, Fountain of the Four Rivers, is centered in the space, not centered with the piazza's Baroque church, Sant'Agnese in Agone, stabilizing the space with a dynamic relation to the church.

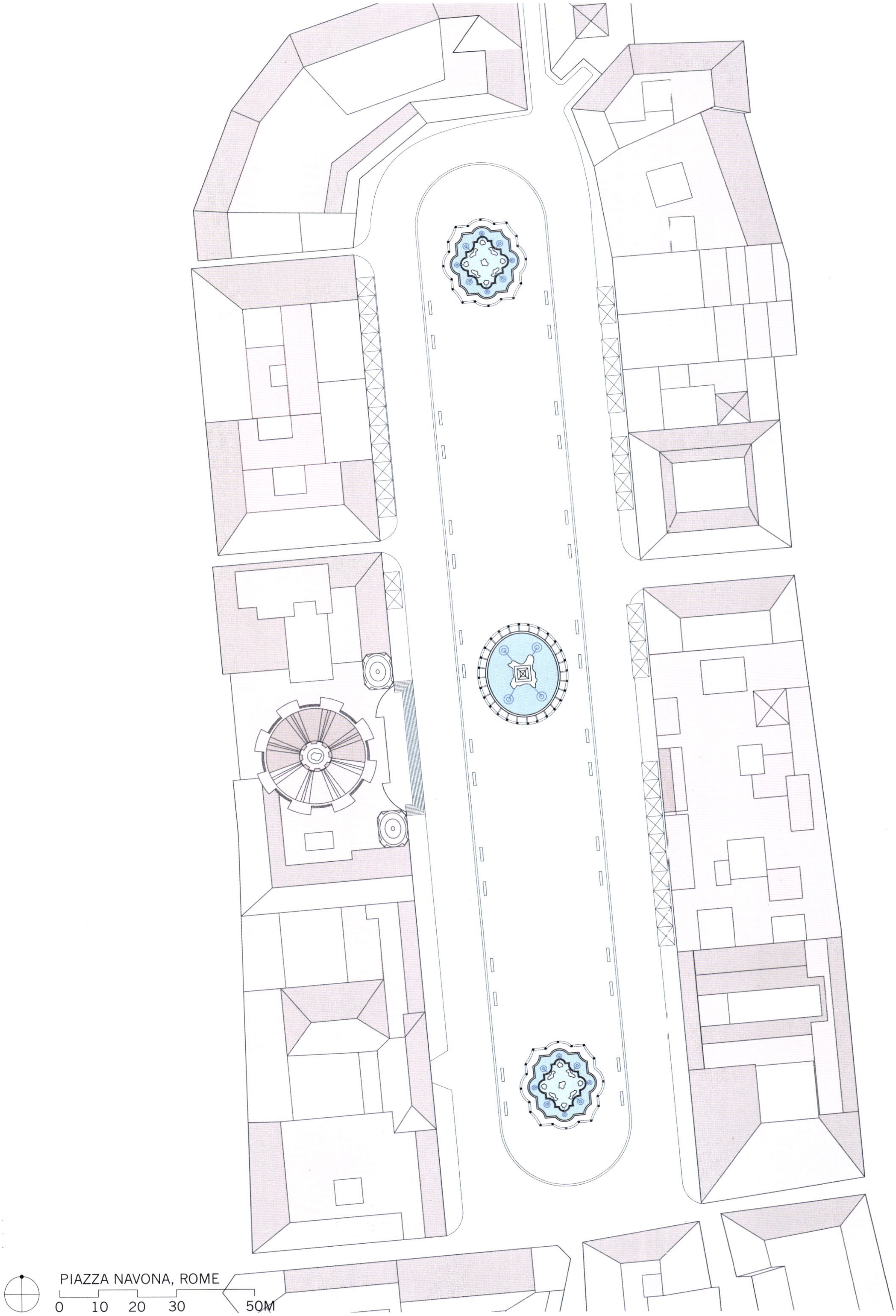
PIAZZA NAVONA, ROME
0 10 20 30 50M

(This page, The Fountain of the Moor; opposite page, The Fountain of Neptune.) The varied, glassy flows accent the dynamic, three-dimensional sculptures, presenting in free space and available to the moving, changing sunlight. In shade, the streams are less effective. (Upper right) The Moor, balanced on a shell with a laminar slim-fan.

(Far right) Neptune toiling with a monstrous octopus and a nearly identical slim-fan jet. A seahorse and cherub sculpture (Far right), positioned on della Porta's ledge in a manner clearly retrofitted; this kind of positioning is regularly incorporated into both fountains on their plan diagonal facets. (Next Pages, the Fountain of the Four Rivers).

RISTORANTE
GELATERIA

Pizzeria

BAR
Pizzeria

RISTORANTE

10 Taormina Fountain

Taormina, Sicily, a small hill-town with an important Roman amphitheater, offers breezy pedestrian streets, engaging, hillside views of the Mediterranean, exclusive tourist diversions, and an interesting fountain in the town's main square. The fountain, built in 1635, is rich in allegorical sculptures, carved in the archaic style from a softly bleached stone. Seahorses spout slender, glassy streams of drinking water at the fountain's four corners, somewhat remotely from the fountain's main form, which stands atop a stepped base in the form of an elaborated quatrefoil. The central fountain body is of three parts, arranged vertically. The base is a little unusual in that it does not incorporate a pool, presenting something like a stage, instead. The steps of the base are over-scaled for seating, amphitheater style. The top of the base is wide enough that it could be occupied by someone making a speech, or by a musician, lending something additional to the feeling of the square as an important social space.

At the fountain's apex is a youthful Sea King merman, presumably Neptune, holding a scepter in one hand and an orb in the other. He is balanced over an adorned, amphora-like pedestal. Below is a garlanded bowl held up by sea Atlases. Below that is the main bowl, raised on the heads of laughing grotesques, one of which is being toyed with by an imp.

The fountain is positioned off-center in the open piazza, organizing the open space for alternative uses. The fountain's many sculpted parts, its scale, spread out anatomy, and its monumental steps invite a leisurely, lingering engagement.

Water actions at the Taormina Fountain are modest, in keeping with the soft, rustic style of its sculptural character. The fountain offers drinking water at four perimeter points, issues from seahorses on pedestals into small bowls. The figure atop the fountain's spindle form, perhaps King Neptune's does not engage water flows, though he does hold a Christian symbol in his left hand. Slender streams (now inoperative) once issued from the upper bowl to the octagonal bowl, which is aloft of the base of the fountain, and as low as water goes until it reappears at the four cardinal drinking water offerings.

11 Barcaccia

An important career opportunity sent Pietro Bernini to Rome from Sicily where he had been working as a sculptor. He brought his family, including his young son, Gian Lorenzo, who in short years would be introduced to the Pope and widely recognized as a brilliant prodigy, gifted in every way. He chose as his life's work to follow his father and be a sculptor though events would press him to also be a painter, to design festivals and theatrical productions, and to be an architect.

One of the elder Bernini's last commissions was for the Barcaccia (the long boat), though current academic consensus identifies it to be much the work of the son, who was twenty-six when the fountain was completed in the late 1620s. Pietro Bernini died in 1629, and his son, with others, went on to establish the style we now call Baroque, and to reconfigure Rome, the eternal city.

The boat fountain existed roughly a century before the Spanish Steps were completed, in 1725. It is gracefully integrated into the sloped paving of the street, with low slung features partly resulting from the water supply's tepid pressure in that area.

The identity of the fountain is reinforced as its subject—a boat—is itself a water-related artifact. The sculpture's formal explorations are unlike common boat contours. Instead, its curved and folded surfaces evoke an in and out, over and under, merging of water and boat. The boat theme is reiterated in its boat-within-a-boat composition, which transforms the main boat into a metaphor of the sea while the smaller becomes a wellspring. It is noteworthy that the sculpture issues flows to its inside and outside, rather than dam water back as hulls are typically expected to do.

The fountain is alleged to represent the ship of the church, or a boat that was washed ashore near that spot from one of the Tiber's great floods. The fountain is also claimed to be a military ship with cannons firing, in accordance with a dream the pontif had had years earlier. This is hard to believe, though loftily attributed. There is also a tale about a bon-vivant wine merchant who operated from a boat which sank from a storm, leaving a community-wide sense of loss. A clinging idea supporting the wine boat story is the claim that the boat's many overflows suggest that the boat is being resurrected, its flooded hull pouring out, the scene cheered by the sun emblems, its moment of salvation accented by the tiny, elegant, boat-like form at its heart.

Left—the view looking up from the Barcaccia through the Spansh Steps to the Trinita die Monti church at the top. The obelisk is not authentic Egyptian; it was carved in Rome during Imperial times. The flows of the Barcaccia (left and right) are modest, glassy and smooth. The sun emblem's fan nozzles are not orginal, though they are likely similar to the original detail. Bernini used somewhat similar, crystaline water expressions at the Fountain of the Four Rivers, at the Piazza Navona.

The waters from the sun emblem are split three ways, a difficult balancing act of flow tension, well resolved with equivalent flows all around.

The central little boat within the boat reiterates the flow character issued by the sun emblem's three-way split. Below, streams from the boat at both ends offer drinking water, accessed from broad stepping stones.

TEA
ROOMS

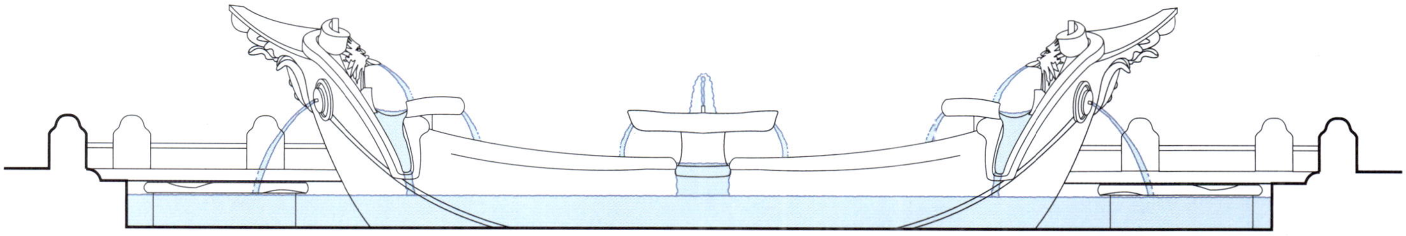

WATER FEATURE SECTION

0 1 5M

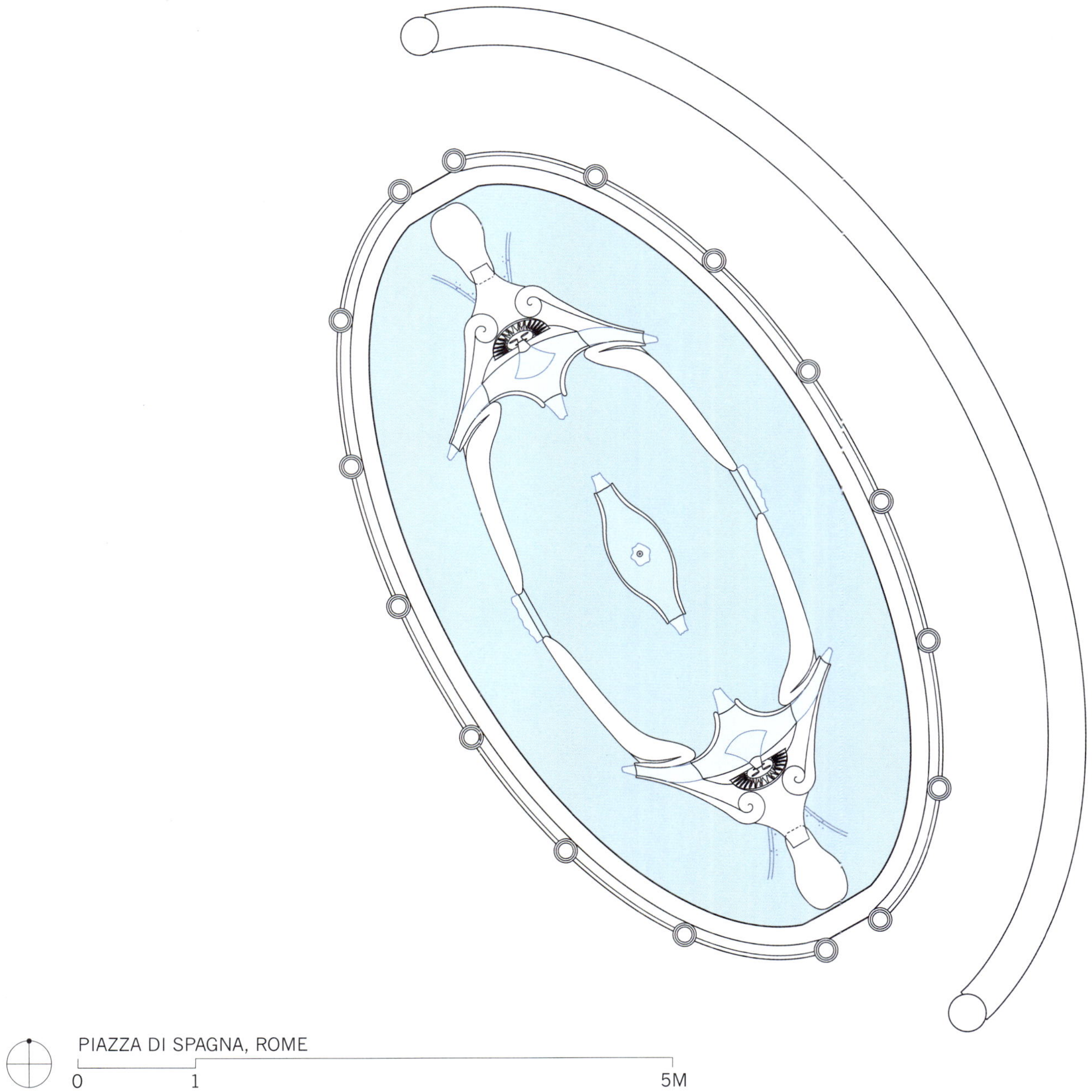

PIAZZA DI SPAGNA, ROME

0 1 5M

The work's transverse section resolves a pronounced street cross-slope by incorporating a dam-like, crescent-shaped bench on the outside, permitting the inner side's paving to be flattened, straightening the ground plane for a level and comfortable formal enjoyment. The space between the bench and the fountain's railing is often a bit crowded.

(Below) the wellspring crowning the boat within the boat, only 250mm tall, represents the water's pinnacle in this fountain, the limit of which is due to the area's low, aqueduct-delivered, water pressure.

(Right) the fountain's swirling waters, streaming, waving, reflecting and counter-reflecting—alive all around—are a signature of the skill level developed in Rome during this period.

Barcaccia offers drinking water, which is known to many of the passers by who fill their bottles from its four hull spouts. Wide stepping stones at the ends provide access to its (cannon fire?) drinking water.

12 Saint Peter's Square Fountains

The north fountain is the original, designed by Carlo Maderno in 1612, who also created the facade of St. Peter's. Under Pope Urban VIII, it was repositioned onto the cross axis of Bernini's oval-shaped colonnade forecourt, with the Egyptian obelisk in the center, and a second fountain to the south, completed by Bernini in 1677 to match Maderno's and balance the composition within the grand piazza.

The top jets in these photos are expressing only to a modest height, which is their normal state. On special occasions, the jets are raised to full capacity, another ten to fifteen meters tall with a forceful character, quite different from these calm photos.

The piazza's compositional strategy of two mighty, double-tiered fountains placed symmetrically about a central Egyptian obelisk, arranged transverse to the site's main axis, was subsequently repeated at the Place de la Concorde, in Paris, influenced by the quality of the composition here at the Vatican.

The design's lower bowl rim and its inverted upper bowl rim behave quite differenty from each other. At the upper form, water flows over a relief of lapped leaf forms, which evenly distributes and animates the flows. The water then rolls over the rim's special weir, comprised of a rounded projection, which gathers the water to the next part, a downward-facing vertical edge, which causes the activated droplets to fall more or less straight down to the bowl below. All this is fairly difficult to get right.

At the weir of the second bowl, the roughened texture of the stone surface and the chamfered projection of its edge divide the pool's overflows in two parts; half of the water sprays outwards and down while other the other half clings to the underside of the bowl, crawling along on something like a ceiling, until it can hold no longer, to then fall, rainlike, and slanting a bit to the interior, to splash into the reception pool around the central, octagonal pedestal. Except during the windiest periods, the managed patterns of water on these tall fountain sculptures do a good job to keep the lively waters within the sphere of the reception pool, avoiding that it might be a nuisance to Vatican visitors. Instead, the combined water actions are grandly presented with energy and proportion.

Shown in these photos with a modest cluster of jets at the peak, those streams are alternatively capable of achieving the far taller height of fifteen meters on special occasions. Note the high, brimming water level in the base's reception pool, which attractively eliminates a more pronounced coping perimeter to provide more water visibility (and connectiveness) for the pool's reflective sheen.

The wellspring grouping at the apex is capable of variable flows, but even at low flow, as shown, the water is sufficient to satisfy the needs of the rim to create consistent rainfall all around. The sloped texture distributes and animates the water. A projecting rim at the base of the slope draws the water, clinging, to the vertical flange below, which releases it to fall in a straight, rain-like character.

That water falls to a subsequent pool, a measure below the higher realm but also aloft. A tooled perimeter weir conducts the flows to the underside of the basin. This surface is textured, causing some of the clinging flows to break away in bunches of irregular droplets.

On the ground, a wide, waiste-high basin captures all water while helping to establish a substantial space and scale for the two monumental fountains, which in spite of their impressive scale, are nearly lost in the vastness of the plaza.

13 Trevi Fountain

The world's most celebrated fountain is Trevi. It is a master work of urban design, architectural proportion, sculptural quality and water action. A product of Vatican decree during the Italian Rennaissance, Trevi transforms an otherwise forlorn nook in central Rome's plan into its most popular destination.

The fountain we see today replaced a previous fountain in order to celebrate a critically improved aqueduct, the Acqua Vergine. The built scheme is the result of contributions from several sculptors and architects working over the course of thirty years. Nicola Salvi was awarded the commission after a design competition (originally won by a Florentine, but then awarded to Salvi, a Roman). He worked on the project for twenty years until his death in 1751. The central sculpture of Oceanus was executed by Pietro Bracci, following a design by Giovanni Battista Maini. The architect Giuseppe Pannini took over the work on the fountain after Salvi, but was quickly released and replaced by Pietro Bracci, who completed the work in 1763 when it was inaugurated by Pope Clement XIII.

Trevi utterly dominates its moderately-sized open space, which is disconnected from the main traffic ways. Trevi presents an immersive allegorical experience. Its edges fuse into the architecture behind it and dissove the sides of its three containing streets. The three-sided pool frontage (something like a thrust stage) offers two teirs of occupation, with passers-by above and steps and seating for dedicated participants, below. The pool's coping serves as a seat-wall. The fountain's rockwork is heroically scaled and lively—especially to the east, where mammoth diagonals of stone splash up the fountain space's container wall. An alcove on that side presents a small, approachable fountain within the fountain.

Trevi's central, cascading waters are every bit as exquisitely crafted as the sculptures that surround them. Flumes, falls, cascades, and the tiny jets here and there populate the urban-scaled sculpture, enriching the realism and power of the central waterfalls. Their thinly textured, subtely lacy, evenly draped flows and sounds contribute significantly to the fountain's scenic power and aura of quality. The main waterfall of the central cascade is especially refined—and perhpas the most ideal of its kind in the world.

The iconic and much photographed, Oceanus, (left), was created by Pietro Bracci. Trevi's three-stepped, central cascade may seem simple, but its flows are virtually perfect, with the final fall especially well-formed. Even the rock sculpture behind the glassy waterfall is superb, offering an attractive backdrop to the waterfall without being a distraction.

CLEMENTIS XIII PONT MAX OPVS CVM
A DOM MDCCLXII

OGGI COME STAI?
VERAMENTE.

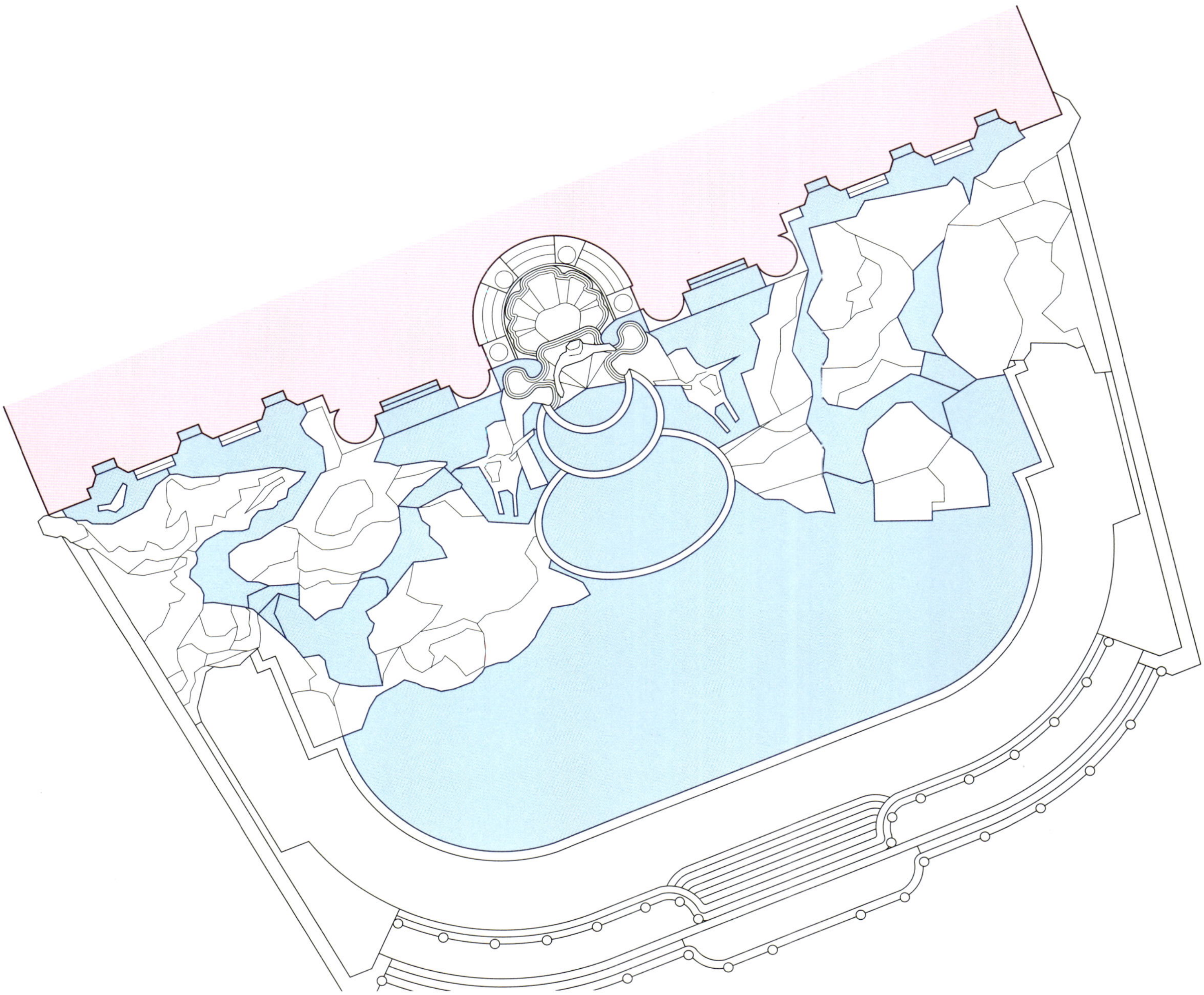

TREVI FOUNTAIN, ROME

0 5 10 20M

Trevi's central cascades are roughly seven meters wide and cumulatively about two-and-a-half meters tall. The upper two steps are much smaller than the main curtain, but all three employ similar weirs, which are level, with square, projecting profiles and rolled backs, perfectly and seemlessly carved in travertine.

Importantly, the upper falls do not simply flow into the pool. Instead, they impact a zone of carved rockery just at the water level, generating a rich, tempered, white-water action, imparting to the pool just the right measure of turbulence needed by the final waterfall's elegant curtain.

Trevi's eastern side offers a generous area where visitors can spend time within the space of the fountain, where a fountain-within-the-fountain may be found. (Top left and right, above, and bottom right.)

Lighting is Trevi's only sour note, improvised and harsh (not shown).

14 Reggia di Caserta

The very large palace and grounds were envisioned by King Charles V in 1750 and designed by the architect, Luigi Vanvitelli, following on the Versailles tradition of large, site-wide monumentality. Before the project was completed, Charles abdicated to become the king of Spain, leaving the work in the south (and his title) to his son, Ferdinand IV and to Vanvitelli's architect son, Carlo. Construction soldiered on for decades until it was finally completed in 1845.

The site axis projects through the acarded spaces at the central portion of the palace's ground level, the so-called, Telescope, across the landscape and up into the hills where a natural spring intiates the water narrative, an impressive 2.75 kilometers away. The clear shot of space is neatly bordered by two lines of trees, a lower inner border and a taller, space-framing edge.

Six noteworthy fountains pace the way from the palace to the water's hillside source, consecutively, the Margherita, the Tre Delfini, the Eolo, the Cerere, the Venere e Adone, and the especially scenic, Diana e Atteone, closely framed as it is by the forest on both sides. In the hills is the Caserta Cascade, landmarked by an unfathomable contemporary sculpture. All the historic fountains are populated by fine figures conveying allegorical content.

The reflection pool from the Tre Delfini is nearly half a kilometer long. It is followed (heading uphill) by two very large scale, cascades which tumble with the changing slope of the land. One set of cascades proceeds from the Cerere sculptural grouping, and the other cascades from the Venere e Adone. The 25-meter wide, 800-meter long cascade, flowing from the Venere e Adone, is comprised of twelve waterfalls, each about a meter tall. The slope changes along the length of the cascade, but the heights of the falls is constant, meaning that the falls become closer together as one approaches the water's source. The weirs are respectable for their scale, rustic texture, softened lip, and the fish-scale patterned rollovers, which evenly distribute the overflows while establishing desirable activation.

Regrettably, at the time of this visit the cascades were covered in debris and operating at a low flow rate. Previous photographs show beautiful water action over clean, expertly carved surfaces.

The axis that connects a spring in the hillside to the Caserta Palace's north facing facade is nearly three kilometers long. The axial waters tumble, visually and conceptually, towards the palace in a nourishing gesture. The flows during this visit were not particularly attractive, but historic photography reveals them at other times to be, heavier, more free of encrusted debris, and quite delightful.

15 Villa Gamberaia

The original farmhouse and garden were built in the early 1500s, changing hands and being revised several times over the centuries, developing along the way the concentrated qualities and special reputation of its gardens.

Almost completely destroyed during World War II, the villa and grounds have been meticulously rebuilt, referencing historic maps and photographs. The parterre fountains examined here were incorporated around 1900, replacing the planted parterres, which were then about one hundred years old. The garden as it stands now is much as it has been for fifty years, a bit overgrown, urbane, stately.

Noteworthy fountains exist at each of the property's extremities, though the parterre fountains are the most importantly situated. Two fountains in separate courts of very different characters are just east of the villa, and a small fountain is incorporated into the property's northernmost garden.

The parterre fountains' longitunal asymmetry (the two pools farthest from the villa are noticeably lengthier than the two closer pools) is proportioned to compensate for perspectival shortening. The geometry works and its logic is rationally elegant, but the actual views of the pools up close are obscured by the varied, dense plantings. More fundamentally, the water features serve as a central organizing armature, simple, clear and interesting enough to permit all manner of eccentrically layered complexity to have evolved over the years, all the while maintaining an underpinning aura of serenity.

(Left) topiary subsumes a lion and pedestal, bordering the villa's forecourt with what has become a signature detail. (Top) The southeast view across the parterre garden and its numerous, varied elements. (Upper middle) an axial view from the villa through the rustic fountain and the south topiary opening. The path is about 1.25 meters wide. Each of the side pools are only about three meters wide, activated only by small jets mounted near their single curved edge. (Lower middle) The rustic fountain. (Bottom) The topiary exedra. The curved plan cradles a water garden with lilies, not visible from this low view, looking southeast.

The main garden's central area is organized by a water parterre of five pools sharing a rectanglular outline, with a circular pool in the middle framing a rustic fountain. Rocky jets (minature rustic fountains) ornament the curved segments of the framing pools.

Especially striking are the innumerable cross-connectioning views stretched between the elements in the crowded space and outward to the landscape beyond, a cat's cradle of invisible lines. The many plantings, sculptures and sub-spaces, each with an aura of gentle significance, multiplied and anchored by the pools, establish a uniquly powerful garden and water experience.

There are seven rustic fountains in this study. Three are in Aix-en-Provence, two at the Villa d'Este, one Hellbrunn Palace, and this one at the Villa Gamberaia, which is the smallest. There are others, though they often pass unnoticed. Their evolving, inchoate or accreted forms challenge presumptions of beauty while connecting us back to nature.

VILLA GAMBERAIA, FLORENCE

16 The Querini Stampalia Foundation

Modern era architect Carlo Scarpa painstakingly intervenes into the Venetian urban fabric with a delicate wooden bridge over the Rio di Santa Maria Formosa Canal, a boat arrival reception hall with a pooling floor, various interior spaces, and a bifurcated rear garden with fountains. All of the designs are performed with Scarpa's customary mastery of detail through the unrivaled skills of Venetian master craftsmen.

The water floor of the reception hall is curiously noisy with rhythmic water sounds delivered by a half-hidden, pulsing pump. A linear water garden in the rear yard plays the role of a runnel, with fresh water supplied through a miniature, marble labyrinth, fed from water flute. The runnel's waters are drained from the opposite end of the living system via a small, angular spout into a stylized spiral drain, carved from pale stone.

A downturned pipe's rhythmic pulses noisily refresh the water floor of an interior boat landing (top left).

What looks like a garden rill is just as much a linear water garden, perhaps 12 or 15 meters long. The water creates no perceptible motion or sound as it moves slowly through the slender channel.

A tiny pair of flute-like sprayers deliver a small amount of water to flow through a marble maze and fall into the linear lily pond (above).

At its far end, the flows are guarded by an antique, carved lion. Water passes beneath into a small papyrus water garden, to weep over an angled spout and fall into a concentric stone basin, where it is taken away. The spout's spill makes only a tiny sound in the planted garden.

Another water garden (right), of perhaps less remarkable character (depleted looking during this visit), draws attention to the back of the outside space and around to another space and more water on the obverse side of its divider wall.

17 Olivetti Showroom

Carlo Scarpa designed and oversaw construction of the exhibition space for Olivetti in 1957 and 1958, creating what is essentially a corporate sponsored art gallery for its products, and by extension, Scarpa's architecture. The showroom occupies a narrow corner unit on the north edge of the Piazza San Marco, in Venice—an extraordinary position with an international prominence.

A small, pleasing (though now partly inoperative) fountain by Carlo Scarpa plays a modest supporting role to the entranceway experience, positioned just left of the entry moment, immediately past the showroom's glass door, almost like a spiritual ablutions station.

The fountain's black stone pool reflects a bronze sculpture by Alberto Viani, which is positioned off-center in the pool, towards the light of the Piazza. Pool waters are fed from a wide metal spout, integreated beneath a horizontal, elaborated, decorative stone panel which incorporates the Olivetti logo, designed by Marcello Nizzoli. A circular opening in the panel frames the small fountain's wellspring, where a tiny horizontal spill introduces water to the spout. The spout's highly stylized design manages to be quite interesting without competing with the sculpture, mainly due to the discipline of its flatness.

The assembly of the ornamental panel with its round opening centered over a panel-formed box is reminiscent of a stringed musical instrument. The axial configuration and round opening is something like that of a Spanish guitar, and likely performed a similar effect in projecting delicate water sounds. This would be interesting, as the restrained, visible water actions could not solely account for the amplified sound character.

The patinaed bar at the head of the design expresses the water's source. A stream directed horizontally, oriented with the design's long axis flows into a shallow tray, leads to a wide spout, half-hidden beneath a mannered stone panel. The water flows gently into the black stone reflection pool to hardly disturb its reflective character.

Place of Places

The fountain collection was part of a complex that had become a World Heritage Site, heavily visited by large groups. This led those managing the situation to institute tightly organized guest schedules with start times and internal gates, preventing overcrowding but putting a dent in the experience. Fortunately, the obsticals could be side-stepped once inside, and there were quiet interludes between the swells.

The architectural chambers were powerfully composed and proportioned, and artfully adorned in loving detail. Poetry was literally carved into the walls and the water wove through the spaces in deft touches. While the chambers were each unique and strong, the relationships between them were surprisingly weak, almost non-existant. And there was no hint what the next space was going to be like, or even how it would be entered, meaning that being regularly surprised and awed was central to the place's choreographic narrative.

One writer likened the wavelets in the pools to the poetry on the walls, suggesting that the living pools, too, were offering poetic commentary. The calligraphic carvings, in seeming response, hinted towards a similarly familiar rythmic pattern, watery, with rolling, regular, crisp prominences. Even the gleaming wood and plaster had a softly finished quality in harmony with the pool surfaces. And there were places that the sunlight reflected from the pools splashed on nearby walls or pedestals, or even plantings, with that fluttering echo of water and light, almost like speech visualized, with the sound of the water nearby reinforcing the communications we would never completely decode.

18 The Alhambra and the Generalife

The Alhambra, or "The Red One," or "The Red Fort" was expanded upon the grounds of a previous fortress, which was underpinned by more previous Roman fortifications.

The Moors arrived in the late 800s and began a series of improvement projects when they occupied the hilltop, re-developing the Alhambra as a palace along with the associated Generalife, its gardens. The Moors thereby created all that is renowned on the site today. More or less continuous improvements to the architecture and landscape were undertaken by them until the complex's 22nd and last Nasrid ruler, Abu Abdallah Muhammad XII, was forced to leave in 1492 by King Feredinand II and Queen Isabella of Spain, by which time the Alhambra's reputation as a deeply enchanting place was long established.

There is a story about the sorrowful royal convoy of Muhammed XII's, finally and slowly leaving the Alhambra complex after its being held by the Moors for eight centuries. Throughout the journey, according to lore, Abu Abdallah had to put up with the unceasing complaints and shaming jeers from his mother, alledged with such off-hand heckles as, "You do well to weep like a woman for what you failed to defend like a man."

The complex was unsympathetically treated for many years, neglected and attacked by variously intervening armies, damaged by new construction, abandonments, military desecrations, even an earthquake.

A long program of incremental restoration, dating from the late 1820s through the mid-1930s, brought back much of the complex's original historic character, and its acclaim. Restorations and modifications continue to this day.

The inlets to the reflection pool at the Court of the Myrtles are chamberized in two elements (opposite, above and center). The small circular basin reflects concentric wavelets from the central jet. The water is then passed through a gate to the second element, a linear chamber, which dampens wave action so as to minimally disturb the large reflection pool's stillness.

The solitary, very simple fountain located just south of the Alhambra, (top) subtly conveys a refined, conceptual clarity. The jet that feeds the basin is not in the basin; it is outside, in a tiny, round pool of its own. The jet's water flows through a small channel before reaching the main pool, thereby assuring its splashes and wavelets hardly disturb the main pool's calm reflectivity (above).

THE ALHAMBRA, GRENADA

0 5 10 20 30M

The Court of the Lions (this page and opposite), a much celebrated space where a specific water design plays an integral role in the architectural statement. The proportions of the space, particularly that of the colonnade, together with the subtly scaled shallow steps, the dark cornice above, and the almost floating roof forms topping the composition, serve to define the space in a manner that speaks to matter and spirit in a richly balanced harmony.

The centerpiece of the design is an elevated, twelve-sided fountain basin over a radial arrangement of twelve, matching outward-facing lion sculptures. The bowl contains a central, vertical jet (not in operation during either of my visits) while the lions release streams of water from their mouths, flowing outwards. These streams flow into a 12-sided reception channel which frames the fountain while creating an island for it. This channel is also fed from the four runnels that bring waters from each of the four cardinal directions, oriented inwards. This leads to an interesting problem: Where is the water going? It seems to flow outward from the lions and inward from the arcades, at which point the narrative stops. The two directions are in conflict, with no obvious answer about where the water goes from the trough. The solution is to quietly sneak the water away through a casually integrated surface weep (left). While this layout works functionally, it is aesthetically unsatisfactory.

In the open space south of El Partal are a pair of axial waterways flowing to the north. The western sequence originates in a grotto nested in a garden facade (top left). Its modest waters spill from scuppers to course through runnels and pools, the highlight of which is their finale, where they split to frame a staircase. At that location the water is more for hearing than seeing, and we hear water flowing in stereo (left). Along the way, a water garden is presented offering a luxuriant display of lush, underwater verdancy (above).

Four massive Italian cypress trees closely shelter the fountain's raised marble pools and glittering, slender streams. The space's dark shade provides an effective backdrop for the sunlit streams and pool patterns.

GENERALIFE, GRENADA

0 5 10 20 50M

This small fountain courtyard fountain (above and center left) presents a delightfully textured pool from eight very tiny arches of water, organized into cornered pairs. These little jets are just large enough to activate the water's surface and create gentle sounds. They are about 10cm tall.

The fountain at the Court of la Acequia (right) was rebuilt in the mid-twentieth century with extremely slender, tall, gracefully arching jets, which create charming sounds and somewhat large splash areas.

A number of the Generalife's similarly-sized fountains (above) explore archetypal variation through simple geometries and restrained, discrete water expression. Small jets are used to activate pool surfaces and tap out sounds. In these designs, the positions of the jets and the shapes of the basins form the basis of the water expressions, particularly regarding wave pattern and sonic composition.

The Generalife staircase's much-admired handrail fountains functional success arises from clever design strategies. The small spinning pools transfer the waters' flow vectors from harsh angles to mild concentric reliefs—dampening splash. The curved landing channels also moderate flow energy. And the straight rails reduce gravity's contribution by unifying two flights with their landing to produce a flatter composite angle.

19 The Royal Palace of La Granja de San Ildefonso

King Philip V built La Granja as a summer palace, influenced by memories growing up at Versailles with his grandfather, King Louis XIV. The palace and grounds were geometrically organized, with the garden planned as the most important part of the estate. The King retired there, handing over the official duties to his son, King Louis I, who tragically died soon after, requiring Philip V to return to the throne, where he stayed for twenty years. La Granja was significantly expanded to provide the necessary facilities to function as the seat of government, including a much expanded garden, with four distinct territories populated by numerous allegorical water features.

The palace is approached from the northwest through the small town of Segovia, near Madrid. A collection of extraordinarily large trees—giants, really—confront visitors at the entrance. The original palace is to the right, and the garden, an exquisite extension of green open spaces richly bordered in plantings and accented with sculptures and some remarkably good urns, points to the southwest and its fountains. A tall, battle scene fountain, Fame, is centrally positioned in the garden, drawing visitors through the spatial sequence. A further fountain, the most famous on the property, The Baths of Diana, draws guests to the end of the garden (or it is supposed to—I missed it).

A lateral pathway extends from Fame to the northeast, venturing into an adjacent, much larger garden, which was part of the royal expansion. It is "The Garden of the Eight Ways," and strikingly composed, employing a distributed plan of fountains as lures and landmarks, inviting visitors through its wide landscape, yielding ultimately to a central space where an epiphany of radial opportunities and realizations are revealed. It may not be the fountains that we fully appreciate today, but their deployment in an ingenius plan.

The fourth garden precinct, to the northwest, is composed in side-by-side symmetrical parades of terraces, pools, falls, etc., ornamented with statuary, retaining walls, steps and ramps, relating back to the palace.

The geometric design of The Garden of the Eight Ways is ordred by a simple grid of sixteen squares, four to each side. The plan incorporates two diagonals transecting the squares through the center of the composition. This intersection provides the "Eight Ways," or directions, in which a visitor might choose to go. Eight framing fountains ring the central space, creating gateways between each pair to the eight terminal destinations, beyond. The first four fountains are spaced one unit outward. Two units outward are the four outbound fountains—two of which are effectively anchored in neighboring domains. All eight are visible from the central plaza. It is elegant that the eight outward fountains define another, larger square, rotated diagonally to the garden's native grid.

The central figure of Fame (opposite page), the large central fountain of the property's original garden is presented in this view looking to southwest. The sculpture is approximately twelve meters tall, six meters wide, in a pool with four smaller sculptures about twenty-five meters in diameter. The fountain is capable of launching a monumental throw of of columnar water up from the top angel-warrier's bugle to the impressive height of about thirty meters. The fountains at La Granja are rarely in operation; turned on one day every several weeks or so.

Two of the vistas and landmark fountains of The Garden of the Eight Ways (above).

The Royal Palace (middle left), viewed from the original garden looking northeast. The design mixes a heady architectural vocabulary organized symmetrically then enhanced with numerous delightful excentricities.

The giant trees at the entrance to La Granja (lower left) may average fifty meters tall. Fame, the central fountain of the original garden, complete view showing all elements (top, this page). The jets are off and the water level is presumably low by perhaps 40cm.

The Plan of La Granja (opposite page) shows the Palace at the upper center position, with the original garden extending to the southwest. The Garden of the Eight Ways is to the southeast of the original garden.

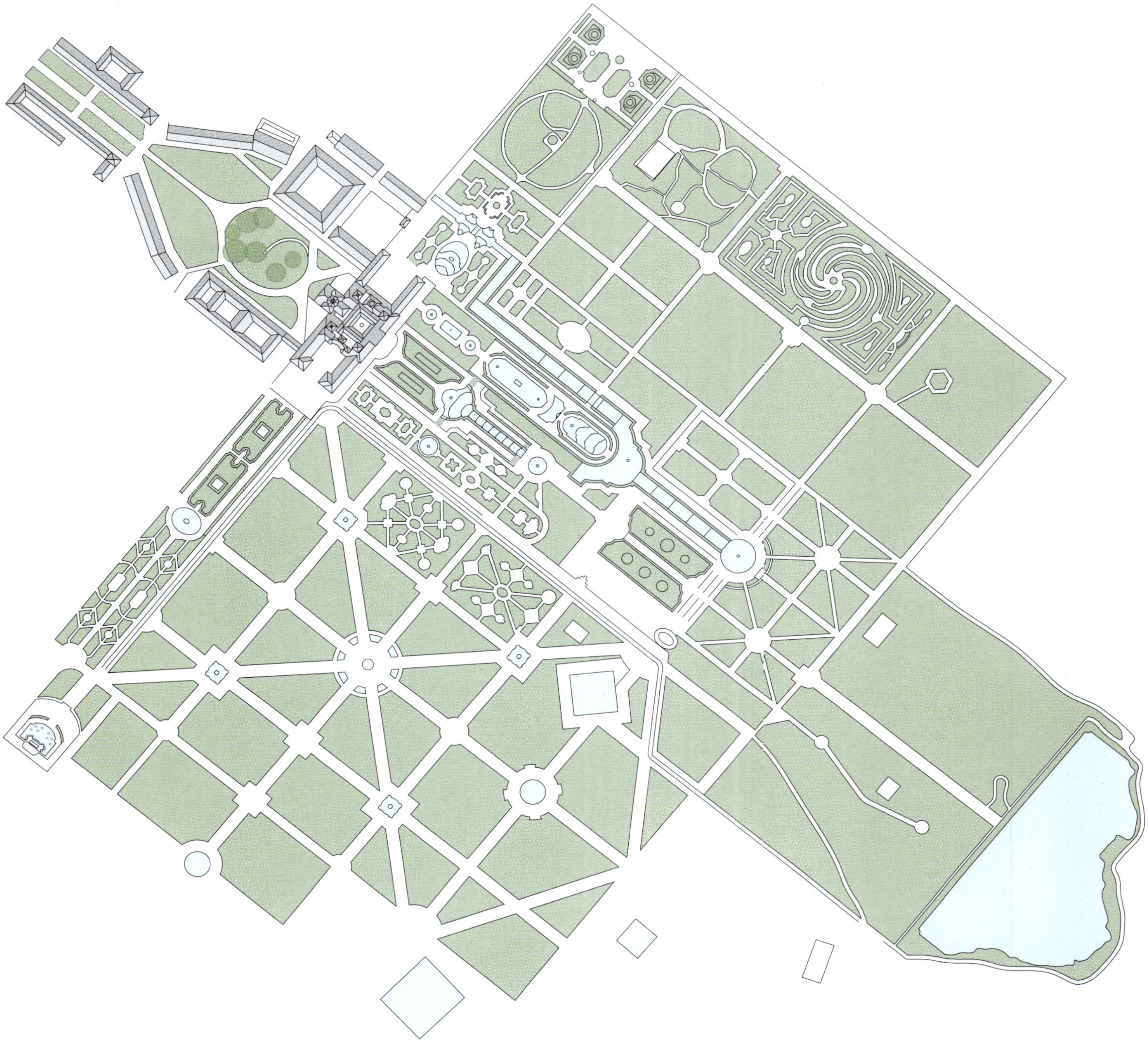

ROYAL PALACE OF LA GRANJA DE SAN ILDEFONSO

0 100 250M

The hub of The Garden of the Eight Ways is seen in the c enter images (both pages), where eight paths with eight gateway fountains encircle the central space. In the distance are elements of the eight destination landmark fountains (shown more immediately in the top photos).

Other locations and fountains in the garden's northern precincts (bottom photos, both pages). The Cascade, dressed in patterned tile (right), is not currently operational, due to wear and tear in its weirs and finishes.

The remarkable plan of the gardens was designed by Rene Carlier.

20 Park Guell

Originally planned as the the centerpiece to a housing development for those who wished to live in the green hills north of the city, Park Guell evolved to serve all Barcelona. Its open spaces are redolent in Gaudi's inventive and masterful ornament. The main entrance is formed of a central staircase leading up to the open, hypostyle hall, above which is the famous wide-open plaza bordered in undulating, mosaic benches affording benevolent views over Barcelona and the Mediterranean Sea. The staircase is occupied by three living system fountains. There are no other fountains in Park Guell.

The challenges of fully seeing the fountains at Park Guell are significant, due to the park's nearly constant crowds.

The three fountains present a compact concentration of water, plantings and ornamental devices arranged on the diagonal of the staircase. Water twists through the separated forms, providing a bit of unity to the group, but they are separate fountains.

At the top, a tiny rustic mound with a wellspring is framed by a triangular honorific from which water seeps into garden planters. A joyful Catalan Dragon rests downslope from the tripod, with waters flowing from its open mouth to a green pond. The ceramics are flawless. The dragon seems to enjoy his attentions and fame.

Water reappears in the second fountain from the city-facing side of a medallion, which is burnished with a Catalan shield mounted with a serpent's head, pouring into another water garden. Plantings, lively and wet, bussle upwards from the sloped basin.

The third fountain, we are told, evokes naturalism, the world, a compass, and a region in the Pyrenees known as l'Argenteria, but its abstration and Gaudi's hermetic language undermine lucid comprehension. The two other fountains are slender, but this one is formed in a wide, V-shape, covered in a mound of plantings with trickling waters flowing into a partly hidden and surprisingly vast subterranean reservoir. From this reservoir we hear the echos of the trickling droplets. Although the fountains tell their story from top to bottom, it is the mosaic seatwall at the base that first greets its many visitors.

A late afternoon view of the fountains from the belvedere (top left). The undulating bench borders the belvedere's two sides and front, partially visible though the visitor thicket (left). The celebrity Catalan Dragon is positioned in the top of the three fountains, water from his mouth pours into a small water garden's pool. Looking down from the top fountain (Opposite top), the charisma of Park Guell's entrance stair and fountain group draws this kind of crowd regularly. Viewed from the base, upwards (right), all three fountains can be mostly, momentarily, observed.

Views of the three fountains on the entrance staircase: the top images (this page) are of the highest fountain, while the images below are all of the central fountain. The lowest fountain encircles an abstract sculpture that serves as an armature for plantings over a pool recessed far below. The plantings are sometimes very dense (opposite top left), though at other times permit views of the armature (opposite bottom).

21 The Barcelona Pavilion

Ludwig Mies Van Der Rohe's influential Barcelona Pavilion was demolished after the 1928 World Expo for which it was built. All the parts were lost. Living in photos and legend for decades, the structure was meticulously reconstructed in 1986 to a high degree of accuracy.

The architecture is comprised of floating rectangular planes, arranged orthogonally to shape space without capturing it, imparting to the space a gentle movement. The proportions of the planes, their edges and interrelationships, and the volumes they almost define, establish the movement's steady cadence, which, for the most part, folds laterally around various corners, under and out from the sheer ceiling plane. The building's two reflection pools extend this folding system in different ways. The main pool doubles the open elevation of the architecture to reiterate the movements in reverse, underscoring the architectural concept. The second pool reflects the spatia play on the vertical axis, turning the flow down into the pool, folding it under the floor of the pavilion, orienting towards the other pool. One can almost feel the energy of the space moving below. At the Barcelona Pavilion, the reflected scenes in the pools do not suggest the other world, rather, Mies has established that the reflections are part of this world, engaging, and in the light.

(Left), the view from within the architecture to the pavilion's unsheltered courtyard is provided with a touch of the infinite, due to the water's reflectivity. A relatively small amount of water is sufficient to the task.

(Upper right), the park is not wall maintained, but the Pavilion is in flawless condtion. It's two reflection pools are not visible until one gets close to the structure and surmounts the entrance stairs.

(Center right), arrival view across the water to the portion of the design now used for a gift shop.

(Lower right), the reflection pool doubless the height of the garden wall, but slices of the trees are seen from afar above the edge of the wall and from below as well, upon close examination. With no expressed water inlets or outlets, and with winds almost completely blocked, an untroubled and silent reflectivity is the pool's singular contribution. A dark marble basin finish idealizes the reflective capacity of the water's surface.

(Top and center left) the pool reflects the architecture's spatial strategy, folding laterally under its flat roof plane, and folding vertically via the imaginary space established by the pool's reflections.

(Above right and below left) the measure of space between the large pool and the building establishes that while under the pavilion's roof, the small pool is the more influential, but as soon as one leaves the canopy's zone, a switch happens, and the large pool becomes the stronger player, carrying the more important message.

(Opposite page) the smaller reflection pool also engages the spatial games of the pavilion, but differently than the front pool. Here, the space projects over the pool, where it is stopped by the courtyard wall, then folds down into imaginary space, and would seem to fold again under the realm of the architecture.

22 The Mercury Fountain

Sandy Calder's Mercury Fountain was commissioned in 1937 by the Spanish Republican government together with Picasso's Guernica to recognize the brutality of the Spanish Civil War. The Mercury Fountain specifically references Franco's attack on the mercury mines near the town of Almadén. The fountain is also interpreted as a tribute to the workers who were sickened and died due to the mines' toxicity.

Mercury, the element, has some physical similarities to water and a host of differences. Mercury is the only metal we know with a melting point high enough to be a liquid at standard tempurature. Mercury is denser than water—13.5 times as dense; pour them both into a glass vase and the water will form a sharply defined layer over the mercury. Mercury has a higher surface tension than water—seven times as high. Mercury beads up a little more than water on a given surface. Mercury is half again as viscous as water. Both materials fall through space at the same rate, which respects gravity, not density or mass. Mercury does not act as a solvent, dissolving so many other materials the way water does. Mercury does not evaporate as quickly as water does; if we watch a shallow pool of mercury in a ceramic bowl on Monday, nearly all of it will still be there on Friday. And its vapor will tend to condense into tiny droples near the evaporative source. Water is transparent, with a reflective surface and an obserable refractive interior, while mercury is opaque, with a bright, silver-colored reflectivity; so, mercury offers light no refractions. Finally, water is the basis of life, while mercury is a heavy metal poison, dangerous or even lethal, whether ingested or absorbed through the skin.

The mercury fountain is isolated from human contact, contained within a glass-enclosed zone at Foundation Miro. We cannot hear it because the glass is insulated, but we can watch the mercury's twirling play in Calder's clever design. Examination of the period photograph displayed above the fountain reveals that it is not fully operational. Slender streams of arching mercury had been used to create a basketweave over the pool. The streams have been removed, no doubt for safety.

Looking closely into the corners of the glass room, away from the fountain's edge, we can find numerous, tiny specks of mercury. At first I took them for evidence of far flung splash, which we do not see with water, but I later learned they were reconstituded from mercury vapor, and physical proof of the danger of this lovely toxic fountain and of the absolute requirement for its sealed enclosure.

(All photos), the mercury is only a little bit eery, in spite of is many physical property differences from water. What it lacks in transparency it seems to make up for in reflectivity. We can barely detect that it has a different surface tension. Due to its sealed glass enclosure, we regrettably do not obtain the experience of hearing flowing quicksilver.

ESPAGNOL
D'ALMADEN

23 Madeira

Portugal's famous port, and its sugar and bananas, come from the three small islands of Madeira, located in the Atlantic about a thousand kilometers southwest of Lisbon. The islands' hills are covered in forest from the tropical rains and fine soils that make the land so good for cultivation. Irrigation waters are brought down from higher altitudes' rainfall collection by way of a traditional network of stone and concrete channels, or Levadas. The use of levadas on Madeira is widespread, an ongoing concern dating back four hundred years. There are over 800 kilometers of levadas on tiny Madeira.

Walking on the gentle slopes cut into the high hills beside the winding levadas lends a quiet, introspective, healthful experience. As the slope is fairly consistant at just a few degrees, the walk is not taxing and the waters, too, do not rush. The open channels function well in the transport of water. Open channel flow is a specific area of engineering study, having to do with the conduction rates of water, based upon slope, friction, cross section and volume. Madeira's levadas are all technically based on a mastery of open channel flow. What I saw in channels a half meter wide with flows 100mm deep, looked to be handling about 300 liters per minute, with plenty of additional capacity.

The levadas are almost all in the shade of dense tree canopies, dimly reflecting diffused sunlight on the water's fluttering surfaces. The flow's sounds are similarly mild, though they permeate the forest experience.

A qualitative water observation is clarified at Madeira regarding the nature of wavelets in the levadas. We are presented with two kinds of waves—standing waves and moving waves. The standing waves set up occasional fixed divots, here or there, together with overlapping diagonal patterns of fixed ridges in the water's surface. The moving water waves, which are quite differen in character, are clearly visible passing through the standing waves. With time, one can see them both plainly. With more time, one wishes the standing waves were not happening. Perhaps the most pure version of the levada display type, aesthetically speaking, would have only the actions of freely moving waves and no standing waves at all.

The 'levadas' of Madeira are concrete forms bringing rainfall down from the hills' higher elevations to the crops growing below. They are skillfully constructed to handle planned water volumes and they are built to last. Relatively shallow slopes conduct the waters steadily to their destination. The mix of standing and moving waves (opposite bottom right) are typical for the character of the water in these open channels of flow.

24 Dubrovnic Fountains

The historic city of Dubrovic is walkable, perched on a plateau over the Mediterranean, and finished in white stone. There is a grandure in spite of the intimate scale, and the main street, the Stradun, builds a generous visual shaft of space connecting the entrance gate beside the Velika Onofrijeva Fontana, to a plaza, three hundred meters to the east. There, another fountain is anchored, the Mala Onofrijeva. They are the large and the small fountains of Dobrovnic.

The fountains were built from 1438-1442 by the Italian architect, Onofrio della Cava, who also built the aqueduct that brought their waters from a spring, nearly 12 kilometers away. They are quite different looking from each other and occupy the two endpoints of the street. Both provide fresh drinking water for the city's residents. Smaller civic fountains dot the town in less prominent locations.

The Velika Onofrijeva provides water from sixteen, constrantly flowing, artfully carved masked stations around its faceted perimeter. The water comes from a spring 12 kilometers away, a significant technical achievement of its day. The top of the central sistern is crowned in a dome with an oculus allowing light and fresh air to the water stored inside. The water feature's design is something like a telescope, with a pair of steps up to a solid, stone railing forming an outside ring, with the cistern seeming to rise from the ground below to where the dome, the next stage, is set back and reaches farther up to where the oculus profiles the sky. A sculpture of a dragon once topped the cupola, gone since 1667.

The much smaller Mala Onofrijeva is octagonal, partially embedded in the face of architecture, and adorned in lavish, dream-like ornamentations by the Milanese artist, Petar Martinov. These include forms of fish, angels, scenes of water carrying, and enriching geometrical flourishes finishing in an elaborate pinacle. It hosts eight serving stations.

The character of the flows from both fountains is unplanned. And today, few people obtain water from public fountains. What these fountains represent—one large and the other small—is a picture of the past when the provision of fresh water from honorably located and sculpturally adorned public basins formed a fundamental part of the life of the community who lived in the white stone city.

The simple, Medieval fuso form of the Mala Onofrijeva, (left), is made into a period landmark by its mature carvings, of which the fish seem begruding (and no longer operating).

The Velika Onofrijeva, (right and following pages) is a cistern with streaming waters from sixteen mask-adorned stations. The masks are remarkable for their inventive variety adeptly balanced with consistency. Each mask tells its story from a different perspective. And its a toss-up if the faces are the more remarkable, or their articulate surrounds.

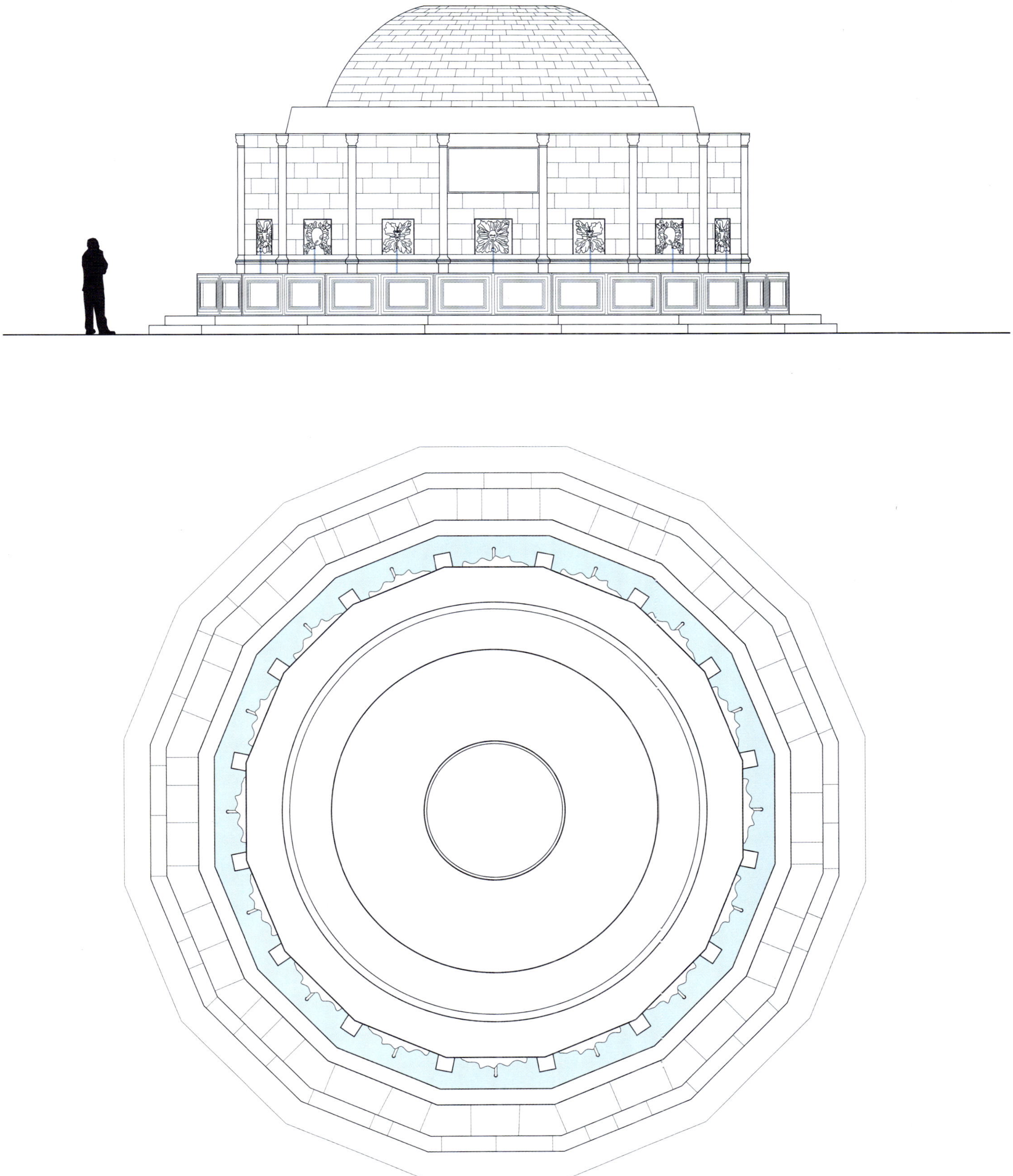

GREAT ONOFRIOS FOUNTAIN, DUBROVNIC

0 1 2 3 5M

Fans of horology will appreciate the clock tower's complications, including a spinning gold orb moon phase indicator (left), which stands above and brings honor to the Mala Onofrijeva (above and opposite). The fountain is sheltered by an arched niche, or apse, which frames its form and reflects the sounds from the streams.

25 Schloss Hellbrunn

Hellbrunn Palace is a day palace, meaning that its purposes included court activities, audiences, socials, and entertainments, but no one spent nights there. There are no bedrooms. The original palace was built in 1615, by Prince Archbishop Markus Sittikus, who conceived of several of its so-called, trick fountains. His architect was the northern Italian, Santino Solari. Subsequent additions and alterations to the grounds and its water features continued until 1750.

At Hellbrunn, there are three categories of water features: ponds and canals, decorative fountains, and trick fountains. The pooling waters reach across the large site, connecting the various areas into a unified, reflective, grounded landscape. They are fed from mountain streams and serve as reservoirs.

The decorative fountains contribute to the liveliness of their spaces, animating with jets, falls and cascades, some of which are unusually refined, even dainty. This category includes the Rustic Fountain, which, like the two rustic fountains at the Villa d'Este, are about as rough and wild as they can be. Some of the decorative fountains are elegantly presented ideas, such as the visual joke of the water chain presented in voids looking like chain links, or the several intances of glassy water domes and waterfalls through which we peer to see tiny, colored figurines or mosaic designs.

The third category—the one for which Hellbrunn is so renowned, is its collection of trick fountains. These are small, water-powered machines, or automata, with clever, remarkably engineered actions, elegantly presented water displays, and nifty or humorous sometimes annoying action ideas. By far, the best known is the Royal Table, a stone dining table surrounded by ten stone stools. The table incorporates a big trough for chilling wine—reminiscent of the one at the earlier Villa Lante, and the stools have little slots in their tops, looking like typical, useful handholds, but actually being openings for squirting water. Such a charmer, that Markus Sittikus.

Other trick fountains include a crown balancing on a jet varying in height (a sophisticated display of Bernoulli's Principle) intended to picture the rise and fall of political authority, occasional fine sprays from an elk's antlers, a grotesque mask in the Neptune Grotto whose eyes roll and tongue protrudes, rotating model boats, and bird whistling sounds. Most technically impressive is the Mechanical Theater, completed in 1750 by the Archbishop Andreas Jakob Graf Dietrichstein, where an entire village is showcased in a cabinet-like building, animated by two-hundred miniature, water-powered automata. The characters represent all the people of a village, in constume and acting out their roles to the accompaniment of water-powered music.

The Royal Table (left), conceived by that estemed local prankster, Prince Archbishop Markus Sittikus. The jets are only about 3mm in diameter, but express over three meters high. Looking into the sun from the exedra brings out their sparkle. (Top), Hellbrunn Palace's arrival court is dry, like Versailles; all the water features are beyond. (Above) the ellaborate garden exedra, offering sunny places to sit as it frames the base of the Royal Table.

(Top left), the exedra and Royal Table. The table incorporates three water features—the squirting benches, the wine chilling trough, and four corner spouts to seashell basins. Garden cascades abound throughout the site; these two examples (upper middle left and right) show variants of progressively scaled steps. (Lower middle left) An interior fountain with chasing figures wheeling around an encrusted mound occupied by a singing dragon. An intriguing mask operates mechanically with an interior, rocking chamber that fills and releases to animate the figures eyes, jaw, and tongue. The nostrils issue slender streams continuously. (Left), one of the many sculptural, decorative fountains on the site; this one in front of the Royal Table.

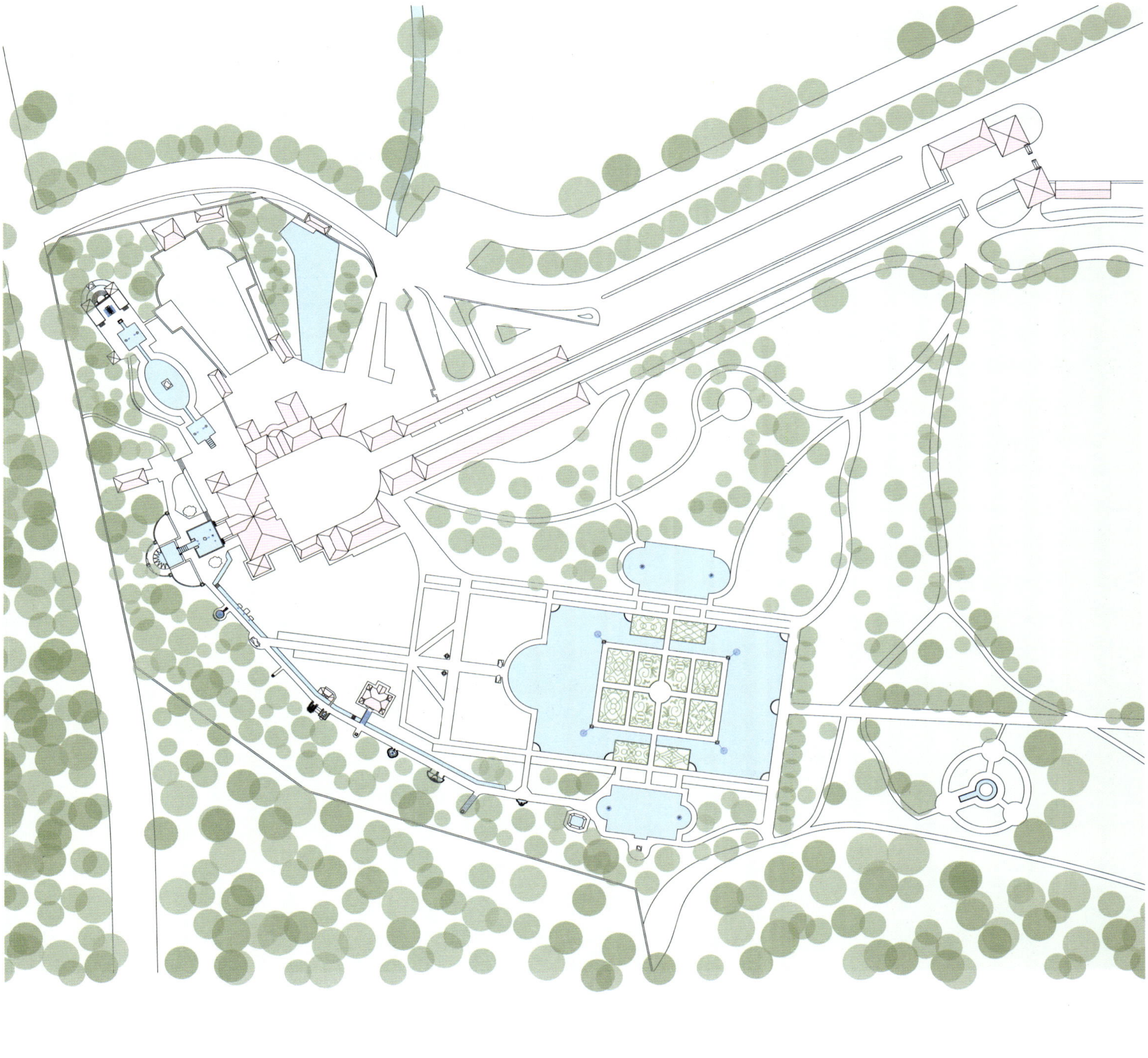

HELLBRUN PALACE, SALZBURG

0 25 50 100 200M

(Top) one of a few cascades on the grounds with this inventive decorated detail. Traditional cascades share the problem of the first fall not being as 'set up' as the subsequent falls, here in white-water. But the first is treated like a window, leading to the clever, layered graphic design.

(Center Left Above) a rustic mound not unlike those at the Villa d'Este or the Villa Gamberaia. (Center right above), The canal incorporates tiny, water-powered automata, like (left) two laborers with a mill; spent mechanical waters flow outward in a slender stream. (Opposite upper), A shallow pool is occupied by a delicate Eros sculpture poised over a dome of water encasing tiny plantings. (Opposite lower) the visual joke of a water chain carved to actually look like chains. The wet/dry duality is superbly controlled, and the slope of the panel functions perfectly; the sound has a very mild twinkling character.

(Opposite), The Village, with its 200 animated characters, all in constumes related to their activities, with aligned movements. (Top left, This Page) The garden building houses a grotto, within which is (Top right) the rising and falling royal crown, one of the better known trick fountains at Hellbrunn, along with the squirting antlers (Above Left). (Upper center right), Surprise tunnel of water and its virtually invisible nozzle detail. (Upper center left), One of the many, very small automata fountains. The southern section of the property presents the pond and island with parterres (Lower center right), which offers a less intensive space for wandering about the landscape.

26 Schloss Linderhoff

The King of Bavaria, Ludwig Otto Friedrich Wilhelm, or Ludwig II, ascended the throne in 1864. The Linderhoff property was at that time the royal hunting lodge. In 1869, Ludwig II purchased lands all around the lodge, and in 1870, transformations began, leading to the completion of the palace and formal landscape, the relocation of the hunting lodge, and the incorporation of other special constructions. Projects for additional improvements were planned until the King's death in 1886.

The site is symmetrically developed along a north-south axis traversing a pronounced, saddle-shaped valley between two hills. The arrangement is such that the low center of the formation is occupied by an articulate forecourt with a large reflection pool, fronted by the palace and the two axial extensions rising in the landscape, above to the south and north. On the south side is a sequence of steps, retaining walls and terraces, completing in a small, stone temple. To the north, behind the palace and beyond its flanking gardens, is a grotto with a sculptural grouping of Neptune, above-which is an axial cascade leading from the interior of the hill, topped by a green-painted lath pavilion. Fountains punctuate the landscape from end to end, several with sculptures of polished gold.

Periodically, the central reflection pool's gilt sculpture will issue a thick, white column of water to an impressive height of more than twenty meters. A copper-finished fountain with mermaids, just south, beckons visitors to climb the stairs to upper terraces. Two matching fountains in the main terrace enliven east and west gardens with festidious, polished, dome-shaped flows. The cascades above the Neptune Fountain use rolled weirs to form activated, glassy waterfalls. A dutiful accounting of water features would also touch on the gilt fountains to the east and west of the palace and the best known of them all—the watery grotto presenting a scene from Wagner's opera, Tannhauser.

These descriptions do not convey the nuanced conviction or dreamlike ideality of Linderhoff, residing in its perfect hills setting, far from the rest of the world. The displays in all the fountains are of an unusually rarefied quality. The white column is exceptionally coherent for so energized a flow. The mermaid fountain's waters spout, swirl, drape and splash flawlessly. The Tannhauser Grotto is the most etheral of places; its internally illuminated still pool works to bend experience to an exotic, alternate reality. The formal cascade's flows achieve a character both strident and gleaming. And the Neptune Fountain presents the water god bursting from his grotto, forcefully and seriously, with the glorious powers to set things straight.

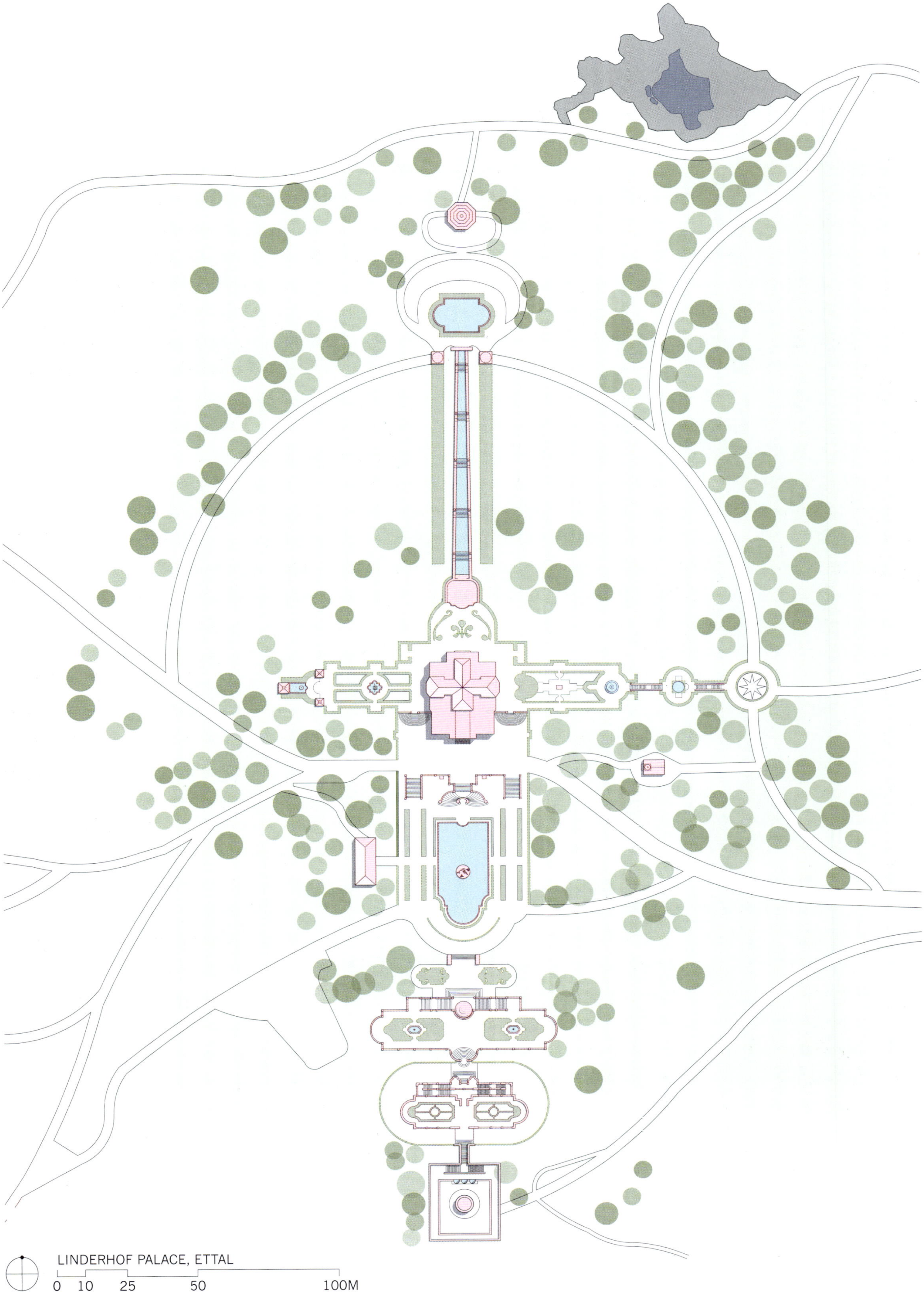
LINDERHOF PALACE, ETTAL
0 10 25 50 100M

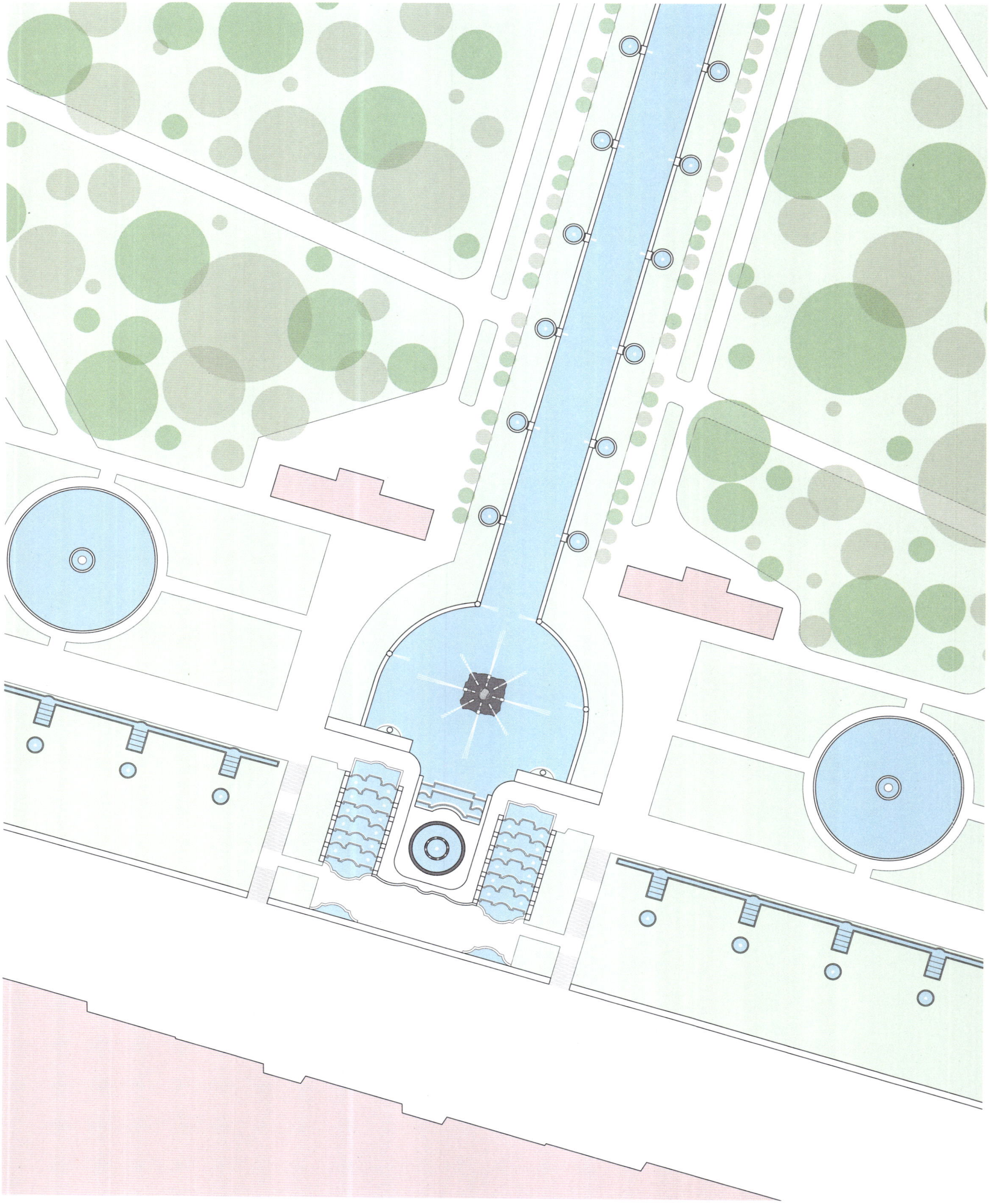

PETERHOF PALACE, ST. PETERSBURG

0 10 25 50 100M

27 Peterhof Palace

Peterhof Palace is comprised of a connected grouping of nine palaces and various gardens in St. Petersberg, the regional capitol. The idea for the composition was envisioned by Peter the Great after he wrested the coastal lands from Swedish control. Construction of the palaces and their significant improvements were undertaken from 1709 to 1756. The palace's gardens were designed by the architect, Jean-Baptiste Alexandre Le Blond, who had previously worked with Le Notre at Versailles. Numerous fountains glorify the grounds and architecture, many incorporating statuary finished in polished gold.

The Grand Cascade takes its inspiration from the cascades built by Louis XIV at the Chateau de Marly, now gone. It is centrally positioned, with two sections flanking an architectural grotto occupied by a circular fountain with vertical geysers enclosed by water arches. The cascades' seven levels of waterfalls are each two meters tall, with pleated flows thoughtfully veiling bas relief artworks and brackets of green stone and gold. Tall geysers line the stepped cascades with superbly controlled, horizontally aligned crowns. (This arrangement of bordering a pool on one side with jets leads to a lot of spray leaving the area of the pools, with almost half the water in transit landing beyond the wet territory.)

Below the Grand Cascade is the fountain, Samson Tearing Apart the Jaws of the Lion, a symbolic depiction of a Russian military triumph. A vertical stream jets from the throat of the lion—its last breath. Water arches, like tributes, spray outwards in all directions from the mouths of fish. All of the figures are gilt, composed on a rustic stone island.

A canal extends north-northeast from the Samson Fountain, six hundred meters to the Baltic Sea in a gesture clearly alluding to Versailles. The solar orientation of Peterhof Palace's axis of symmetry is a bit different Versailles', but it shares somewhat similar afternoon sunlight, which plays across the axial view from the left.

A trick fountain is to be found inside the palace, near the Grand Cascade. It takes the form of a dining table, laden with food. The visitor reaching for a piece of fruit is squirted with water. Another joker having a field day.

A visit to the Palace's fountains was not possible during the time of this writing due to Russia's war with Ukraine; hence, the missing photography and detailed examination of the designs.

28 Prague Castle

The large and complex Prague Castle surveys Prague and Vltava River from its position atop the acropolis-like, Hradcany Hill. The formation of the castle's components includes eleven interior courtyards, four of which have interesting water features, but it must be said that the marvelous, general composition lends distictive energy to all its constituent elements.

Kohl Fountain occupies the first, large courtyard. It is eight meters tall in a three-tier composition, favoring sculptural expression over water action.

Figures at each level are busy holding things up. The water is expressed in the slenderest of streams, aimed to low, downward angles, with a finely trickling stream from a ridged and rolled upper level weir. Water streaming from eight, tiny ports at the seond tier bowl land in the reception pool to find itself contained by a basin rubbed free of detail, and held at a low level to handily dispense with splash stains. As a result of all these decisions, the fountain marks space with a measuyre of resolution while the water statement involves a least possible attitude. The totality of the installation, however, receiving the graces of Prague Castle effect manages to survive with its dignity intact. A nearby, royally protected water well contributes to scenic character.

The bronze statue of St. George, in the next courtyard, also presents water in the tiniest manner, here with a heroic and impressivey detailed, flying bronze railing serving to protect the unwary from its ten centimeter reception pool.

Another courtyard's Cerrati fountain, which used to be located elsewhere (which shows) and is claimed to have once held the statue of St. George (which doesn't show), is augmented with a grotesque, mysteriously combining the scroll of an ionic capital with the mask of a lion. The lion mask offers an expression somewhere between the perplexed and the bemused. A small slim-fan spout is starkly below, with the deft touch of a tracheotomy's breathing tube. The tube's flows are conducted at an order-of-magnitude below its designed rate.

(Opposite page) The main fountain at Prague Castle presents a central column with two elevated bowls over a base reception pool. Water does not overflow the edges of the bowls, but is highly controlled through just a few very slender streaming spouts aimed at sharp angles into the bowls below. On the visit day, the sun was up in a clear sky offering good visitility of the small scaled streams, which would otherwise be nearly invisible. On this beautiful day, the delicate displays fulfill.

(Upper opposite) the sculpture incorporates an integral spout made of three tiny tubes extending from a landscape protrusion. The reception pool is shallow and courtly, with a minimal curb. A circular railing contributes notably to the composition with a machine-age, riveted character. (Lower opposite), a stone basin oncorporates a lion mask with a crimped spout below, perhaps to generate a slim-fan jet. (Top) the main court's caged well proudly exhibits a distinguished pedigree. (Above lower right), the finest common workmanship is exhibited in a simple brass pipe, support stem and mannered spout with another crimped tip. Waters flow into a basin configured as for animal drinking.

29 Tivoli Gardens

Tivoli Gardens, an urban amusement park of roughly six hectares, is located downtown, in the city of Copenhagen, Denmark. The hugely popular park was conceived and built by Georg Carstensen, an army officer. He opened the park in 1843 and it has been in more-or-less continuous use since. The park is planned with numerous winding pathways, gardened open spaces, and pleasurable distractions, including dining, drinking, shopping, amusing rides and theatrical venues. The park is never finished, with alterations and refinement projects regularly underway.

Especially inventive and well-known water features have been incorporated into the park; most notable are the fountain incorporating glass columns of animated air bubbles at the Nimb Hotel and the transforming fountain in the garden in front of the Tivoli Concert Hall. The thirty-two wooden bowl fountains integrated into the garden on the park's north side are unique in their constellation-like scattering and surprising materiality. The park's lake, with its intricately developed perimeter, is skillfully done, surrounded as it is by labyrinthine walks, steps, ramps, decks, artworks and trees, all of which frame and present the criss crossing views to numerous, internal landmarks. The lake currently hosts a show fountain curiosity at night with laser and colored light. A small fruit tree and boy fountain is charming and finely made, though without special water expression. One of Tivoli Gardens' rides incorporates a ring pool ornamented with fan jets, referenced as the model for Disneyland's Dumbo ride fountain. Tivoli Gardens was the prime inspiration for Walt Disney's groundbreaking project of the 1950s, Disneyland.

One end of the amusement park is given over to colorfully painted thrill rides, and the water features populate this area in ways that embellish the ride experiences. (Top right) visitors are threatened from below by tall geysers. (Center right pair) the pedestal for a spinning ride incorporates waterfall-like fans arranged in a skirting over a circular, blue pool. At this moment, they look a bit rough from a maintenance short-fall, and a little dull under the overcast sky, but on an attractive day we can envision them sparkling warmly. (Bottom right) a traditional fountain is enterprisingly detailed with a miniature figure atop a raised bowl with a perimeter of dentils, providing the modest overflows with a measured cadence of fall segments. The segment theme is reiterated in the design of the bench's radial sections, which share the segments' scale. The upturns on the bench segments' water side gestures to the nearby falling water.

(Upper left and middle left) the bubble-activated glass cylinders were an innovation when the fountain was installed. Nearby, this painted metal fountain of the young man with a lemon tree provides a small landmark for an orientation spot/rest area. (Lower group) the bowls look scattered, but they are organized through a garden arranged in parallel green swaths and permeating brick paths. The bowls are fabricated in wood, with a rough, hand-hewn character, each with a central jet. I counted twenty-nine bowls—many more than a visitor sees at any one time.

(Next page) nighttime views of the water features and the lake. The park is surprisingly dark at night, with elements in space appearing to float in isolated illumination.

TIVOLI GARDENS, COPENHAGEN

0 10 25 50 100M

30 Neptunbrunnen

The idea for this fountain in Berlin is attributed to the respected architect, Karl Friedrich Schinkel, but it was Reinhold Begas who designed and sculpted this monumental work in 1891. Bronze is the principle material, and here we are presented with a large, highly articulated casting. Due to its scale (the central form is about eight meters tall and ten meters across) it must have been cast in sections, welded together, and the markings refinished to invisibility. There is great skill here in the modeling and the casting.

(A restoration of the bronze, stripping it of the mottled, brownish patina and refreshing the original surface finish, would do wonders for its physical presentation in the city. For the time being, it looks a bit decayed and untended; no fault of the artwork.)

The composition is energetic and detail is remarkable. All of the figures are good, but the clumped fish nets, numerous infants, rearing lobster, climbing octopus, and the benign Neptune at the peak are standouts. Positioned on the reentrant corners of the quatrefoil basin are four monumental, solemn and impressive female figures.

The water action at Neptunbrunnen (we must imagine) plays second string to the power of the sculptures, compromising the expression of the fountain, as a fountain.

Neptunbrunnen could be compared with Fontaine de l'Observatoire, in Paris. They are both about the same size with sculptures and water setting up assertive fields of self-referential formalism. There are differences. The Paris fountain shows us superior flows over a raised pool with a more spirited energy and a stronger dialectic between the sculptures and the water. The Berlin fountain
is fiercer, darker, more complex, brooding, more physically accessible given its lower reception basin; perhaps spiritually deeper.

It might be argued that the Neptunbrunnen needed its thinner jets, narrow falls, and a tepid pool to be in balance with its more articulate sculptures. But the qualitative shortfall of its waters are not so handily disposed of, fine as the sculptures are.

The heroic casting is itself rewarding. Probably the greatest of the world's many Neptune fountains—or at least in terms of its sculptural presence, in spite of the degraded state of the sculpture's current finish. Regrettably, the fountain was not observed with its water active. Published photography shows a handful of thickened streams spraying in the space around the fountain, and overlfows from the two horizontal clamshells.

Trapped Goods

The famous fountains presented a little bit of a surprise when I made it up close to get a good look. They were, well, less favorful than might have been presumed by their celebrity, or by their carefully proportioned promises when viewed from afar.

The fountains' sprays and falls were adequate in design and skilfully delivered, though perhaps a touch dutiful. What effected me were the countenances and body language of the sculptures, which seemed trapped, frozen and quite dispirited about their lot. The figures were superficially beautiful, but they were uncomfortably posed and woe-begotten, like water gods in a funk. Perhaps there was a poetic clue to decode the scene, but I didn't have the wit to see it. And while I watched, each of them, the tritons and naiads, mer-rulers and mer-helpers, stood fast.

After a while I was almost impressed by the gods' resolute dedication, and it struck me that maybe the problem was in me; that the sculptures were fine. I was making it all up. It was a dreary day; I should come back another time and look again. Which is exactly what I did, two years later, when they were all waiting for me, unmoved, sorrowful, the same.

31 The Fountain of the Innocents

A photograph from previous decades shows the water on the steps performing far better than today. The thin, crystalline flow in that image appears to be interwoven with open patterns of white-water lace from the upper step's agitation, and the two water characters, the clear and the frosty, mix to create some kind of idealized bunting. A very effective visual event, indeed.

Today, insufficient maintenance starves the steps of their previous glory, but the dynamism of the spring in the cupola remains a marvel of chandelier-like richness. The overall proportions of this dignified fountain building, centrally positioned in its aptly proportioned square plaza establishes the Fountain of the Innocents as not only the oldest fountain in the City of Lights, but perhaps the most refined.

Some interesting history and mythology shrouds the fountain's identity. Its name arises from a legend that the fountain was originally part of a special cemetery, solely for infants. Archeology has not provided confirmation. The sad and beautiful name endures.

The fountain was originally a wall fountain, built in a three-sided projection and later moved to the center of the plaza in which it currently stands with the fourth side added. Although surely true, close examination suggests the structure's evolution was a bit more detailed.

There are two marvelously carved bass relief nymphs on each face of the cupola, for a total of eight, and they were clearly carved by the same hand, at the same time, and they fit so well into the four elevations that at least portions of the upper structure was probably part of what was invented when the fountain was rebuilt. We might also conjecture that the sheltered chalice was incorporated at the same time, as it is so fine and perfectly suited to its current task. The idea of the steps may be from the original construction, with a wellspring on top to feed them. The original fountain was probably no match for its masterpiece decendent, located a mere stone's throw from the Centre Pompidou and the Stravinsky Fountain in the Fourth Arrondissement, Paris.

One of the eight muses posted around the fountain (left), this one pouring from an ornamented vase. All of the muses take different poses, sharing a water theme.

(Right) The cascades are hybrid-elliptical in plan, with slightly complex profiles relating to how they were built up in segments. Today the flows are stretched too thin and barely cover the steps, but in their heyday, they intersperced lacy white-water strands through shimmering, clear sheets. By the look of it, the cascades feed on the leavings from the superb challice on top, and a second pump meant to supply them what they need for success, is not in operation.

The chalice's flow (above) may be the best example of its kind in the world, where a simple, and not too large water form (less than a meter tall) is transformed by spray device, steps, a transition pool and surface textures into an outstanding water presentation.

The fountain's cascades (left) berift of their previous rich flows, has become too transparent to be visual effective.

Seating around the fountain (lower left) is part of the fountain design, organized on four sides of a square plan with shade trees.

FOUNTAIN OF THE INNOCENTS, PARIS

0 1 5 10M

A valuable shot of the chalice dry (left), waiting for an even more informative image, closer and from above, which would explain a bit how its vibrant flows are achieved. The cascades (above and below) may be starved, but they still show quality in their threadbare mode.

32 Place des Vosges

The immaculate square of Place du Vosges, built by King Henri IV as a speculative real estate concept based upon the creation of an ideal open space framed by symmetrical architecture, is fortified by a quartet of matching fountains, approached diagonally from the square's corners or its center.

The water design begins at the top of a four-level composition, perhaps five meters above the ground, where a spring from a thin spindle's wide nozzle creates a glassy, slightly textured veil, in a fine, beret-like, saucy style. This water stages in a small upper bowl with a rounded rim, which directs its overflows to a wider bowl below—without the distraction of wide splashes—which is achieved by aiming the water inwards. Such inverted waterfalls are usually a prime signal of clumsiness, but here the effect seems right, partly because its tall, tiered design is prevented from looking chubby or top-heavy by the trim waistline the inversion creates. The backward-flowing falls are also sanctioned by the very good character of their flow, which is textured and animated in spite of the weir's rounded profile. Rounded weirs without special detailing will usually dampen water character, but here the water's flow rate and the breakaway detail at the rim's underside manifests in a nicely feathered outcome.

The main bowl gathers the waters from above to send it to the basin at grade through the small faces of twenty lions mounted on the bowl's underside, not far from its leaf-textured, dry rim. The flows take the form of slim-fan streams, which are difficult to achieve and expertly crafted. The slim-fans convincingly unify with the mouths of the lions and stream outwards with notewor-thy lateral energy. The impacts from the many streams create much activity on the basin's water surface, sparkling under the sun, and splashing only a little onto the gaged, rounded profile of the basin's stone coping.

The four fountains of the Place des Vosges are identical, and each is somewhat perfect, though conservative in format and maybe not fascinating. The crown is created by a heavy flow with a low head, leading to a well-controlled, slightly thick, glassy veil at the peak of the jet. This creates a vibrant syncopancy to the top pool's waves, which we can't see. But though the waters overflowing the upper bowl's rim are evenly distributed about the bowl's perimeter, they do present the action of the wavelets above and behind them, which we can see. The falling water, however, doesn't drop straight down as it normally would be expected to do, which hs to do with the detailing of the bowl's rim. The lion masks that spout water around the second bowl's underside projects surprisingly far outward, which looks energetic and keeps stains off the central pedestal, but also results in wet crushed rock paving around the perimeter of the fountain's extent.

33 Luxembourg Gardens

Originally a Royal Palace, the project of Marie de Medici and King Henri IV; today, Luxembourg Palace is home to the French Senate, with the gardens open to the public.

The gardens are spatially generous, beautifully groomed, peaceful, and host several excellent water features. Most notable are the Octagonal Basin, the Medici Fountain, and we will admit to the group, *Fontaine de l'Observatoire,* named after the nearby observatory, and located in an adjacent landscape immediately south of the gardens. The park dates back to 1612. The Medici Fountain, early in the program, was built in 1620.

The Octagonal Basin's wide, low pool is framed in an over-scaled, molded coping which serves as more than a curb when on weekends, visitors comfortably lay across its rounded profile to gamely interact with the rented miniature sailboats for which the fountain is famed. Mostly, though, the reflective pool, with its faceted perimeter serves as a central, formally inspiring element about which wheel a wide social setting, populated by visitors, standing, walking and seated in the countless signature metal chairs, all painted in the specific gray-green color, which is thematic and shared across the Gardens.

The Medici Fountain has been altered several times over the years and was even moved eastward for the construction of the Rue de Medecis. Today, the fountain presents an hypnotic, iconic scene, shaded by two rows of mature sycamore trees. The linear design, open on its narrrow, west end, is flanked by curiously sloped side terraces, which operate subtly to distort the perspective of the long view and to push down deeply the level of the canal. The east end is terminated by a fountain building adorned in a neoclassical scene depicting the cyclops, Polyphemus, in bronze, spying on a pair of lovers, Acis and Galatea, in white marble. These superb figures, by Auguste Ottin, replaced an earlier sculpture in 1866.

The Fontaine de l'Observatoire, located just south of Luxembourg Gardens in a small park of its own, is dominated by bronze figures of the monumental scale, artfully modeled and finely cast. Horses and sea creatures occupy the main level with four maidens of the world holding up an armillary sphere with celestial markings at the top. Below, eight turtles generate the fountain's main arching sprays. The pool is imposing, with its level lifted to waist height. The north side of the fountain faces Luxembourg Palace. Here, the least successful element in the fountain is its waterfall, tepid, and in shade most of the time.

The Fontaine de l'Observatoire was beautifully employed in the film, *Gigi*, around which Gaston reckons his emotional fate during a lengthy soliloquy, at first during the day, then later at night, for which it was specially and romantically back-illuminated.

(Top) the octagonal basin, the grand reflector, centrally positioned in the Gardens, is almost the pond-mirror in the center of Paris, and about which its visitors sit or stroll in a near-continuous wheel, and people perpetually arriving and leaving. The scene is most alive on Saturdays and Sundays when the sailboat rental carts show up and the pond becomes alive the pretty, boats, each color coded and insigniaed in the countries of the world.

(Right) Plan of Luxumboug Gardens, just less than a kilometer long from L' Observatoire on the south to the Palace gates on the north.

(Following pages, left and top right), the Medici Fountain, original to Marie de Medici's era though moved and transformed with new sculptures at the front, and a new architectural fountain, obverse.

(Following pages, bottom right), the L'Observatoire fountain, partly shaded, looking north.

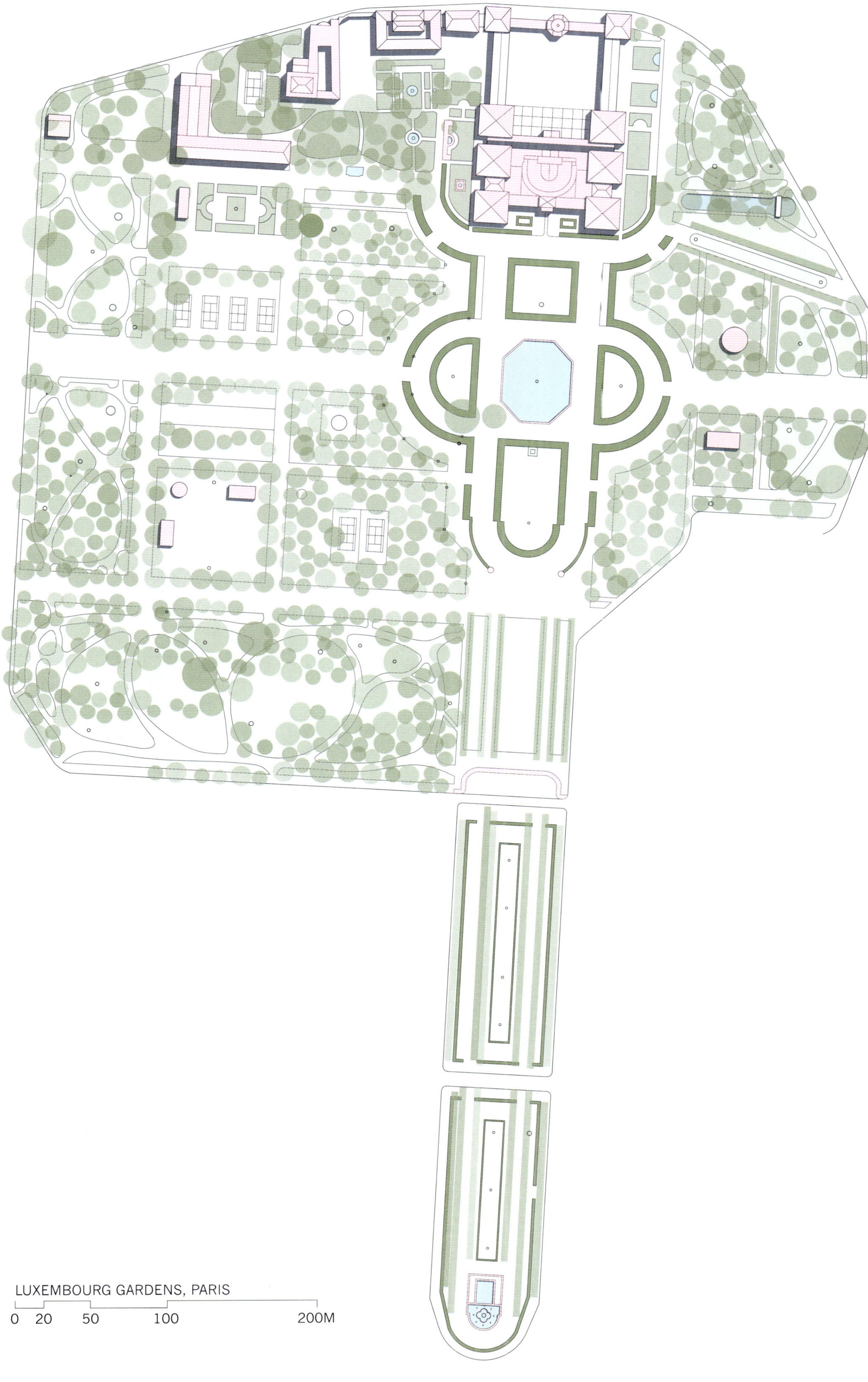

LUXEMBOURG GARDENS, PARIS

0 20 50 100 200M

(Both pages, left and right) the L' Observatoire fountain's patinaed bronze finishes have diverged in character over the years to become either perpetually dry and chalky or wet and polished-looking. The sculpture is deftly signed by the artist on one of the horse's front left hoofs. Women of four races hold aloft the amilary sphere. (Europe is represented by Northern and Southern women, who are joined by their caryatid sisters from Africa and Asia.) The sprays from the turtles and sea monsters are especially good, particularly when looking through them into the sunlight. The pool waters are green and subtly alive with algaes. The waterfall to the back (opposite, center right) is a bit hamstrung by its almost sunless northern orientation and its frankly unattractive reception pool, but its waterfall, which flows perfectly straight down in a clean dive, is masterfully wrought.

34 Vaux le Vicomte

For the creation of Vaux le Vicomte, Nicolas Fouquet, superintendent of finances for King Louis XIV, spent the rest of his life in prison, accused by his enemies of embezzling state funds, which appears to have not been true. The residence's unified architecture, landscape, and decorations, conceived in 1656, firmly established a new chapter in design. The work was performed under the talented encouragements of Fouquet, who assembled the key participants. Louis Le Vau created the architecture. Murals, paintings and decorations were by Charles Le Brun. And Andre Le Notre authored the landscape architecture, the vision of which proved to be especially influential and longlasting. Each art category was vibrantly polemical, independentaly superb, and interconnective with the other two. After jailing Fouquet, Louis XIV called all three artists to his property west of Paris, where they then collaborated on the Versailles we know today.

A central axis organizes the elements of the domain. The axis is oriented north-south, with the entrance on the north side, in shade. The sun warms the south side of the residence, which faces the length of the garden, backlit by the sun. A monumental, golden statue of Hercules is in the far distance. The path to the vista's terminus is experienced in a sequence of definitive compositional elements, which also engage topography. The main axis is transected by cross axes, offering lateral place connections.

Water plays a major role in organizing and punctuating the landscape though the employment of a moat, canals, reflection pools, activated retaining walls, and jetting fountains. The water features serve to guide circulation through the property by drawing visitors towards strategic destinations, bordering paths, and embellishing the value of places in the landscape.

Specific fountains merit special attention. The central, round fountain is simple, but well positioned and effective. The Crown fountain is ridiculous and resplendant. The east axis terraces adorned with three levels of activated retaining walls employing mask motifs are engaging. The monumental wall of fountains, on axis but hidden from the palace by the major transerse landscape recess is an impressive discovery. The pair of iron fountains on the far side of the transverse canal are skillfully detailed for finely controlled displays. And the stepped, rustic fountain which terminates the entire landscape's formal composition before the walk uphill to Hercules, is skillfully made for its type.

The garden's central pool was in operation while all the other elements were dry (they are rarely all on.) The central fountain is well proportioned, stately, and simple. It's water level is just below the that of the surrounding turf, with an elegant stone coping framing the pool. The pool offers a fine reflection. The special cast nozzle (right) aims a six-meter-tall stream perfectly vertically. On approach from the chateu, the sun illuminates the jet from behind and the presentation brightly sparkles.

(This page, lower images) the east terraces are outfitted with upper and lower basins, left and right. Numerous masks, which are to spout waters, decorate the faces of the basins. Each of the masks are unique, though they share much in family resemblance.

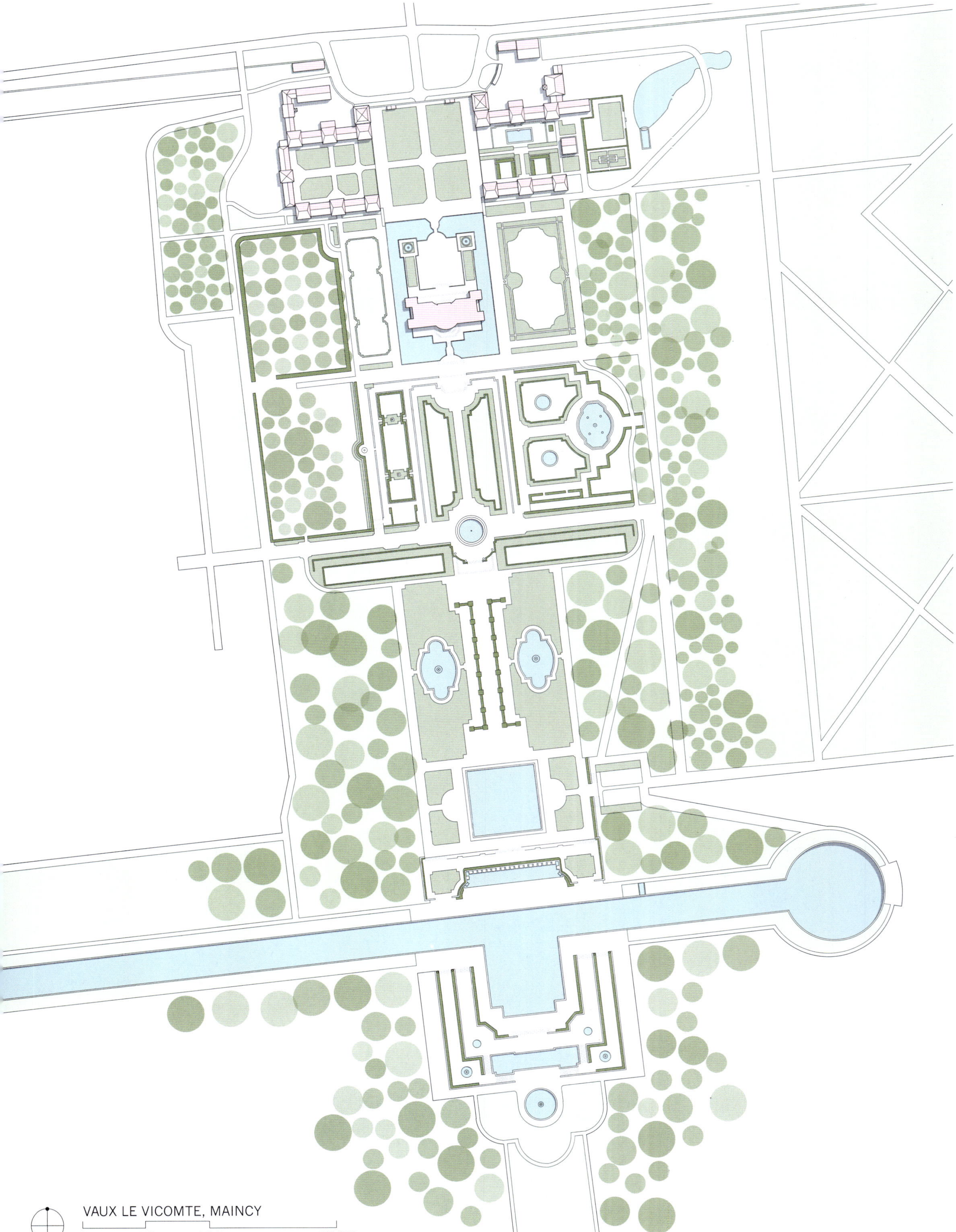

VAUX LE VICOMTE, MAINCY

0 50 100 200M

(Opposite, upper left) the view of the Chateau from the south rise, where we note the compositions disparate architectural elements unite into an idealied whole. (Opposite, upper right) access to the south rise is via this arcaded retaining wall, with fountains in its seven niches. Small, ornamental fountains (opposite, left) flank either side of the retaining wall. A rustic fountain at the base of the rise is hidden from this view.

A transverse, recessed canal separates the south rise from the central lawn, whose massive retaining wall is articulated is activated by tiered pool fountains, each topped by varying masks nested in each of the fifteen crenelated niches, with variant and more robust expressions in the wall's two end reentrant angle formations (above). The Chateau's impressive west elevation (right).

35 Versailles

Versailles is the holder of the largest collection of major water features in the world. None exist on the great palace's entrance side; they are all on the garden side, to the west-northwest, where guests are invited to explore and linger over the superlative garden's collective statement.

As we know it today, Versailles was built under King Louis XIV in the mid 1600s. The King was closely involved in the curation of the grounds and wrote a detailed guide to the design and its meanings. Garden forms and several fountains have changed over the years, but the basic concept of Versailles's landscape is intact from the time of its authorship, by André Le Nôtre, with clarification revisions under Jules Hardouin-Mansart. Le Nôtre, together with architect, Louis Le Vau, and painter-decorator, Charles Le Brun, were engaged as a group to design Versailles after their joint success in the creation of the paradigm-shifting Vaux-le-Vicomte.

Mammoth as the landscape is, it is well organized with a comprehendable layout and it is given consistancy by certain repeating patterns. The largest gesture is the Royal Alley, or Cour de Honneur, that central, columnar vista extending from the doors of the Château to the horizon—a visual axis under complete control for three kilometers. A pair of large pools with border sculptures dominate the terrace from which the grounds are surveyed. To the left (facing the vista), the South Parterre and the Orangerie. To the right, the North Parterre, the Triumphal Arch Grove and the Three Fountains Grove, with the Dragon Fountain centered beyond and the Neptune Fountain terminating the sequence. Immediately forward of the terrace is the superb Latona Basin, an elliptical stepped form with water expressions second to none amongst golden statuary. Looking southwest, a group of six carrés (something like a square city block) of gardens collectively establish two precincts of gardens with fountains, which are symmetrically reflected about the principle axis. Within these two precincts are most of the signature gardens and fountains of the domain: varied, inventive, expertly crafted, charmed in allegorical content and linked via a geometrical system of pathways and view connections. In the central, medium distance is the partially submerged sculptures of Apollo's Fountain, followed by the Swiss Guard's Canal, in which is the forty-meter tall, Jet d'Eau, the apex of the panorama.

To the property's northwest, the Versailles landscape statement is extended and complimented by the additional gardens of the Trianon Estate and the Petit Trianon, where more water features may be explored, including the Water Buffet and the emerald-tinted pond, reflecting the Rock and the Belvedere, art-directed by Marie Antoinette.

The Cour de Honneur (left), the Latona Basin (upper right and following page), Apollo's Fountain (lower right).

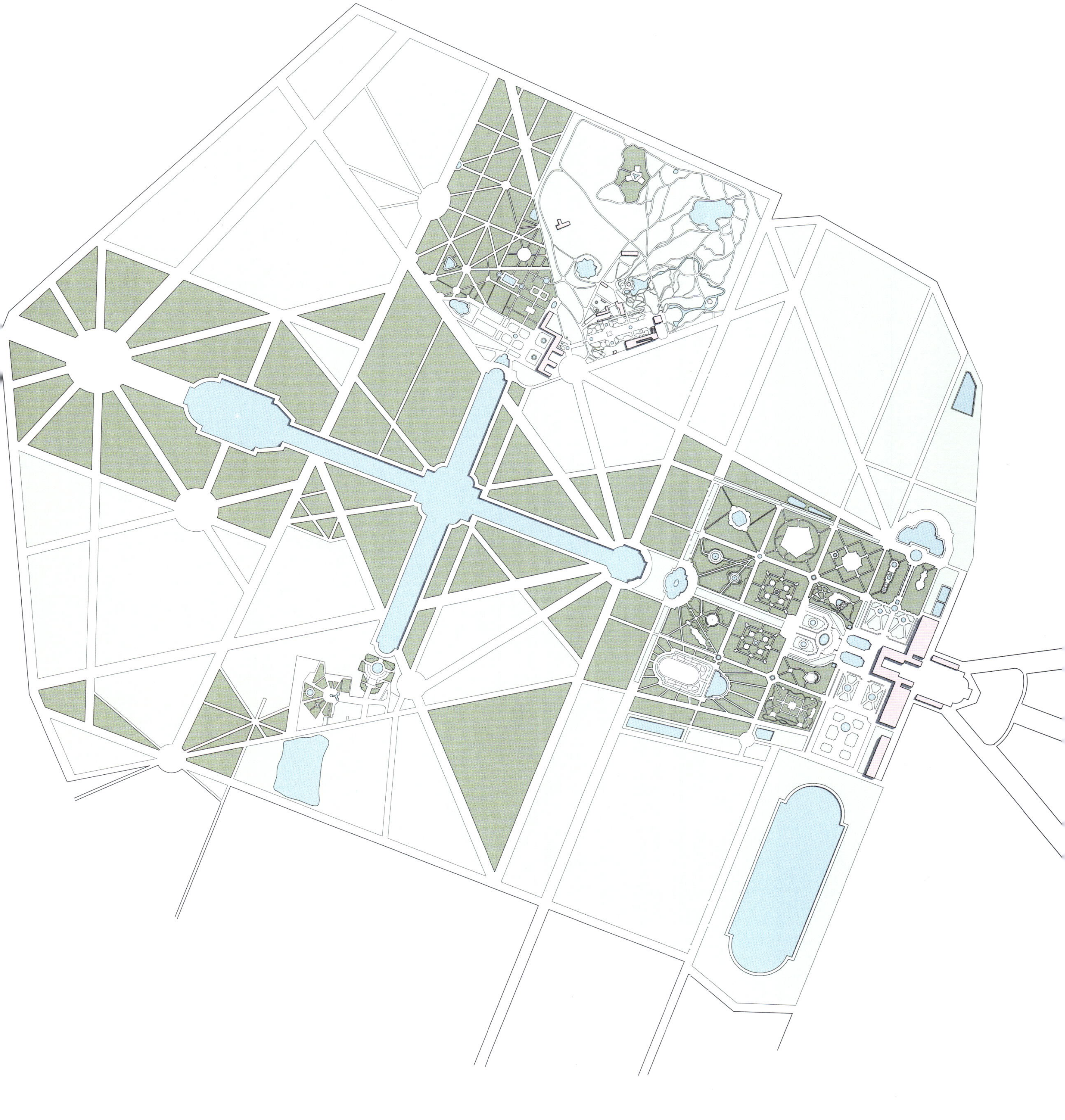

VERSAILLES

0 100 200 500 1000M

If the visit is carefully planned in accordance the with published operation program, the fleet of foot can see all the fountains at Versailles in operation—just barely. All the fountains have surpassing qualities.

Night Fountain (opposite, top) presenting an exquisite waterfall before a strong design of veined marble in dark green over dark red. (Left, upper center) one of the small fountains in the parterre beyond Latona, with a 'bouquet' of jets, a repeating idea at Versailles. (Left, lower center and bottom photos) Collonade Grove, where garden design, architecture and water features are integrated. (Left near), the peak of the Latona, celebrated by its sparkling sprays. (This page, upper right) framing element of the Swiss Guards Canal. (Top left) small fountain near the Chestnut Trees Room. (Above) The Girondale Grove Fountain, where light plays delicately over the white-water jets in the shaded space. (Middle and bottom right) the Water Parterres and their sculptures.

(Opposite, top) the fountains of the Marmosettes Walk. The top geysers and rounded, cornice-like weirs create inflected rainfall around the cherub pedestals. (Opposite center left) fountain at the Triumphal Arch Grove with fine its sheet waterfall above rollover weir cascades. (Opposite center right and above, and center lower right) the Pyramid Fountain's open design functions reasonably well as a sculpture when off. When on it is an intriguing display that transforms greatly regarding view and sun angle conditions. (Opposite bottom) a cascade detail from the Three Fountains Grove. Bits of gleaming, colored glass accent rockery and seashells. (Top) the Ceres Fountain's gilt centerpiece combines the energy of its mixed jet upthrusts with the sparkling veils of falling droplets, activating the air and splashing about the the sculpture. (Right) view from the Pyramid Fountain looking west.

(Opposite, top) a fountain of the North Parterres. (Opposite center) the Obelisk Grove Fountain's perimeter cascades overflow with raindrop-like falls, with attendant fine sounds. (Opposite bottom) the Dragon Fountain presents an allegory of several elements. (Above top, center and right upper center) the Domes Grove Fountain is one of the very few fundamentally flawed installations on the site, where the glassy waterfalls that flow from the railing's nested trough flutters unattractively (a not uncommon waterfall failing). Cleverly, the same waterfall provides a guard preventing sprays from dampening the walk surrounding the installation. (Above lower centert) large rockery at Marie-Antoinette's garden. (Right) a maintenance person manually turns the fountains off via a simple mechanical valve accessed from a plug in the walk.

36 Aix-En-Provence

Aix-En-Provence, City of a Thousand Fountains, hosts more than simply a high count, as their quality and character are special in the way of gentle icons.

The community is idyllic, just off the Mediterranean in the south of France, with a comfortable climate, a leisurely lifestyle, and a pedestrian-oriented urban texture. The artist, Paul Cezanne, grew up here. Water features of all kinds are as prominent in its grand boulevard as in its out-of-the-way alleyways. This sets up a repeating and pleasurable pattern of accidentally discovering very good water features, often in unexpected places.

On the Cours Mirabeau, a wide, historic street in the center of town, are four fountains in a row, spaced in two-block intervals, two of which are spring-fed and thickly veneered in greenery. The street culminates to the west at the impressive and monumental, Fontaine de la Rotonde, which has no trouble commanding its hundred-meter diameter context.

(Opposite) Cours Mirabeau, a central pedestrian street populated with four noteworthy fountains, two of which are sheathed in greenery and mosses. Their stories are matters of lore. The second in this view is explained as two historic stone column capitals, one over the other, over which the fountain is expressed. Waters from the aquifer support the greenery. (Above right) typical street fountain. (Center) the Dolphin Fountain, in the Place des Quatre-Dauphins, something like a back alley piazza, is one of the city's better known fountains. (Right) One of the many drinking water fountains. Note the common twin bars upon which jugs or basins are placed for receiving water to be carried away.

(Both pages) the Fontaine de la Rotunde, at the terminus of the Cours Mirabeau, performs admirably in the center of its circular space, which is steadily wreathed in traffic and bordered with various perimeter plazas. The horizontal sprays from the sea monsters about the base of the pedestal are the main display concept, but these are supported by numerous attendant flows and, of couse, by the many sculptural figures, themselves, not the least of which are the three monumental maidens at the formation's peak. The copper-finished upper bowl is well proportioned and elegantly detailed, unfortunate revisions to their masks' original spouts notwithstanding. At the base of the central composition (opposite, top), between the pedestals with pairs of lions are steps over which its not difficult to imagine water should be cascading, but that action, which would help anchor the large reflection pool to the central element, was never meant to be.

(Both pages) a church's bell, marvelously strapped in place.The city's many fountains are woven all through its urban fabric. (Above center right) a fountain offering water for horses on one side and for humans on the other. It's bronze decorative figures are very finely detailed. (Opposite bottom right) the fourth fountain in the sequence on the Cours Mirabeau.

Fountains of Aix-En-Provence's Cours Mirabeau (opposite and above).

37 Parc des Buttes Chaumont

In Paris' 19th arrondissement to the north, Parc des Buttes-Chaumont offers a green and quiet wooded oasis in emphasized contrast to its densely urbanized surround. A central, small mountain, crowned in a neoclassical cupola, is banded by a mote, and given access only by an elevated bridge and a thin ismuth. The steeply sloped land around the mountain is arranged with open space pleasures. Naturalistic water features populate the scenery. A lengthy, slender, convoluted stream cascades down a gentle slope through a sequence of spaces. A sculpture of Pan watches over a particularly twisted section of the stream. A tall waterfall occupies the 'mountain's dark interior cavern to emerge into the sun and greenery. The water below is alive with fish and birds. Another cascade, wider and rougher, flows from the pinched, northwest corner of the site, binding the park space to the streets outside, while mitigating traffic noise.

The park occupies the site of a former stone quarry. Its horn-shaped, 19th-century plan is lush with plantings and curving pathways ideally contrasting with the dense Parisian urbanism flanking its sides.

Although visually recessive, the cascading stream is unusually well fashioned of sculpted concrete, integrated with rocks, which in some places become quite elaborate. The stream's various switchbacks, braids, little ponds and rivulets carve through an open lawn, a tree-shaded glen, and an area bordering sidewalks and ramps. In places, narrow channels cut across the paved walk to relieve the stream to pick up again on the other side. The water character throughout is subdued, even slightly starved looking, though in places it manages to be just vigorous enough to make a good sound.

(Images to the right) an artificial braided stream is artfully made along one of the curving pathways located directly south of the fantasy mountain. The water moves through channels of every variation, cascading here and pooling there.

The stream is impressive, partly due to its surprising lengthiness. A bronze of Pan the Piper frolics over a section of the stream (center left).

(Opposite upper left, this page center and right side images) the pond that frames the mountain in the park. (Opposite top right and bottom) a lengthy, braided stream, sculpted in cast-in-place concrete borders much of a path that weaves through the park. (This page above) the waterfall within the mountain has not been in operation for some years.

DAME TARTINE

38 The Stravinsky Fountain

Sixteen kinetic artwork fountains are scattered in a large rectangular basin located in Place Stravinsky, between the Church of Saint Merri and the Centre de Pompidou. Completed in 1983, the basin's polished stainless steel perimeter offers continuous seating on all four sides, which is often occupied. The installations were created by Niki de Saint Phalle and Jean Tinguely (they were married) to represent musical works by Igor Stravinsky, including *Ragtime, The Clown's Hat, The Heart, Life, Love, The Nightengale, The Mermaid, Death, The Diagonal, The Frog, The Serpent, The Fox, The Elephant, The Spiral, The Musical Key of G,* and *The Firebird*.

Both groups of fountains are humorous. Tinguely's black fountains explore cleverly staged mechanistic exhuberance while Saint Phalle's sculptures, which also operate mechanically, orient aesthetic appeal mostly towards their colorful representational identities.

None of the fountains show significant water presentation of the kind that forms the basis for this examination, but this is more than compensated for by the raptuous delight so many of the sculptures convey. They are alive by more than by their sculptural integrity—which is respectable, or by their flippant water actions—which are entertaining enough. It is for their clickety rotations, bizarre mechanical intrigues and happy swaying—and by the unequivocal human joy these movements engender in their visitors, for which we salute them.

The red lips, left, rachet back and forth, blowing kisses to visitors. The snake, right, spins on a vertical axis, spraying water in a spiral above while two little tails spray at its base. The blue derby spins as if tossed into the pool and coming to rest. A redheaded mermaid reclines, floating and spraying jets from her breasts. A heart spins, two-faced—but both sides are positive. The black sculptures' wheels turn chains, linking to other mechanisms with sprays related every which mechanical way.

39 Fondation Louis Vuitton

The foundation's Frank Gehry-designed museum building was completed in 2014. Nestled in the Bois de Boulogne, in Paris, the architecture is presented in a surround of mature trees, with close access to the energies of Paris, with all its high fashion connotations.

The building's lower level gives access to a platform over a reflection pool, contained by parallel side walls with a long cascade reaching down from the ground level. The arrangement of the stage-like platform and the cascade places the water in the audience position of a theatrical format, with visitors on the stage.

The cascade offers an especially elegant, almost slow-motion, rolling, gliding, folding water action. The special character of the water results from precise proportions and finishes of the steps together with a subtly manipulated flow angle. The flowing poetries are not communicated in photography.

The steps of the cascade are roughly a bit less than a meter wide and perhaps 100mm tall. The energy in the water is carefully gaged in the angle of the wide dimension, which the author guesses to be about 2 percent.

Experience in the Square

The renowned architect leaned from his seat next to me in the black cab, pointing, "There's the pair at Trafalgar. Too small for their space, obviously."

I took his comment at face value until I could return for a private visit to study them. At the time I filed it away. When I finally got back to the square two evenings later, the realization of their genius was a shock. I have since visited these fountains more than any other in the world. I've read about their creation, their author's artistic career, and what occupied the square before. Those fountains provided my first inspiring taste in history and they continue to instruct me to this day in the subtleties and complexity of water craftsmanship.

Superficially, the two fountains aren't unusual. Their twin Neo-classical forms are symmetrically arranged transverse to the space's major axis. Their ornament would appear commonplace. They employ wide quatrefoil pools with central stone bowls, topped by simple jets in a fleur-de-lis bouquet. There are extraneous sculptures in the pools.

The fountains' generic appearance belies their profound water performances while hiding the tremendous skill required for their achievement. There is greatness in their undeclared superlative quality.

Ripley's
MUSEUM

40 Shaftesbury Memorial Fountain

This cast bronze fountain with its boldly scaled, upper masses and cast aluminum top figure occupies a broad sidewalk at Piccadilly Circus to command its busy surround, though this was not its original location.

The work was sculpted by Alfred Gilbert in the late 1800s in finely detailed Art Nuveau panels and devices. The fountain is particularly interesting as a fountain in that it employs small amounts of water. Only the tiniest streams emit from small ports just above its basin. The superliative quality of the work, its terrific location in London, and the excellent steps formed all around its base have worked to ensure the installation's popularity as an outward looking urban amphitheater. The fountain is vacated only during the harshest weather.

It is the Shaftesbury Memorial Fountain. It was built to honor the Londoner by that name, a philanthropist. Eros Fountain is a widely employed misnomer and misconception, made only more interesting by the fact that it isn't Eros at the top, but Anteros, representing love returned back to the sender.

In the world of fountains, the Anteros Fountain is much more important than might be presumed. It has no equal, really, in terms of its urban powers in relation to its format and the amount of water involved. We might point to the Fountain of the Innocents, which is something like the same size and maybe quality, but is not as commanding, or the fountain in Taorimina, which similarly uses very little water, but is scaled and sculpturlaly softened to be less forceful. The Anteros Fountain is in Picadilly Circus an intensely visited place, located in an influential coutry's capital city, significantly raising the network of issues about which the fountain must successfully contend.

The Anteros Fountain is one of the great landmark fountains, perfectly situated, artfully sculpted, contributing inescapably to it's place's identity and experience. Picadilly Circus' special vibrancy is infused by theater-related content, heavy vehicular and pedestrian traffic, and a walloping dose of western culture commercialsm, all framed in the downtown architecture of a previous era. There is a palpable, heady energy there quite like no other place in the world, and the Anteros Fountain is its cultural totem, offering a special place to stop, be protected, witness, reflect, and connect. The fountain handily manages all this responsibility with that English culture aspirational idea, with the effortlessness of gods.

(Opposite and right, center) fountain as amphitheater. (Upper right) fountain as landmark.

41 Trafalgar Square Fountains

Designed by Edwin Lutyens in 1936, near the end of a long and illustrious career, which included his work with Gertrude Jeckyll and her creativity and skill with garden design, when he was a young man. The fountains replaced earlier fountains, which were passed along to two cities in Canada, Regina and Ottowa, where they are installed today. The original basins were retained. Embellishing mermaid sculptures are by William McMillan. The water action of the two chalices is of the highest quality.

The water performances of the chalice are designed to function in a dynamic, interconnective anatomy, where each action is physically linked to a neighboring action and all lead to something greater than they would as individuals. Trafalgar's anatomical design is the most intricate and successful of which I am aware.

The geyser in the center of the design is peaked in a canopy that randomly spills about its center. These spills land upon the bases of the tall, arching water streams, causing abrasion and the presentation of a staccato arch formation. The arches are aimed to fall down upon the upper bowl rim, creating three simultaneous water effects: first, is a spectacular, clumpy spray, which is active all about the upper bowl; second is a torn or dappled perimeter waterfall, which dissolves and animates the percieved rim of the bowl; and third, the water cliings to the underside of the bowl to roll along until it meets the stem holding the bowl aloft. This clinging action is performed perfectly, and there are no dry flaws under the bowl. The water that gathers at the stem is then redirected to the sloped, clamshell-profiled radial flume, which conducts the flows to a perimeter of spout-edges where they all pour into a lifted marble basin. It should be noted that the underside of the clamshell-flume is absolutely dry, with not a patch of wetness, anywhere. This is an impressive exhibition of a fundamental aspect of water design, the dialectic between wet and dry. Water in the basin is alive from all the sprays above, and it overflows the basin, unevenly. These uneven flows are made more lively by complicated molding treatments, leading to a complex blending of falls and clinging flows. All the waters ultimately land in the wide, quatrefoil reception pool. The slim-fan streams from the remote mermaids enrich the scene without complicated the central water display concept.

The fountains are difficult to fully appreciate from any single view, due to an optics fundamental. When observing a fountain with the sun behind us the form of the stone chalice is ideally presented in light and shade, though from this view the water is a little lifeless. If we move about the fountain to look at it from the other side—towards the sun, then the chalice becomes a dark silhouette while the water completely changes; dazzling the eye from thousands of sunlit airborne sparkles. So, we can stage to see either the chalice or the water to good effect, but not both.

(Opposite, above, and following page) the operatic variety and intensity of the water actions initiates with the pinnacle geyser, whose canopy splashes irregularly onto the nozzles of its perimeter of tall arches. These arches are improved by the geyser's texturizing. In standard setting (we see variations, occasionally) those arches impact the bowl edge to 1-spray, 2-waterfall, 3-cling to and fully wet the bowl's underside. The flows are coursed over a clamshell-formed stem flair to issue from spouts in the round to the next pool. Water overflowing that pool flows over a richly mannered side, which creates a variety of effects. Finally, the water lands in one of the great quatrefoil reflection pools, where it is joined by slim-fan streams from the aquarian sculptures.

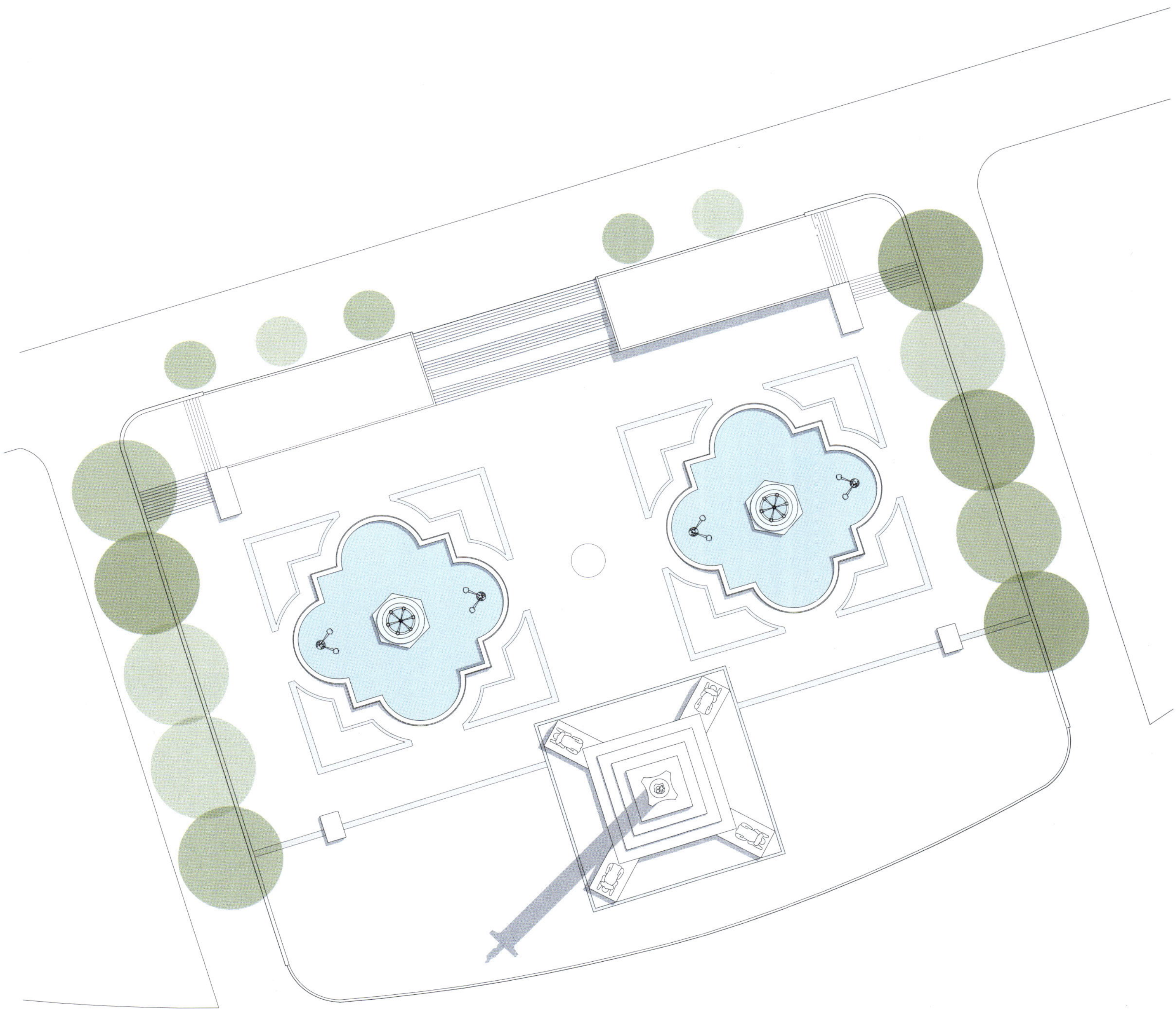

TRAFALGAR SQUARE, LONDON

0 5 10 25 50M

(Opposite page) seeing the fountain dry can be informative, and sometimes details are visible that are not typically so, such as the simple and fine proportion of the upper bowl, or the elegant seashells arranged under the radial clamshell flume, and even the tiny, recessed square carvings circling just above the clamshell. When these hidden details are rich enough, they can offer some substitute for the missing waters.

(Top) the aquarian sculptures. (Above, center) a windy day's perimeter overflow and actions with the lavish architectural profile.

(Right) difficult to see in any photograph, is that in this stormy moment under the fountains, with water splashing seemingly everywhere, is that the underside of the clamshell is bone dry—the intentional result of the same great skill that brought all the other superlative displays.

SOUTH BANK
SOUTH BANK

42 Revolving Torsion

Busy saving lives or whatever, when I asked the St. Thomas Hospital receptionist to contact the staff member who oversees the fountain in the square and turn it on for me, she made the call, but I was refused. Too bad, laddie. Come back another week.

Sometimes they get away from you. In spite of all the planning, checking ahead, having the lenses professionally cleaned, and attending to Karma, it can happen. In this case it was a regrettable blow with the parched consequences notably absent from these accompanying photographs.

Naum Gabo, the acclaimed mid-century sculptor, had scored a terrific commission in the early seventies via the Tate Gallery, the outcome of which was loaned to St. Thomas' and installed in its current, Thames-side garden. Gabo's portfolio, particularly well known for his organic/geometrical explorations in space and light, often showed evenly spaced lines tensioned along straight and curved framing edges—much of which translates without too much trouble into the realm of water.

Gabo's innovative sculpture, *Revolving Torsion*, literally spins around on its base, which is centered in a round reception pool on a square green. The artwork revolves six times per hour.

When the sculpture is operating, two arrays of slender streams energetically spray outward from curved edgest to converge towards two points in space, where they continuously crash and spray. These points in space, with the sculpture, spin about the sculpture's central vertical axis.

The sounds should be in two tones, the first created at the two stream group impact points, and the second as their splashes hit the pool.

The sculpture's treasured site—a genteel courtyard across the Thames River from the Houses of Parliament (left), where the river, the adjacent bridge and the hospital's generous setback establish an open area with good air, sunlight and fine view connections.

By walking around the (at the moment) fixed sculpture we can gain some suggestion of how the armature's silhouete transforms as it spins. The wing-like, spokes of water would collide in space from the sculpture's two, upright curving arcs (right, top to bottom), and when moving, the convergences parade before us, to then orbit to the far side; given the transparency of the sculpture, the opposite waters will remain visible.

According to a piece in the blog, The Art Story, an interplay of shadows takes place at the base of the rotating artwork.

43 Princess Diana Memorial Fountain

The variously cut granite panels, freely composed in a large, asymmetrically curved loop, rests elegantly in the contours of Hyde Park, London, just south of the Serpentine. It seems at first that the water wheels about in a continuous direction, but instead, water rises from within the channel at the rounded form's south side, to flow in two directions, northeast and north-west, drifting over sculpted surfaces with loose associations to nature, such as mud flats, shallow cataracts or rocky shoals—abstractly presented. The two flows rejoin under a bridge on the north side. Water flowing over the various textures takes on different responsive characters and sounds. The sculpted channel also changes in width and slope, so there is much for which the water to show a range of expression. The looped basin is a skilfull armature for water action, but it is also a visually successful monumental sculpture, wet or dry. The fountain is unique for a memorial in many ways, one being its tolerance for visitors who wish to wade through its waters.

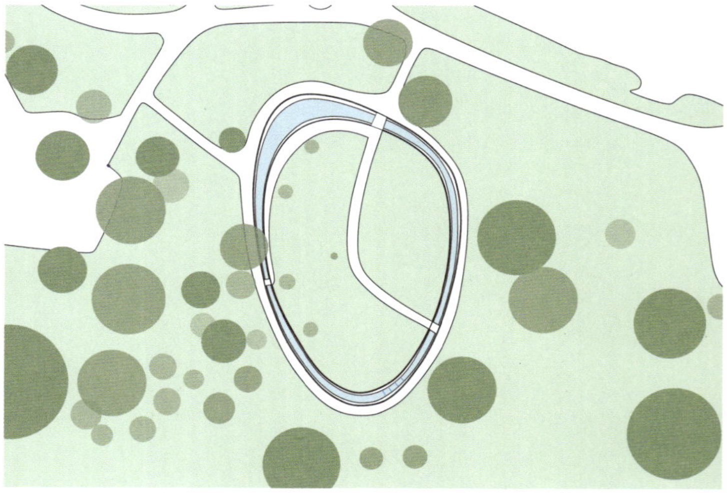

The progressively cut, rolling cascade (upper right), is perhaps the work's most mesmeric (and most photographed) texture, though there are several other expressive textural moments about the installation. The shimmering waters pooling behind the falls are also attractive, carrying a certain calm expectancy.

The stepped ridge area (lower left and right), generates sunny highlights across its full width. The linear mudflat-like wave carvings (left center) channel the water more subtley. This memorial fountain was not conceived for the kind of popularity it now enjoys, with dense crowds in bathing suits that sunny days bring, but the gentle curves are tolerant.

Not Empty Space

The list was getting long. For every exceptional location scouted and visitied, three more would turn up in the reasearch; not second-tier examples, but fine works of the first rank, simply not so well-known. It was not exactly as if there were masterpieces hidden all over the world. It was more like a secret society's thin, pervasive evidence. Maybe research projects are always like this.

There was water integrated into the much-published, small work of architecture. It used sunlight and water to create deft highlights reflecting up into its dark interior conducted through hidden, low level windows. The concept was alluring but the effect in person seemed over-celebrated. The interior was simply too dark and the effect was too faint. Maybe it would work better at a different time of day, but I looked at the sun angles and was skeptical it would ever be much better. Maybe. Nice idea.

The way out was back through the entrance corrodor which was built like a glass-enclosed bridge over a wide pool. I noticed it was pretty good on my way into the main space, but I had been rushing. There was nothing in the books about that part of the building.

The walls of the bridge were sheathed in small panels of pale, tinted art glass outfitted onto evenly spaced vertical rails. Sunlight reflecting from the water broadcast ripples of light migrating upward on the colored glass panels and through to the ceiling. The corridor was an uplifting experience, even if the main interior volume was just a little disappointing, with respect to the water and light realization.

The bridge reminded me that the best experience was the journey, not the end. It was wonderful spending time in that glowing, kinetic corridor.

44 Bethesda Fountain

The angel atop the Bethesda Fountain was created by the artist, Emma Stebbins. This sculpture was the first major public art commission awarded to a woman in the history of New York City. The bronze sculpture is eight feet tall. The rest of the fountain was designed by Jacob Wrey Mould, a Central Park architect. The fountain was inagurated in 1873.

The figure of the angel is depicted purposefully striding over an unruly mound issuing small sprays in every direction, establishing a connection between the angel's movements and the water's. The flows from the streams are gathered in a shallow bronze bowl, shown here overflowing a lapped weir with a smoothly trimmed edge to fall straight down in fine rain. (When operating according to the original design, the water does not overflow the basin edge, but rather slips behind a perimeter flange to fall as attentuated triangular ribbons, traces of which can be seen here partially dissolved by the unintended overflows.)

The falling water veils the central pedestal, which is braced with four cherubs in a scene of cattails, before splashing into an octagonal, granite bowl with spouts at each of its vertices. Stout granite columns uphold the granite bowl while water from the spouts flows down approximately three and a half meters to the fountain's thirty-meter-wide reception pool. Lost here is a previous crenelated edging, which used to issue fine streamers of rain between the spouts, but these are not missed. The reception pool hosts a water garden dotted with lily, lotus and papyrus plantings.

The fountain's top streams, middle falls and base spouts form a cohesive water presentation in three tiers. These elements define a wrapper around the fountain—with the exception of the area around the angel—which is above the water actions, thereby free and open to the enfolding sunlight, space and views. This composition empowers the angel, while the water plantings in the reception pool soften the design and integrate it with the living landscape of Central Park.

The vertical composition organizes four significant water elements. The twenty or so small streams at the top form a cloud-like plinth for the walking angel (upper right and upper center right). The clouds, then, rain in a cylindrical, architectural form, with very finely made straight falls. This water is not overflowing from the pinnacle pool—rather, water is slipping down through perimeter slots (lower, center right), which is part of how the water falls so straight and true.

Midway down, the water is captured by an octagonal pool and directed to eight bell-shaped spouts, which issue glassy, sunlit streams through cross-shaped slots.

The reception basin hosts various, similarly scaled water plantings.

(Upper left), view from Bethesda Terrace, overlooking the fountain and the lake, beyond.

(Left and above), the bronzes of the angel and the putti share a smoothly robust muscularity, unmarked by splash, as they are arranged above and behind the flows, and well cared-for.

The fountain (opposite), looking southwest in the afternoon lit by the sun behind, grounded by the woods. The top pool's weir often misbehaves from clogging debris, as is shown in this image's ragged top effect. The clever design calls for the pool's water to flow behind the leaf-decorated cladding into numerous down-pointing spouts to create a straight waterfall of closely spaced vertical streams. The splash on the middle pool is well-scaled, and the water from the vertex spouts is channeled to create glassy volutes, which give over to slender streams to land in the reception pool's water garden.

45 Seagram Building

Mies van der Rhoe's 1958 twin reflection pools demark the wideopen space of the Seagram Building's entrance plaza from corner positions along Park Avenue's east side. The pools are rectangular, and fairly large, measuring roughly 21m x 14m, with the short sides fronting the north-south sidewalk. Eight feathered geysers, just shy of 2m tall, are arranged in a tight, 2 x 4 grid, paralleling the avenue, off-center lengthwise in the pools, biased to the front. I have seen another jet layout in the pools, and it was just as simple.

According to Phyllis Lambert, who represented the Owner (her father) through the designing of the building, Philip Johnson had drawn up designs for elaborate fountains which went so far as to have some of the building's columns residing in L-shaped pools. (Later and coincidentally, Charles Moore created a somewhat similar approach to Philip Johnson's, with water channels and pools bending around the open plaza and, seemingly improvisationally, exploring the architecture, submitted as part of his PhD dissertation.) Mies was not sympathetic to Johnson's idea. The clarity of the architecture and the freedom of the space would not be impinged by adventurous waterworks.

The two reflection pools at the Seagram Building have little in common with his two at the Barcelona Pavilion. Barcelona's pools present still water, serving as mirrors. They draw the spatial system of the architecture to fold down into their silent, reflective windows, facilitating dual visual and philosophical inquiries.

At Seagram, the pools are activated by jets, creating water sounds and rendering the pool surfaces glittery. The discipline of the forecourt's geometry and the restraint of its few forms release the visitor to more purly enjoy the freedom of the space, and the independent society to which the space correlates. Seagram's pools are for sitting beside at lunchtime, in the warm sun with a sandwich and an apple, thoughtful and relaxed, restoratively.
The sounds of the jets mingling with that of the traffic place the city at bay and reinforce the message that all is reasonably well in the world.

The pools are less about reflection than the establishment of calming energy. As such, the jets activate the pool with propogating and reflectiong waves that evenly and mildly pattern the pool's wide surface area. The basins are finished in the same stone as the plaza, as if their depths were carved away. Sunlight entering the pool is refracted by the waves to create a second action of wave-shaped shades and highlights.

46 Paley Park

Paley Park presents us with a dramatic wall of water at the end of a slot of space with buildings to either side and an appoach from the south, on 53rd Street, in Manhattan. The water is a torrent, flowing against the slightly sloped surface of a rock-textured, concrete panel. Today, there are many such 'water-walls', though Paley would still be judged by most to make the clearest statement. The park, designed by Zion & Breen Associates, has proven to be consistently popular since it opened in 1967.

The water feature is six meters tall and twelve wide. Its waters flow at the rather heavy rate of over 500 liters per horizontal meter of weir—or understood in another way, to a depth of about two centimeters over the top , which is a lot. Steps lead up to the wall, which are always wet from spray. (The display is every bit as loud as it is splashy.) The wall is made of concrete, and has a surface texture seeded with rounded river stones, ranging in size from four to eight centimeters in diameter, closely spaced. Water rushing down over the texture rapidly entrains air to create thick streamers of white-water, with a bold, curtain-like character. A large step at the base receives the flow and turns it over to a very turbulent reception pool. Almost unnoticeable side wall valences bracket and clarify the view of the water-wall while hiding its ragged side splashes and providing an effective location for mounting light fixtures.

I met Robert Zion some years ago. He explained that the wall of water idea came to him while vacationing in Mexico. There, he was impressed watching a hotel gardener making an arrangement with rocks in a line and water overflowing from the top. This observation led directly to his design for Paley Park.

A south-facing wall of water (opposite) is flanked by ivy-covered brick side walls of a public space, open to the street; the first of the so-called, pocket parks. Sunlight on the wall is filtered through leggy acacia trees, which scale and shelter the space. Movable white Bertoia chairs and Saarinen tables provide the space's sole, tasteful furnishings. The water is loud.

The water flows over a concrete panel seeded with silver dollar sized river stones to create its signature, thick expressions.

The display has interesting complications. The weir is shaded by a capstone, hiding what otherwise would be an attractive, gleaming highlight. A step at the bottom sorts the wall of water before overflowing into a turbulent reception pool. The steps, and the bowls of flowers (right) are soaked from spray.

There is a graceful, urbane tolerance about the space. The straightforward grace and power of the water feature, and the delicacy of the trees create a balance that seems to be particularly right for the formidable scenes of midtown Manhattan.

47 Chase Plaza Sunken Garden

Isamu Noguchi created the Sunken Garden artwork at the Chase Manhattan Bank building in 1964. The installation occupies a cylindrical void, cut into the tower's plaza, down to the level below where a branch bank looks across to the space. The space is about fifteen meters in diameter. A very large Dubuffet is positioned not far away on the plaza deck; it is an emphatically physical form, arranged sensitively with the void of Sunken Garden, not so close as to suggest a dialectic, though it's hard not to compare the two.

The installation is abstract and modern. It begins with a historic reference to Zen raked gardens via its white stone cobble paving pattern and rustic rock formations. But Noguchi departs. His paving is underwater—and undulating, and the waters are active with waves and splashing sounds. The seven rocks are as much like freestanding, naturalistic sculptures as suggestive of faraway mountains. The rocks are of remarkable character, almost black in color, and powerfully textured. They also seem foriegn, something like large and very heavy meteorites. The six rounded voids in the basin floor are overtly contrapuntal to the rocks and a purely modern move. The grouped collection of slender jets draw from Western sources. The piece reads as much like a surreal landscape as it does a work of art, a little like a Yves Tanguy painting made real.

The installation is not just part of a building, but part of Manhattan. Its offering is such it may be appreciated from any of the nearby towers which look down into the plaza.

The undulations of the basin, reiterated in the paving design, crest into the air in places. Jets cluster over the larger pronouncement. The pool is activated by the jet grouping. The surrounding glass walls reflect the water sounds.

The rocks are all of the same dark red-brown material, which has neither veining nor grain. They are textured in places and smooth elsewhere; the surfaces showing no toolmarks, though obviously some of nozzles and piping bored through them. Still, their aspect is such that they appear to be found and placed with sculptural intent, rather than manipultated to mimic natural finishes, but we do not know and this is part of the question they pose. None of the rocks are completely underwater. The circular voids in the basin, which are fully underwater, seem to the conceptual opposites of the rocks.

The monumental Dubuffet, positioned on the opposite side of the plaza (opposite top) provides an interesting dialectic with Noguchi's recessed artwork.

48 MIT Chapel

This nondenomenational chapel was built in 1955 by Eero Saarinen, with a sculpture by Harry Bertoia. A shallow pool, or moat, surrounds the cylindrical form. Sunlight reflects from the water's surface to enter the dark interior through low, hidden windows. The water then glows over the interior walls' undulating surface. A bronze Harry Bertoia artwork of floating small rectangles catches light from a skylight floating over a white marble altar. The fixed light of the artwork and the dim, kinetic light from the reflected water establish a dialog in the dark, textured space.

The entrance bridge is brighter and more demonstrative in its use of light, though its space is also calming and introspective. Light reflecting from the pool in this area animates art glass panels and the ceiling in migtrating wavelet patterns.

Dappled sunlight from the chapel's wind-textured moat is reflected up into its dark interior (above). The effect is subtler than the idea. More emphatic are the same reflections cast through art glass panels which line a bridge leading to the chapel interior. There, the light is more direct (right), casting colored animations in the glass and to the ceiling the projections on the floor are direct from the sun, relatively fixed, and do not mingle with water action.

49 Longwood Gardens—Main Fountain Garden

Industrialist, Pierre S. du Pont, Jr., an MIT-trained engineer, was inspired by Chicago's Columbian Exhibition and the many important European gardens he visited to build something along those lines at his home near Kennett Square, Pennsylvania. This ambition developed into something of a hobby for the busy corporate leader.

Du Pont began incrementally, but soon enough he had personally engineered his own large-format, transforming display fountain, completed in 1932. State-of-the-art at the time, the design was influenced by combined interests in French Neoclassicism and advanced technology, which still today fairly sums up the Main Fountain Garden. The installation has received successive improvements since its opening. Du Pont's home and grounds were eventually recast as a non-profit institution showcasing horticultural gardens, with the centrally positioned, Main Fountain Garden serving as one of its most popular features, along with numerous other fountains in what became a vast fountain collection.

A thorough reconstruction of the Main Fountain Garden in 2017 restored the water feature's original expressions, with an updated landscape architecture by West 8, a reconstruction and expansion of the fountain building by Beyer Blinder Belle, and fountain refurbishments and enhancements by Fluidity. The latest round of water expressions include robotic jets, flowing basketweaves, next generation changing-color lighting, and flaming water geysers. The fire was the last to complete the Garden's exhibition of the primal elements. The 'basketweave' composite jets suggest a landscape's harvest, referencing French style haystacks. Longwood continues to upgrade the Main Fountain Garden to this day.

(All) Images by photographer, Daniel Traub, except the three upper right. Longwood Garden's Main Fountain Garden in the late afternoon looking north (top left) with various jets operating monumentally but not in water concert mode. (Lower left) alternative water presentation with large-format fans and lateral geysers. Here, two superimposed fans are in operation, a low, wide fan together with a tall, narrow fan just behind. They visually unify into the large, triangular form. (Upper right) image of the fountain building from the central portico and its small-format fountains. Shoulder patch landscape tapestry from security guard's yellow jersey. The fountain building from the upper level walk (center right). Romantic interpretation of the Basketweave jets, created to convey 'harvest' associations of the landscape. (Next pages) images of the Main Fountain Garden during nighttime music, light and water exhibitions. The reconstruction restored all the original jets then added contemporary technologies and custom-designed nozzles. Lighting was expecially formulated for wider color ranges and more nuanced expressions.

Night Fountain

It was unusual for it to be so foggy at night, and when I boarded the ferry at Algiers Point the boat lights incandescing colorfully in the thick air were all we could see. It was a rowdy crowd, and a rowdy time of year. When we landed and the mooring ropes were secure they let us off over the boat's big iron drawbridge, whose clang sounded even louder in the misty darkness. The bunch of us at first headed in the same direction, and I watched individuals fanning away until it was my turn.

A blind man carded me at the door and pointed me in with his head. I ordered the signature drink and headed straight for the courtyard to see America's most unusual fountain pair. These are nothing like the pairs at the Place de la Concorde or at St. Peter's. They are not monumentally scaled, but they are monumental in experience, at least to me. I enjoy their hypnotic attributes.

The fountains seem haphazardly plugged together from common parts. They are not pretty, but they are succinct. There is even a confidence about them, an engineer's clear-mindedness; nothing is extraneous. Even their surrounds of plantings and their iron railings are part of their rational formula. Well, perhaps one aspect of their glory comes from the Hurricanes, the notoriously whollopping drinks that were invented steps away and in their presence.

Who, on this wide earth, would not be dazzled by the strange and complex combination of flames dancing in the sparkling, spraying waters; waters which fly up and over into the small bowl, where a little pond reflects the fires, and in that watery-flaming sparkle certainly also gleams, for flashing moments, the countless flung droplets. All the while below, the streams shooting up and the underside of the aloft bowl soft-lighted from modest, changing-color sources in red, yellow and green. All of it goofy, raw, without any refinement, fitting, and wonderful.

50 The National Gallery of Art

The National Gallery of Art is located west of the Capitol, on the Mall's north side. The institution is comprised of two buildings configured to either side a wide plaza cut by a cross street, beneath which is a fully activated below-grade level, joining the two buildings. The west, neoclassical building was designed by John Russel Pope and the later, well-known, East Wing was by I. M. Pei, who also designed the plaza. The fountain is integrated into the plaza's elemental composition, which notably reaches down into the level below, bringing daylight, water action, geometrical expression, and creative energy.

Plaza elements are freely composed within a large circle of evenly spaced bollards. Triangular shards sheathed in mirrored glass are clustered with a row of white-water jets and a triangular slice tilting down to the lower level. The row of tall, frothy geysers rise directly from the plaza to emulate a white wall while generating flows to tumble down the tilted surface, which is developed as a cascade of compact steps. The steps are textured and rounded, and the water's frothy character is effected. We could say it's dented, or even blobby. The character of the white-water jets is crisp, while the cascade flows are less so, though they are both white. Several geometrical inventions result from the design's triangular composition. These tantalize and create confrontations with various levels of closure or openness when viewed from any angle or either level.

The introverted character of the plaza level water presentation opens up on the level below where a glass wall showcases the final triangular presentation. Here, the turned-away cascades from above finally flows toward the viewer. At the lower level, we see the sloped flows directed to the interior space, and then fold diagonally to create a vertical, ribbed wall positioned just behind a large glass view panel. Daylight brightly illuminates the tilted plane cascade, which is framed in shadow to form the triangular statement, made of light.

The fountain is made into something of an inert, subordinate artifact on the table-like plaza, part of a larger composition of elements. The wall of frothy geysers are of good quality, with a rich texture and fine whiteness. The flows tilt over a closely stepped, triangular cascade generating a sudsy character. Two interesting things then happen, one is obvious and one is not. The cascades flow energetically toward the lower level space, to then fold sharply down, bringing the water in immediate proximity of the downstairs space in the form of a waterfall mere centimeters behind the glass partition. The row of potted plants—a sure signal of a problem at any fountain—serve as a barrier to a moisture zone. The interesting hidden item involves geometry. the cascade flows diagonally into a side wall; normally, flows sliding into a wall like this would create an unsightly gutter-like pile-up which would become thicker and more evident towards the base. That doesn't happen here because of a clever gap, which drains away the excess flows. The gap is knowingly done. Its 1.5cm width is architecturally unnoticeable, but sufficiently wide to perform, hydraulically (bottom right).

51 The Park at CityCenter

The tree-shaded plaza and its pair of large fountains serve as a key social anchor for a neighborhood of Washington comprised of a newly developed mix of office buildings and housing. The plaza does a good job of bringing social depth and environmental quality to a locale without much in the way of history or formal character. Notably, the space is bordered on its long side by New York Avenue and its several lanes of traffic, which the plaza manages to place at bay with palpable aplomb. The fountains play a role in this achievement through their scale and various intrigues.

The comparatively low fountains, designed by GGN, are more about strategic spatial framing than presenting a champion figure.

The fountains are bordered by large wet and dry sections. The dry volumes are of veined, white marble with slightly raised paneling. The wet zones are interstitial, made up of dark gray granite finished in topographic micro-grooves sculpted akin to low, rolling waves.

The water action over the grooved granite masses is mesmerizing with its stop-action-like, lensing flow dynamics. The fluttering-crawling-bulbous character of the water mostly is that way in order to make an expressive statement, but it also performs unusually well by its helpful sideways water migrations. The sideways flows are necessitated by the intervening, white marble masses, which sometimes create triangular, leeward zones where normal cascades would be unable to reach, leaving those areas dry and forlorn. But the shallowly sloped, finely grooved texture serves to slow the water so much that it can follow the little horizontal ledges laterally. The technique is successful even in the most acute and lengthy lee conditions.

A little time spent on the plaza is further rewarded with the dawning awareness that the flows over the surfaces vary, sometimes heavier and louder and sometimes thinner and quieter. The variations provide a savy extra dimension to the plaza experience.

The larger fountain hosts a grouping of thin, vertical jets. These are arranged geometrically and their heights alter in coordinated fashion. The slender streams rise from attractive, polished metal pots and the peaks of the jets have little, glassy canopies. The wide fountain masses do not make a great deal of sound; the jets provide much of what we hear. The overall sound character of the fountains is aptly suited to the urban open space with its vehicular traffic border and perimeter of sonically reflective buildings.

The chief display for this large and important, Washington DC, pair of fountains operates at the very smallest, finely crafted scale, where water flutters in lapping wavelets over subtly micro-grooved dark stone, though the collection of vertical streams from custom pots plays a minor but integral role in the compostion (right and opposite).

52 Clarence F. Buckingham Fountain

Buckingham Fountain is an iconic landmark and symbol for the city of Chicago. Its perimeter lawn and plaza are exceptionally large, encompassing a space as large as a traditional city block. The monumental fountain is prominantely located in Chicago's Grant Park between Michigan Avenue and the lake, though view connections today are limited by legions of mature trees. Buckingham Fountain was designed by the École des Beaux-Arts trained architect, Edward H. Bennett; built in 1927, making it at the time of this writing just shy of 100 years old.

The fountain's mammoth, 80-meter diameter quatrefoil pool, plus the surrounding lawn and fencing, strategically captures much of the jet spray on this wide-open, windy site, with the trade-off that visitors are as set back from the fountain as any in the world. Another example in its range is Paris' supermassive, Trocadero.

The design is chiefly composed of a stepped formation of three waterfalling levels with thickly flowing arching streams lofting water back upwards. At its peak, a cluster of vertical jets organize a culminative gesture, with a central jet periodically activating to a height of 40-50 meters. This figure is then complicated by four associated seahorse group sculptures in corner positions—which are good sculptures, and a thicket of other jet-clusters and cattail lighting valences which clutter the design (to contemporary eyes), and undermine clear views to the central statement.

Most effective is its composition of heavy waterfalls together with upward thrusting arches and geysers. These two categories of kinetic elements are fundamental in water design—those which flow up and those which flow down. This duality might intuitively seem automatic in any water display, but it is not. At Buckingham, the curated energy balance establishes an unequivocal statement of mighty forces acting in harmony.

The central formation's three tiers of heavy, outwardly flowing waterfalls (top left and opposite bottom) are visually balanced by numerous, inward and upward flowing, thickly streaming arches and geysers. This balance is the central gesture in Buckingham's design statement. The weirs are expertly crafted (left upper center) where water is conducted to a lower, flinging ledge, incorporating two intermediate steps enlivening the fall effect.

(Left lower center) detail of one of the four seahorse groupings. The sculptures are excellent, while complicating the views to the central formation. The reception pool is huge enough to offer a significant water presentation of its own (left). Without scaling elements nearby, and the public held far back by its wide perimeter, the very large scale of the fountain is difficult to ascertain. The central geyser is nearly 50 meters tall over a pool 85 meters wide (opposite top).

53 Water Tower Place

It was determined that the water in this stepped location should not simply cascade downward; that would be mundane. It was also thought that the water should not jump up from tier to tier, since that would be an obvious and goofy alternative. Instead, the design concept calls for the water to flow smoothly from one level to the next, through openings in tray-like, candilevered pools. The design would then be founded in the tradition of water chains, such as at the Villa Lante, but interpreted as a modern, three-dimensional design.

At Water Tower Place's entrance escalators, the water evenly flows through the circular cuts in the pools to create rows of laminar vases, each quivering from flow, but sharply holding their forms. The vases are a little elss than 30cm tall and 15cm in diameter. The cantilevered pools are about a meter wide.

At the base of each of the vases is a metal cone with an opening in the top from which occasionally leaps small baubles of water, about 2cm in diameter. The water jumps vertically, through the opening in the cantilevered pool above it, into the air to a full height of about half a meter above the nozzle. The marble of water then falls back down into the vase to spash inside. The flowing waters of the vases absorb the marbles' splashes to prevent visitors from being irked by spray. The squirting from the nozzles explores complex choreographic designs through the water feature, patterning up, down, and in other ways.

Barely perceptible is the subtly flared plan of the escalators—which are not parallel. In order to avoid the railroad tracks perspective view upwards that the parallel arrangement conditions, the space's original designer, Warren Platner, slightly tweaked the plan. This effect is more overtly visible, once one is aware of it.

The design is configured in two flights of escalators. The main section (opposite, lower) presents a water chain with three vases per tier. The upper chain (opposite, top) is composed of a pair of chains with a staircase in the center. These have two vases per tier, each.

The anatomy of the water feature's display concept recalls the nature of anatomy at Trafalgar Square, in that all the elements are intentionally interconnected to create synergetic results. At Water Tower Place, water from each small reflection pool flows through round openings to create glass-like vases of water. The vases serve to contain splash from the water marbles launched upwards from nozzles at the base of each vase. The marbles pursue choreographic patterns in the air, sequencing up, down, and side-to-side. Without the containment of the flowing water vases (left top and lower center) the splash from the marbles would be intolerable to passersby on the escalators.

ADVENTURE

Water Tower Place
MAGIC PLAY

54 Crown Fountain

A famous work of public art that happens to serve as a fountain, the 2004 Crown Fountain was concieved by artist Jaume Plensa especially for Chicago, starring monumental video clips of Chicagoans in their characteristic, multicultural variety. The two glass brick video towers parade slowly through the faces of residents, each face taking its turn to spray a jet of real water from pursed video lips. Waterfalls from the tops of the towers contribute subtely but significantly to the energy of the installation.

A monumental membrane pool receives the flows from lips and the tops of the two structures, while creating a large, magnificent space for participatory experiences. The pool is about seventy-five meters long and a little over twenty meters wide. A nicely judged, 5m border frames the pool all around. Rustic timber seating continuously lines the fountain's length on both sides. The pool's highly reflective, two-centimeter-deep water over dark gray stone paving engages the park on one side, Michigan Avenue on the other, the two video structures with their water actions, street trees, and all the visitors.

The installation parallels Michigan Avenue and is closely positioned to the avenue's sidewalk. Because street trees and traffic noise obscure approaching awareness, one suddenly happens upon the impressive scale of the glass video monoliths and the wide reflection pool to surprising, positive effect. The closeness of the artwork to the street also enhances the concept's formal delivery.

After the spouting video faces, the great membrane pool is the artwork's chief water display (left). The wide space of the pool establishes a generous space with visually dramatic views in every direction.

The famous, pursed lips' issuances are created from custom-made, transparent nozzles. The are formed something like a showerhead, with numerous, closely spaced, small openings for the streamers of water. The streams are off most of the time; we have to wait for them, expectantly. When they come they are strong and hold for a while. A few beats after the streams quiet away, the great waterfalls are reestablished from the tops of the structures (left bottom and next pages).

The video faces are clearly the stars of the show, but each of the design's major water elements, the reflection pool, the pursed lip sprays, and the waterfalls, are strong and integrate with the video structures, and the general concept, in a pursuasive, unified design.

The waterfalls of the video structures (above, opposite and right) are important to the installation's energy, while being the most subtle aspect of the concept.

The five-meter-wide border with the continuous, timber seating provide an ideal relationship between the space of the participants in the pool and those who prefer simply to watch (above).

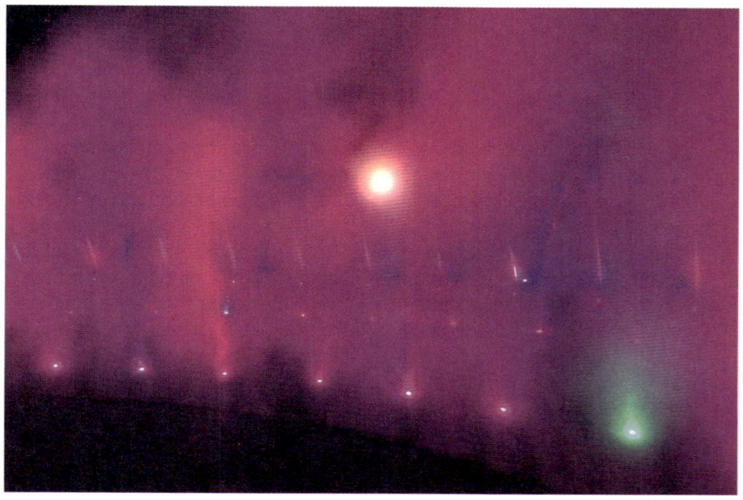

55 Polk Bros Fountain

The circular fountain is centered in a square plaza at Polk Bros Park, the entry point to Navy Pier, a Chicago destination. The park was built as part of a property-wide transformation effort, completed in 2016 by James Corner Field Operations. The strong geometrical gestures of the water feature seems appropriate for Chicago's erudite and commanding architectural context.

The fountain's most distinguishing feature is its ribbed horshoe-shaped hillock, which organizes countless, densely packed, constantly fluctuating, streaming arches. Water design theory holds that people are naturally drawn to water, which works here truely enough, but once in this fountain participants are then just as surely drawn to the textured embankment. It's a fun play element and an unusual maneuver in the urban scene; more abstract than Halprin's Lovejoy Plaza or Forecourt Fountain, built a generation earlier. The ribbed, texutured element also provides a positive statement for the space during Chicago's colder months when the fountain is dormant and waiting for the next, warm season.

The fountain has a calm perimeter and open end which faces the Navy Pier entrance doors. The calm areas compliment the active sections amongst the heady—not to say dizzying—turmoil of the jets around the embankment.

Fountains that are explicitly designed for play are conceived with people in mind such that the people in the fountain are part of the fountain, and therefore a part of its design—part of its visual statement. Which is almost to say that the people are the fountain's sculptures. Bernini's nearly alive fountain sculptures are then replaced by real, living people, who have become dynamic, figurative elements in, or of, the work of art. Their invovement with the water and the space and forms of the fountain are both compositional statements and interpretive responses.

The ribbed hillock with its tangle of ever-flexing jets wrap around a calm center, open to the east. The night character is very different, with the ribbed form becomeing less assertive and color and mists becoming dominant (left). A slender, curving path, finished in water, loops around the installation's open side, completing the plan geometry of the hillock (far left bottom). Based upon the idea that Bernini's sculptures are replaced by real, living people in immersive fountains, such photography as these (opposite center right, opposite far left bottom, and the three to the right) document not only visitor responses to the water, but authentic, even intentional, compositional expressions of the fountain.

56 Vizcaya

Located in Coconut Grove, Miami, Florida, the former house and gardens of James Deering, now a museum, is distinghishable for its outstanding collection of numerous water features integrally woven into a landscape plan of rare richness and complexity.

Once again, this chronicler must admit that the photography does not do justice to the feeling of the water features or the deft skill of the landcape plan—except perhaps the images of the barge, which is so photogenic that a rooster with a camera taped to his comb could deliver a creditable job.

It is easy to be distracted by the plan's Baroque ordering systems. If the plan has a weakness, to modern eyes, it is that it over-relies on symmetrical compositions for scenic coherence and distant element focusing. However, the symmetries certainly help to make the plan's complexities comprehendable. Along the way, spaces are nested within spaces, countless place-to-place sequences are offered, numerous spots present cleverly composed panoramas, and all destinations deliver rewards without fully consumating desire, leaving energy and interest for the next.

Vazcaya's labyrinthine shell game of regular forms and diagonals is complemented by an easy-going rustic texture in the material finishes of its architectural and sculptural elements, which contributes to the environment's restorative tone.

The fountains and plantings are fundamental to Vizcaya's spatial character and experience—though none of those elements are more important than the general scheme. This is Vizcaya's gift. Its plan is a dazzling armature, organizing all the many parts and pathways.

A good example of the plan's many potent strategic intricacies occurs at the two small, round islands, planted in simple turf, located at the villa side of the twin diagonal promenades that run to the southwest. The simple act of walking around the little islands while looking forward offers a wheel of perhaps ten different opportunities. Where to go next?, seems to be explicitly asked by the tiny roundabouts. And the little island to the south makes completely different overtures than its mirror to the north.

(Left) Axial view to the upper terrace from the garden's central island. The apex, white marble fountain and its cascades are regrettably not in repair. (Upper right) The approach drive to the villa follows a subtle slope down, bracketed by local stone stepped water channels with pools and jets emphasizing both ends with a little pomp. (Upper middle) A wall fountain elaborated in architectural flourishes. (Lower middle) the mote around the central island. (Right) The marble fountain overlooking the gardens to the villa.

(This page) not in very good shape and inaccessible at the time of this visit, the stone barge was once in use for the moorings of visiting boats, and as a destination in itself. Even today, as an almost-ruin, it is majestic. A group of four cascades bordered its stairs that led up from the central arrival deck to the overlook prows to the northeast and southwest.

The barge plays an interesting role in stabalizing and anchoring the views from the villa and the garden's nearby edge, though the main garden spaces have no view of it.

We would be remiss to omit this barge's assertive background role in the important Missy Elliot music video, Take Away, which for some intuitive reason added a Chinese baldaccino into the barge's architectonic composition.

VIZCAYA, MIAMI
0 5 10 25 50M

Vizcaya was art directed by art curator and interior designer, Paul Chalfin, and designed by the young New York architect from New Orleans, F. Burrall Hoffman, who trained at the Ecole des Beaux-Arts. Hoffman is credited with generating the plan of the house, the outbuildings, and the preliminary garden layout. The garden's development and plantings were by Diego Suarez, a talented Colombian, who had been trained in Florence and was new to America, living in New York City.

James Deering, the owner, was very involved in the project. He purposefully sought a promising architect, early in his career, rather than one with a more established practice, with the idea that such a person would be more collaborative. Chalfin was the first engaged, and it was he who recommended Hoffman and Suarez to Deering. There were, reportedly, artistic tensions in every direction over the course of the job. For all three of Deering's top talents, Vizcaya would prove to be the most celebrated commission of their careers.

A more detailed portrait of authorship can be conjectured, but because of the dovetailed relationships between the participants it isn't straightforward. Chalfin, more artistically developed and older than the others, guided the project, but he did not hold a pencil. Deering, the strong client, located the house on the site and managed the process to specific detail. It was Hoffman who conceived of the barge, which was then drawn and developed by Suarez, after which Hoffman refined it further. The great garden plan seems to be the work of Suarez, who wrote persuasively about how the plan was significantly reworked by him after his visit to the site and his apprehension of the strong local sunlight which required address to avoid a ruinous glare. The planting scheme was Suarez'. Hoffman and Chalfin continued to participate in the garden layout and its fulfilment.

Begun in 1914, the project was completed in 1922; a demanding process for all involved.

(Top) the historic sarcophagus is made into a fountain with contemporary frog-jets, incorporated into the house's patio, facing west, with the main garden showing beyond. Its slender streams catch the bright afternoon sun and create gentle sounds from multiple sources. (Upper middle left) one of two simple, pedestrian roundabouts which prove so effective to the plan's circulation. The main basin with topiary island is beyond to the right, shaded by live oaks. (Lower middle left) a subtle axial shift sharpens a view connection through a basin side aisle, glimmering gently under the oaks. (Bottom) the rustic cascade, with course lufa panels beneath hand-tooled, bowed weirs, if operating, presents in thin streamers according to a period photograph.

(Top Left) one of two semicircular basins which frame the first section of the garden from the villa. The historic columns are repurposed artifacts.

(Right top and bottom) the clamshell fountains (jets not operating) receive and punctuate the thrust of the diagonal promenades. (Above) a recessed, segmented water garden occupies a faceted perimeter within the Rose Garden, which is dominated by a white marble fountain, with a compositional format employing volutes a bit like those at La Granja (right center).

57 San Antonio River Walk

The River Walk is a four kilometer stretch of flowing water which winds through the city of San Antonio a full floor below street level. In 1926, the city was planning to pave it over and transform its channel into a sewer, but the San Antonio Conservation Society objected, and lobbied hard, ultimately winning rights for its beautification.

The local architect, Robert Hugman, developed a concept for managing the waters' flows and activating the lower level with commercial frontages. His plan was approved, and his office was an early occupant of the recessed riverfront level. Slowly, he was joined by others. In the early 1940s, the spaces became more articulated with terraces, planters, bridges, stairs and so forth, much of which was funded and built under the Works Progress Administration. As a result of improvements, restaurants and lounges moved to the increasingly attractive River Walk.

Contemporary developments along the river edge areas continue the now common policy of incorporating entrances at both the street and river levels.

The lives of our cities ebb and flow. I have visited the River Walk when it appears lackluster and bleakly commercial, and other times when it feels authentic and ringing with enchantment. It has proven to be durable; at the time of this writing, the River Walk is over eighty years old and as popular today as ever.

Like West Lake, in Hangzhou, the water body is something of a given here at the River Walk. It is the garden detailing of its many edges and details that bestows to the water its high level of appreciation and care. Some water details do exist, such as the stepping plank bridge's overflowing slots (left lower center), and the occasional side fountain.

58 Fountain Place

The tower was designed by Henry N. Cobb, with urban landscape architecture by Dan Kiley and Peter Ker Walker. Mark Fuller and Alan Robinson at WET delivered the site-wide water features. Numerous innovations were developed to make the vast water design concept practical for this commercial real estate development, which opened in 1982.

The urban site is sloped, which contributed to the generation of the terraced pools and waterfalls, enlivening the design. Testing led to the creation of a special double-weir, which accellerates a minimal overflow to then fling it outward energitically. So, a relatively small amount of moving water creates a robust effect.

The pools are vibrant, with jets creating surface turbulence. Wide orifice pipes, positioned centimeters underwater, function with high flow rates to created the thick, frothy geysers without requiring nozzles to project into the air and compromise the presentation.

Small islands regularly spaced across the watery landscape are planted with bald cypress trees, establishing a natural, light-filtering canopy to shade the open spaces from the hot, Texas sun.

On the south side of the plaza, a square grid of vertical jets rises from the deck, flush to its surround. Achieved for the first time in the world, this design showed a way for a fountain to engage a plaza without being hemmed in by a pool or coping. The innovative approach, countlessly copied in subsequent years, allows visitors to move through the space of the fountain, a radical idea for its day. Further: each of the jets operated under individual control; the resulting choreographies play through various geometrical patterns, offering kaleidoscope-like shape changes when viewed from the tower. (The fountain was replaced in the 2010s with a similar, though not as striking, version of itself.)

At Fountain Place (opposite), the landscape, architecture and water each engage eachother to merge as a grand idea, supported by numerous, finely crafted details. (This page, top right) the concept continues its expression to the interior, where a tall ceiling plane and frameless glass panels supports an inside-outside connection with the landscape and its water.

The site's noteworthy topography is interpreted to yield energetic waterfalls activated by water-accelerating double-weirs in stone and metal (right center).

The innovative—and first example—of the pool-less, flush deck, immersive fountain.

Fountain Place's pool, jet and cascade details (this page).

(Left and above) the waterfalls' double weir involves the upper and lower elements of a rounded granite edge which gathers the overflows and accelerates them to a lower step, or ledge, fabricated in metal, where the waters quickly roil and fling outward, achieving the rich flows presented. The roiling in the upper pools, established by the jets and their underwater nozzles, contribute to the richness of the falls.

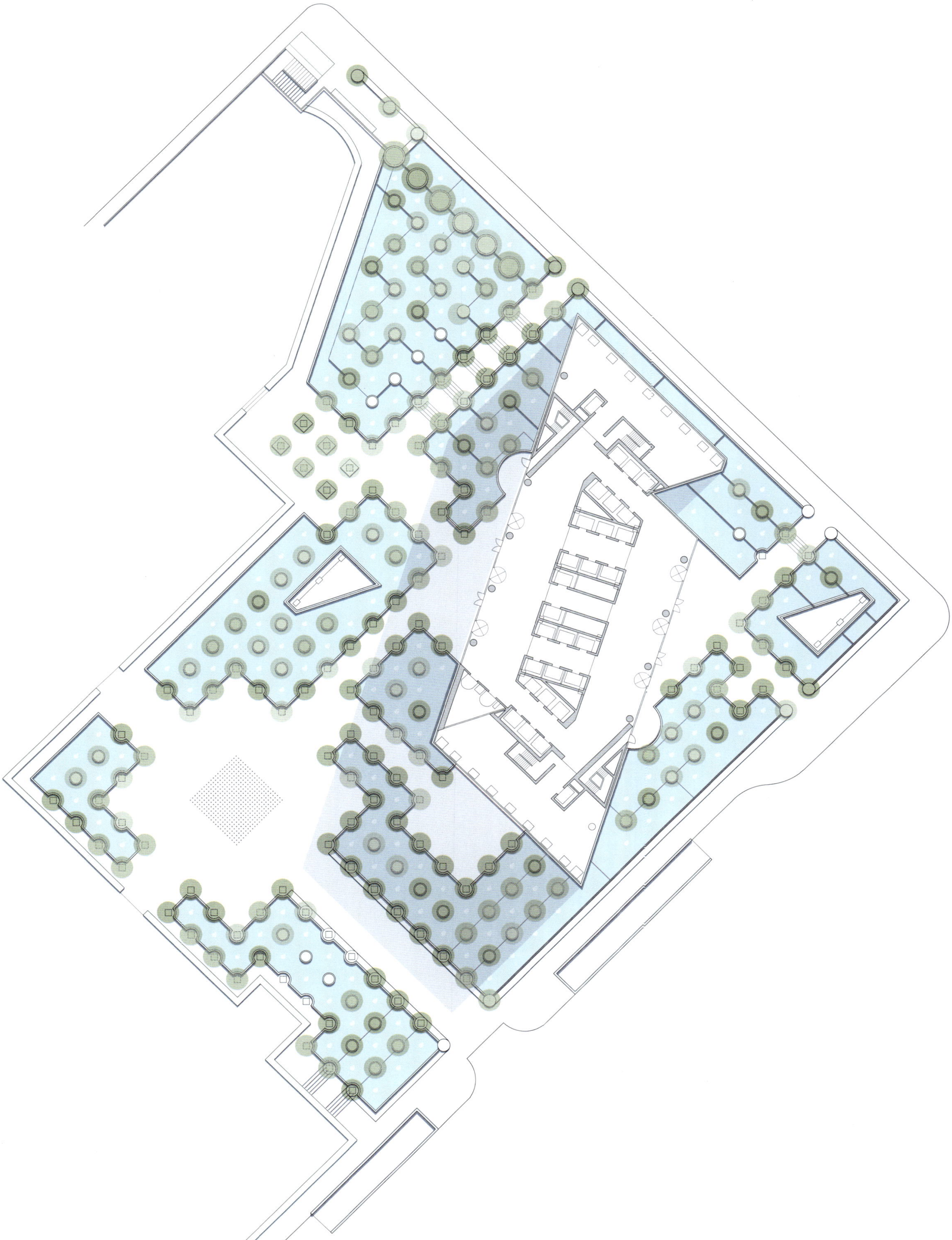

FOUNTAIN PLACE, DALLAS

Past Master

A symposium was organized to celebrate and futher investigate the works of the highly regarded landscape architect who had passed away some years before. I was asked to prepare a paper on his work with water. There would be other speakers, all experts.

I was hardly an expert on this indivudual, while there would be many in attendence who were, and others who were old friends. So, I doubted that a clever feint was going to be sufficient. I flew to Oregon to re-visit what I thought was his best work. And, I looked again at a few others.

The famous urban critic, Ada Louise Huxtable, once referred to his project in Portland as the most important public space design since the Rennaissance. This was an interesting statement. What could it mean? Perhaps, if taken at face value, it could be rephrased to mean there were relationships between this new, Ira Keller Fountain, and Trevi Fountain. She surely meant more important things by her statement than my narrow comparison, but looking at the two was still telling.

Both are oriented to the south, slightly off axis. Both are monumental with developed seating areas to the front and sides. Both are about teh same size. One is glorified by spectacular Rennaisance sculptures, but the other is delightful with its abstract reference to nature. Both have environmental experiences deep on the right hand side. One is hard and urban, the other is green and verdent. Both flirt with architectural paradigms.

After my lecture, which was frought with hypotheticals about what he was thinking and what he knew, his daughter, who I didn't know was in the in attendence, was introduced to me and suggested that all the congecture was correct, that her father had made her and her sister draw, in situ, over and again Trevi and the other fountains of Rome. She said Trevi did influence Forecourt Fountain. She was kind, enthusiastic, and maybe it was true.

59 Lovejoy Plaza

This 1966 public space and its superb water feature were co-created by Lawrence Halprin and Charles W. Moore. The design was based upon theories about importing nature's energy into the city's open plazas, the abstraction of Pacific Northwest mountain streams, empowering the movement of the human body through space, place activation via the choreography of events over time, topographic representation by artfully staggered straight-line segments, continuity and infinity, and other such lofty and pragmatic motivators.

We might hypothesize the provenance of the staggered segment shape grammar, which is special and fundamental to the expression of the fountain and open space. The storyline would begin with the late 19th-century Finish surveyor, Johan Henrik Aalto, whose large working table of unrolled topographic drawings would use this surveyor's technique, and captivate and inspire his son, Alvar, who became a pioneer of modern architecture. At Saynatsalo and the Maison Carré especially, Aalto manifested the segmented line contour into a stylish design expression. The motif was taken up a generation later by Moore, an architect and a colleague of Halprin's and a fan of Aalto's work. At Lovejoy, the specific details of the fountain likely came from Moore, via Aalto, while the vision of the bursting, open and accessible fountain with the provenance of Pacific Northwest mountains and streams, was Halprin's.

The Lovejoy water feature is a composition in three movements, the wellspring, the cataracts, and the lake. The pools of the wellspring and the lake are framed in seating ledges, while the central cataracts are open to the sides, inviting visitors to walk through the cascade area, or even climbing up into its gorge.

The design's accessible, naturalistic formation was revolutionary. Articles in the news media of the time commented specifically about how popular the plaza and fountain had become with young people in particular, with photography showing teenagers climbing all over and sitting in its wet forms, something almost unheard of across previous centuries of fountain visiting.

The fountain represents topography through the abstract visual language of facets—a system appropriated from a surveyor drafting technique.

(Opposite and this page top and bottom) cataracts details. The wellspring pool (right upper center), with a portion of the cataracts, beyond. A curiously mute block, like a massive talus dropped into the scene, is composed at the base of the cataracts (right top and lower center).

The seeded concrete, like at Forecourt Fountain (Keller), was originally gray, but shited to this color due to iron staining, likely from the fountain's mechanical equipment.

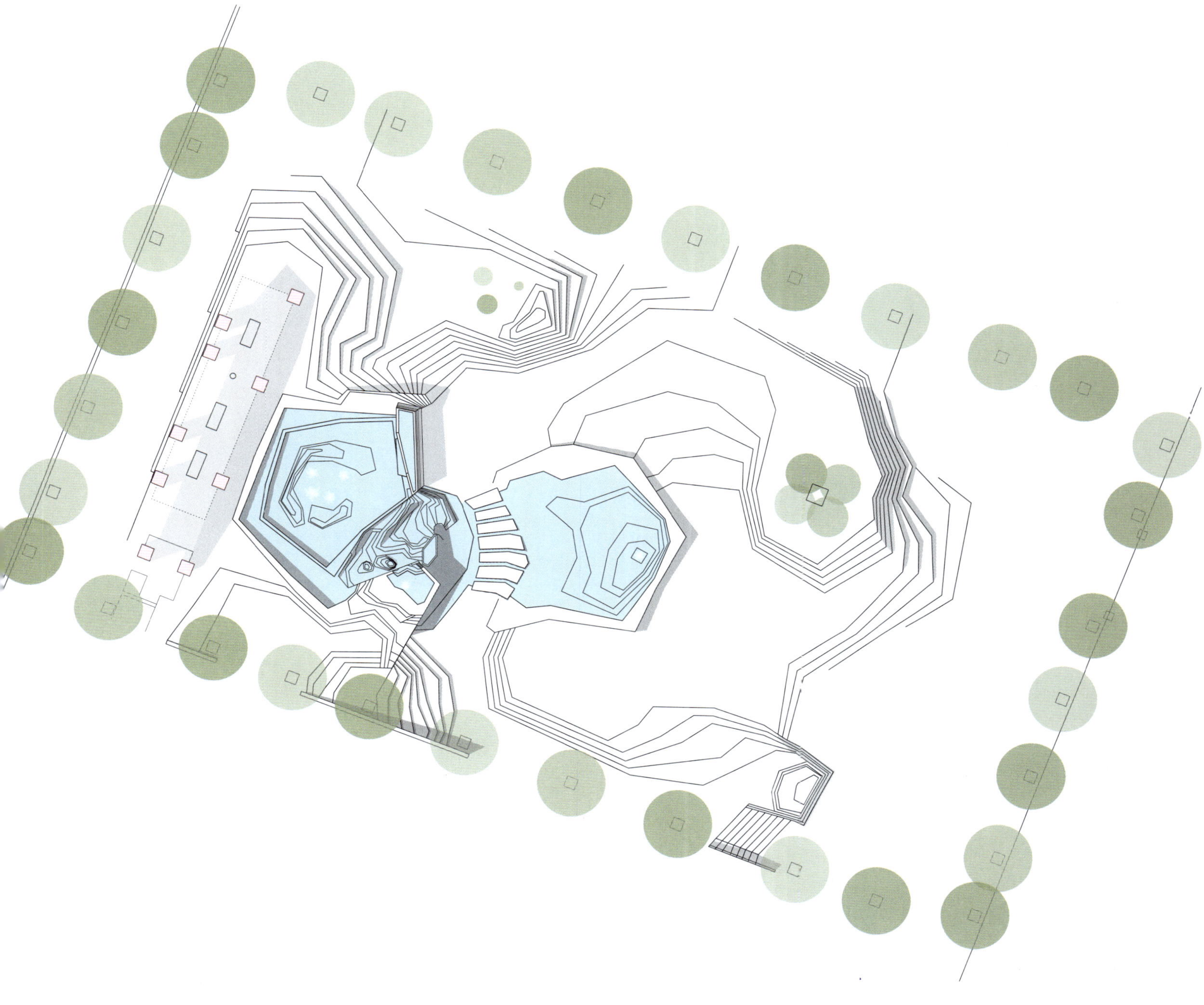

LOVEJOY FOUNTAIN, PORTLAND

0 5 10 25M

Water from the cataract flows into a calm lake, but not before contending with a dressed stone stepping panel walk (opposite, left and above). The slots between the stepping panels conduct fairly high flow rates, they hold that energy, then release it into the lake. The turbulence at the slots' exit points relaxes quickly into the large, welcoming body of water.

60 Ira Keller Fountain

The Ira Keller Fountain, or Fourcourt Fountain, as it was originally known, was completed in 1970, some years after the nearby Lovejoy Plaza. Both are part of Portland's Urban Sequence, a group of conceptually linked open spaces in the southwest area of downtown. The park was designed by Lawrence Halprin and Angela Danadjieva. Ms. Danadieva was a Bulgarian architect and set designer, who worked in Halprin's studio. Danadjieva, not without some controversy, is credited with the design's signature character, while Halprin's involvement is undisputed as the author of its guiding principals and general format. This business of who designed the fountain is a source of squabble to this day, though it is obvious both were engaged participants.

Approaching from the block's west side, walking mildly downslope in the direction of Portland's Willamette River, one might not even know that one of the greatest water features in America was mere steps away, but three narrow, V-shaped slots in the seeded concrete paving introduce fastmoving flows in channels hinting that something is up. The burgeoning waters expand in sculpturally abstract streams and pools, widening to much of the width of the city block before tumbling over a chasm, which, when seen from the south looking back and upslope, present a dramatic formation, monumentally scaled, thick with white-water flows. There is none of the facets of Lovejoy here, only four years later; a new visual language is created for Forecourt Fountain.

The fountain's warm, cinnamon color is a serendipidous gift from the plumbing equipment's rusting, as at Lovejoy.

A few years ago, I was asked by Charles Birnbaum, leader of the Cultural Landscape Foundation, to participate in a symposium regarding Lawrence Halprin's contributions to the field of landscape archtecture. In it, I suggested that the Ira Keller Fountain was intentionally related to Rome's Trevi Fountain. Both fountains faced an angle just off of south, receiving the midday sun (Keller tilted a bit to the east, Trevi tilted a bit to the west. Both fountains were about the same size. Both fountains had spaces to the right where visitors could access the space of the fountain. Both fountains had block-wide steps down where people could sit, sheltered from traffic to absorb their iconic presentations. And both fountains were gestures of culture, built as environmental landmarks in prideful cities. The fact that one was expressed through Renaissance sculpture and the other was based upon abstractions of nature seemed, to me at least, secondary. The values they share seem more pertinent than the values they do not.

The visual language is unique, and uniquely effective. The textured, cast-in-place concrete finish abrades the sliding water flows to froth up in thick white-water panels, while other waters that leap off the rustic weir edges are glassy and densely ribbed. Both work well against the medium-dark value concrete to present water in sunlight.

STRENGTH AND BEAUTY COME
IRA'S
DEDICATED BY

The waters that feed the mighty falls begin modestly enough, from three springs, like this one (upper left). The waters stagger outward, gaining in volume and energy (top right). The water becomes calm enough just before tumbling over the installation's signature, monumental cliffs, where it sizzles on the aggregate-seeded concrete faces.

Like Lovejoy before it, the concrete and exposed aggregate finish material has been stained by iron from the fountain machinery, and like Lovejoy, the fountain is probably improved by the accidental coloration, with its warmly burnished orange blush.

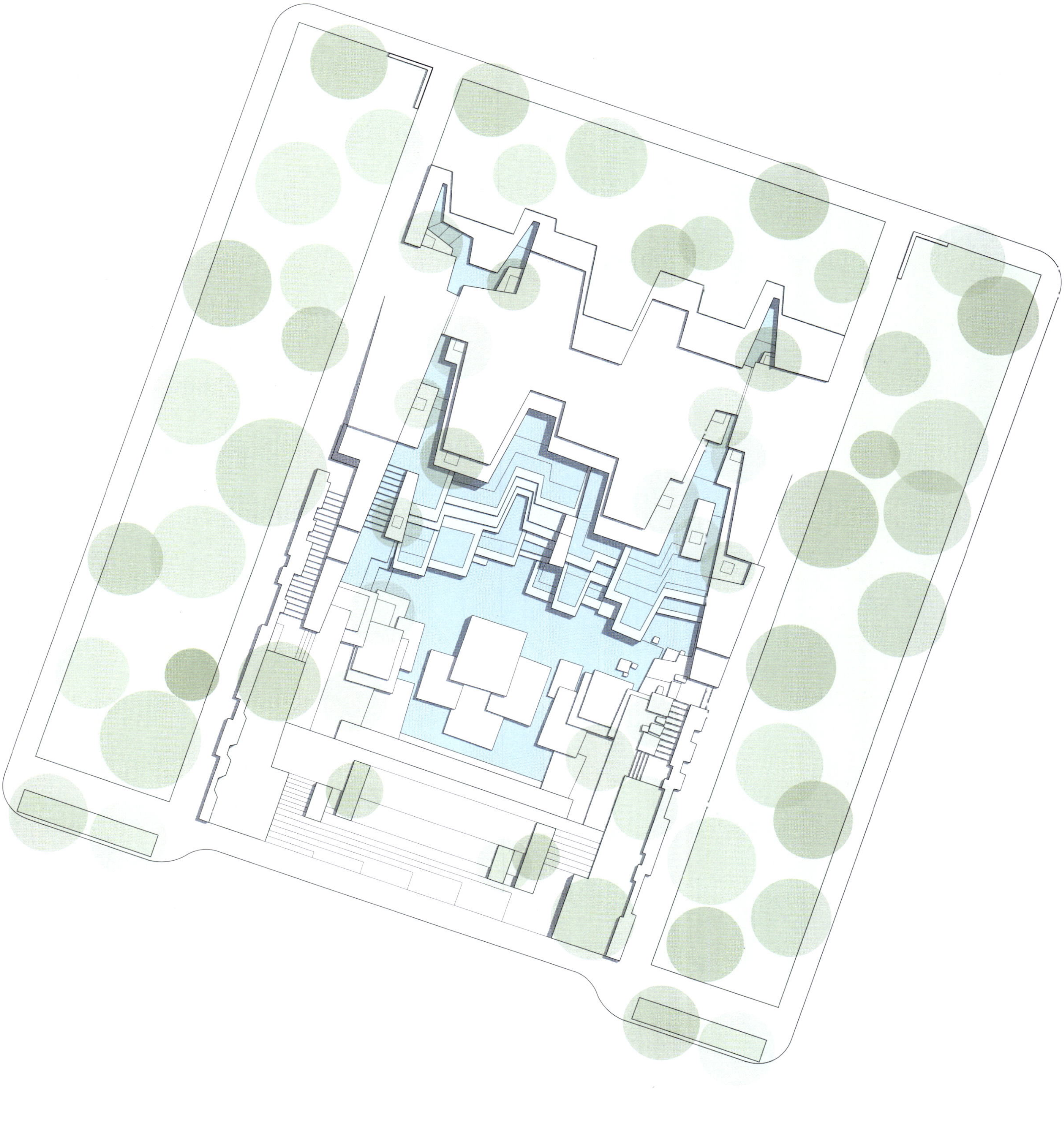

KELLER FOUNTAIN PARK, PORTLAND

0 1 5 10 20M

The north side of the cliffs give passage to a behind the waterfall experience (opposite center right, opposite center left lower, and above). At Trevi, the congruent space to the right is a small patio, with a fountain in the fountain, offering drinking water.

Amphitheater-like seating (opposite bottom left) cascades down from the adjacent street to the recessed pool area with its various internal terraces. A heady, white-water cascade is partly hidden to the left of the fountain's main elevation (opposite bottom right).

61 Jamison Square

This one-block urban park is developed with a transforming, immersive water feature as it centerpiece. It mostly serves neighborhood families who benefit from the play it provides children. The bow-shaped water feature is positioned in the center of the park, facing west, receiving the afternoon sun and with its back to the busy street to the east. A lawn with canopy trees along the block's fountain-facing zone offers a shady place to rest and keep an eye on things. The park and its fountain was designed by Peter Walker.

From the perspective of water craft, the cascade is unique. Cascades, as a class of display from antiquity share the condition that the intitial, or top fall is clear, undeveloped, leading to subsequent falls, which are textured and consistent. At Hellbrunn this is cleverly turned to advantage with the incorporation of artwork panels to be incorporated only at the top fall. But Jamison manages to make the first fall look much like the others. This is accomplished by pressurizing the source. The water squirts out quickly and frothily, pressing past top and bottom rough stone surfaces. The top slot is not so much a weir as it is a roughened linear nozzle.

The cascade's flows are not merely consistent—they impressively deliver a unique blending of churning white-water thickets with striated glassy streams. The expanding and retracting pool, too, functions well as an engaging, spatial reflector.

The water feature plays through a cyclical display sequence, transforming from a dry space, then activated by the cascades, a pool appears and fills to a depth of about 25cm, then the cascades taper off and slow the pool drains to emptiness. The narrative repeats over something like a twenty-minute cycle.

The east edge of Jamison Square is dressed in a finely detailed wooden sidewalk which connects the park to Tanner Springs Park, an identically sized but very different urban amenity, four blocks to the north.

The 'Sense of Immediacy' (Charles Moore's phrase) that water can bring about is evident at the cascades at Jamison Square (left).

The special character in the water steps is created by a pressurized top throw from a chamber under the capstone, which works something like a slot nozzle made of rough stone. The resulting flows have a marvelous visual character and rich, sonic signature.

The fountain's has a choreographic narrative which transitions over time from an all-dry environment to active cascades, which creates the pool and raises its water level, then the cascades transition off and the pool slowly drains away, to be re-created, soon enough, to the reviving pleasure of the fountain's visitors and participants.

62 Vaillancourt Fountain

A fair candidate to be the most disliked good fountain in the United States is San Francisco's Vaillancourt Fountain. Located in the Embarcadero area, the installation was created by the artist, Armand Vaillancourt in the early 1970s. Its concrete forms were conceived in visual relation to the Embarcadero Freeway, which lumbered above, titanically, just behind the fountain. That is, until it was destroyed in the earthquake of 1991, and, as it was generally detested, never rebuilt. Starker today without the freeway backdrop, the fountain still manages to withstand occasional calls for its fate to follow that of its inspiration and meet the wrecking ball.

The fountain is underestimated. The spouts which issue from square openings in the ends of the cranked, concrete forms, are robust and good looking. It's jetting actions are pleasingly volumetric, lively, and in excellent proportion with the overall composition of the design. And they make a terrific noise.

There are nine functioning spouts, pouring on average about a half a cubic meter of water per minute each—which is a lot. The broad reception pool receives all the flows and establishes a proportionate space for the appreciation of the dynamic sculpture. Stepping stones behind and under the sculpture offer more intimate, and even louder, experiences. A raised coping surrounding the pool does a good job containing the action while establishing a sharp visual frame for the large-format urban set piece.

Although the sculpture's system of boxy girders would seem to be modular, each of their nine jets presents a different water design problem with each handling their differing situations uniquely and appropriately.

The twisted, horizontal box (lower left) acts as a gigantic spout to pour a grand volume of white-water. High above, another box issues water that seems to fill its entire cross section of opening with spray. The down-pointing box, below, is a little thin in a way that looks like a maintenance shortfall rather than a design slip.

Two of the boxes (upper right, second from top) offer clear, flowing streams in a paired event, framing a third waterfall between and below.

The pool (left) is a little wild, deep and dangerous looking by contemporary standards, but it pairs well with its muscular sculpture and jets.

65 BATTERY

63 Levi's Plaza

The fountain is made memorable by it's centerpiece rock, perhaps, but its design is complex and many of its parts showcase a variety of superbly-performing displays.

The plaza was designed by Lawrence Halprin and completed in 1982. The landscape architect, Steven Koch, who worked for Halprin later, relayed the anecdote that Halprin had seen a rock in a quarry and asked the quarry to hold it for him. Halprin liked that rock very much. He had no place to put it at the moment, but felt the chance would surely come some day. The quarry was obliging to Mr. Halprin. After something like ten years, Halprin called them back, and yes, the rock was still there, held for him. This is the rock placed at Levi's Plaza.

The rock is somewhat two-dimensional, with an obvious front and back. The back side of the rock (to the north) faces the fountain's more articulated elements, leaving the simpler and stronger presentation facing south towards the sun and the plaza's open space.

Within that semi-hidden, shady north side, stepping stones and small open moments establish a meander through and around the fountain. To the east, a linear cascade with nine textured, sloped steps frame a vigorous rush of water. The rock is in silhouette from this position, but its corona-like outline of water gitters in the midday sun. The crenelated lower reaches ground the fountain in a water skirting remeniscent of the base falls of the Neptune Fountain at the Villa d'Este. Looking up, we are presented by left and right cascades. Those on the left are thick in layered white-water. Those on the right are glassy, and fed from a central geyser and waterfall such that—and this is a bit subtle—at each subsequent terrace, low waves glide sidewas to a side wall and then reflect back through the step's pool; the effects here are like watching someone play the piano, moving their hands back and forth over the keys, while the flows step down and through. All the pools are fed from the various sources above them and they are all lively with reflecting wave patterns, except the one in the center, which is calm.

The special rock of Levi's Plaza, due to its scale, character, coloration, and form, has no trouble playing the alpha role in the hierarchy of elements in the space. Smaller stones are dropped in like talus at the base of the front steps (Opposite and top right).

A variety of delightful nooks and water exhibits are almost hidden in the small space to the north of the rock, including the stepped flume (right upper center) the spring and cascade (right lower center), the low falls (right), which are composed in uneven plan crenelation, another cascade, which steps from thre rock (right—deep in the image, left side), and various pools, stairs and stepping panels.

The north side of the design can be accessed walking through the composition, just east of the rock (top left). The cascades that flow from the rock's terrace, roll over textured cast concrete, each ledge about 450 mm tall, to generate a water action looking almost like a crisp ink drawing (top right). The stepped flume (far left), similarly presents a markedly textured water action. Two geysers are part of the design. This one, to the west, presents an uncomplicated action from a standard-issue nozzle, but it is a good nozzle, with a rich effect of glassy, textured streamers (left).

Waters from the nozzle are well behaved, do not splash too much for the pool, and generate—with the pool—a lively wave action that is transferred to the cascades below it (above center). In this photo we can see that the flows immediately from the pool's channel, which feeds the cascade, leave the two sides of the cascades in shadow, and less lively. In reality, this is not so true because interesting sideways wavelets reflect back and forth at each level of the cascade, establishing a playing the piano sort of activity, overlaying the downward flows.

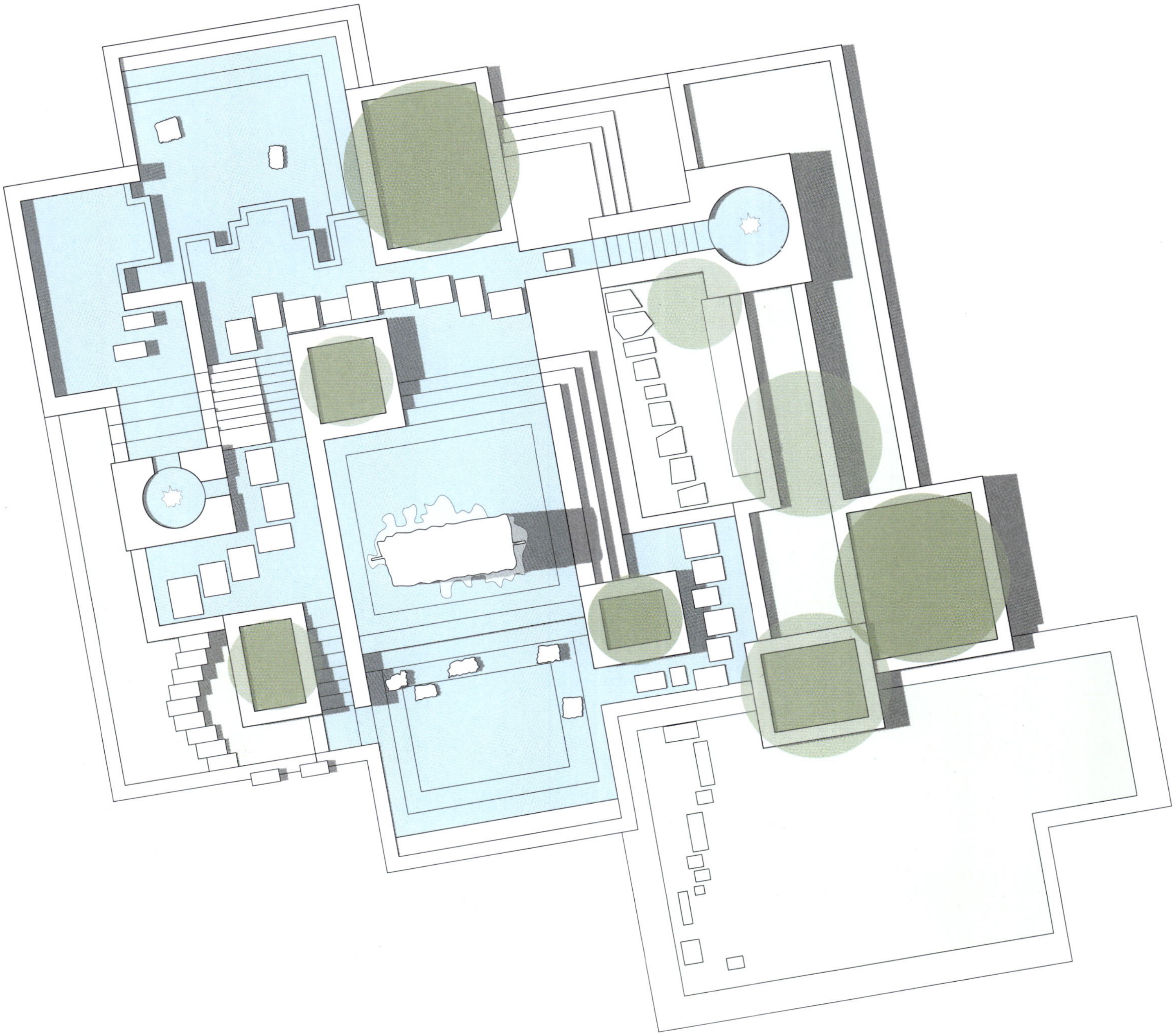

LEVI'S PLAZA, SAN FRANCISCO

0 5 10M

64 Hearst Castle

The swimming pool that Julia Morgan designed for William Randoph Hearst's Castle in central California shows us underwater finishes in dark blue glass mosaics with gold mosaic ornamental accents. The result is a highly reflective water volume undistracted by refracted underwater imagery. Just enough light reaches the pool's internal surfaces to yield a feeling for its considerable depths. The room's walls are also dark from matching mosaic finishes, which serve to modulate and focus the bright beams of daylight to high-contrast, dramatic effect.

Strategically, there are no skylights over the main portion of the pool. The iconic reflected sunlight visual statement is performed solely from a generous alcove, into which the stem of the T-shaped pool extends. This arrangement prevents the sunlight from overlighting the main pool, which would decrease the water surface's reflectivity and spoil the effect of the diagonally beaming sun's play.

Electric torcheres parade about the perimeter of the pool, presumably creating a quite different nighttime effect. We can imagine the lanterns' soft lighting hardly effecting the blue walls while causing the white marble standards to glow and reflect in the dark pool's surface, challenged by little other than what light manages to reach the underwater gold mosaic filigree. The carved, Carrara marble ladders are an additional, nice touch, and at night, and they would glow reassuringly brightly in the dark, torchere-lit space.

The other thing common visitors do not see is what the pool is like when people are swimming in it. We can imagine the back wall still lit in the strong diagonal light, while its reflection is broken by waves into flickering shards. The pool might be as impressive with busy waters, though very different.

The T-shaped swimming pool's main space is dark. Light is introduced from a skylit alcove stemming away from the main room where the bright sunlight plays and reflects to create an illuminative focus for the main space. This energetic light effect is balanced from two calmer groupings of three arched windows centered in the narrow walls of the rectangular main room. This secondary lighting prevents the main light source from being a source of glare. This complex and effective light strategy is the primary device, the secondary being the dark blue mosaic finishes, which combine with the pool to create the drama of the space.

65 Disneyland Water Features

I learned from Disney personnel that there were, at that time, 84 water features in Disneyland (there are more now, in the ever expanding Magic Kingdom). This is roughly the same number of water features as in the gardens of Versailles, though those at Disneyland are smaller and very different, naturally. Both places share lofty aims even if only one of them was an actual seat of government.

Water is employed throughout the park to contribute to the quality of the guest experience. Much of the water craft is well done, aside from the artifice in their sculptural accessories.

The waterfall at the Matterhorn is unusually well-behaved for such a large, attenuated fall. There are two other significant waterfalls; the Jungle River Cruise offers a boat tour behind a fall that used to be stronger, but has been subdivided, weakening its power. The other, at the submarine ride, is actually better, but far enough away that it is reduced to a scenic background element, one of many. The moat around Cinderella's Castle is carefully scaled, as is the river that loops around Tom Sawyer's Island. The fan jets around the Dumbo Ride, with their fanciful, golden nozzles are so good that the water feature design community once saw them as a touchstone. The three-teir Mickey Mouse fountain at Tunetown (no longer existing) is an accomplished exhibit of craft, while water becomes the path at the Its A Small World ride, providing a tactile experience while keeping things moving along. The water road at Pirates of the Carribean is a more vigorous experience, particularly with its eyebrow lifting climb up the rushing flume.

The most charming and inventive water feature in the park is The Magic Fountain, in the Enchanted Tiki Room. It dates back to opening day in 1955 and benefitted from Walt Disney's personal involvement. It shows water effectively in a variety of ways; it is colorful, with displays including a clever mechanical action which behaves rather well for a fountain in a small space. It interacts with other show pieces in the room and performs in time with the music and other charming scene of graphic animations. The Tiki Room's musical show is delivered with a nice artistic touch and an easygoing sense of humor. The space could hardly be imagined without the Magic Fountain.

Looking at any of the water features at Disnelyland is to understand them as elements in scenic environments, with the exception of the Magic Fountain in the Enchanted Tiki Room, which is the focal point of the space. But generally, the water features at Disneyland are subordinate to wider concepts and proportioned for those roles. Throughout the park, water is employed for ambient, atmospheric effect (left), and as characters in scenic narratives, such as at the Matterhorn (right center) or at the Jungle River Cruise (right).

EXPLORER

The rockery may not quite look real, but the water action is convincing (opposite top left). The waterfall at the Jungle River Cruise used to be much greater, before it was broken into three parts, for reasons unfathomable (opposite center). The faraway waterfall at the Submarine ride is more successful (opposite upper center right). The Magic Fountain of the Tiki Room (opposite bottom row) includes an impossibly tall column of water, which elevates to a chandelier and draw it down, with attendant singing birds. The fan-shaped jets at the Dumbo ride employ nozzles finished in gold, contributing greatly to the water's sparkling actions. Mickey's fountain in Tune Town imploys a challenging, vertically attenuated cascade of glassy petals. Water forms the path in the It's A Small World ride, as guests explore from boats (fundamentally, a crowd flow management technique), more felt than seen, the canals provide the experience with a boyant, tactile grace, which mates well with the briliant, Mary Blaire-designed color schemes and imagery.

66 Salk Institute for Biological Studies

The central space was orginally a Lawrence Halprin project. Halprin had conceived of a green refuge framed by the great buildings overlooking the ocean. Then while working on the architecture, Kahn visited Barragan in Mexico City. A letter written back to his office testified to Kahn's enthusiasm about what he found. Barragan was subsequantly invited to see the site. His response, "Not one tree, not one blade of grass," was only learned about relatively recently. It is rumored that Barragan was not paid for his time, which is hard to believe. The project is officially listed by the Barragan Foundation for the years 1965-1966. The actual courtyard design work was performed in Kahn's office in Philadelphia. Because the construction was so far along, the final drawings were performed quickly. An associate of Kahn's executed the work.

The poetic unity of space, light and water in the courtyard may have no superior anywhere. There is a subtle echo of the Alhambra or the Agra Fort. Kahn and Salk's achievement went far beyond the creation of honorable workplaces for hardworking scientists. Many decades after its creation, the institute is still among the most respected and successful scientific enterprises in the world.

A modest, but monumental wellspring is positioned at the east end of the courtyard. Arranged into a U-shape, three cojoined clear sheet falls intersect and weld into a fixed but energized form. The waters pour into a channel. The flow rate is about 200 liters per minute. The conduit is lined in panels of open-cell travertine. Water moves steadily in the direction the Pacific Ocean, beyond.

Funnily, because the wind is typically strong and from the west, waves on the west side of the runnel tend to pattern back to the east, as if the flows were backwards, even though the actual water flow walks steadily westward.

The clarity of the diagram gets a little diffused at the west end of the courtyard. The water from the runnel flows into a pool nearly as wide as the courtyard. It then pours from a heavy U-shaped spout into another pool, which is symmetrically met by a pair of stone staircases. That pool yields to another, which is framed by a geometrical arrangement of travertine club chairs. The last waterfall is an unusually large, clear sheet behaving with remarkable stability. A tribute on the face of the weir is hidden behind the waterfall.

The water is almost crystaline, flowing in the Southern California sun over finely dressed travertine panels. The intensive double-waterfall is unique and effective. The purity of the initial compositional elements loosens up towards the western edge of the court, where various pools and falls play with variation and surprise. The final waterfall presents as large an unbroken clear sheet as I have seen anywhere. It hides a commemorative inscription on the face of its weir (right).

67 The Getty Center

The Villa's grounds encompass divergent attitudes to the experience of space and water. A vehement aesthetic argument between the Richard Meier, the architect of the Getty, and Robert Irwin, the artist who designed its center garden, received a fair amount of press when the completed work was unveiled. The water features other than that in the central garden were developed under the Getty's landscape architect, Laurie Olin.

An axial pool in the main courtyard takes queues from the famous liinear fountain at the Generalife. A continuous stone bench biases the water feature to the eucalyptus trees side of the fountain, away from people, curiously. And there is another problem with this otherwise very fine fountain—its elegantly arching streams are nearly invisible due to the light-toned context (mostly of cream-colored travertine) and some complexities of the play of light in the space. There is some glare from the bright Southern California sun and the sparkles we expect to see in the streams and pool are never brought to life because most of the time we are forced to look at the fountain from the wrong angle.

A nearby fountain of interrelated pools at the south end of the courtyard incorporates a frame-breaking composition select stones with a randomized disposition of glassy jets. There is someting antiquarian about this fountain, though it is unapologetically modern in design and construction. Additional fountains can be found in the approach terraces; there is another in a northern plaza, and a very quiet one near the visitor transit system's lower terminal incorporating a fair-sized bronze by Henry Moore.

Robert Irwin's installation begins with a stream through a sloped, green lawn, flowing over fitted rocks while cuting through leafy vegetation and under bridges to penetrate a slot and cascade down a purple-tinted, stepped stone wall. The floor of the rotunda is designed with a labyrinthine interweave of plantings and water, where many of the garden's plants were selected by their capacity to change colors through the seasons. Regrettably, as alluring as this area is, it is inaccessible. The water serves Irwin's garden as a principle player, activating the pedestrian circulation areas and celebrating the terminal rotunda.

The linear water feature's jets are not as visible as they are audible due to solar orientation and the light value stone finishes all around (top). The interplay of naturalism and architectural geometry is played out at the courtyard's south fountain, and there is a mythic, almost allegorical character in the scenic posing of the rocks and jets (center).

Water flows through the length of the Robert Irwin-designed garden, finally cascading over a textured flume to come to rest in a labyrinthine garden, where the design seems to float over a sea-green reflection pool. The sculpted plantings seem to float on stone pontoons while the water seems to glide below in a shiny, cool and dark backdrop layer.

Expert Guide

I met the private architectural tour provider at the agreed-upon time at her car, which was large and comfortable, and there was plenty of room for me to situate my photography gear and notebook. We had previously discussed the sites to be visited and together we reitereaded the sequence. Her knowledge of the subject was profound, even personal, as she apparently knew all the owners of the properties on our list very well as well as the special complications of the pubic spaces. One location was no longer available at the last minute, and she offered a serviceable alternative with which I was perfectly comfortable. Other than that, everything was set and we headed gamely out into Mexico City's concatenate urban traffic. We started early, on a beautiful, sunny day.

68 Casa Gilardi

Located on a quiet, well-heeled neighborhood in Mexico City, is Louis Barragan's Casa Gilardi. The house is comprised of satisfying, well-proportioned rooms, simply made, assembled with a courtyard in a complex plan. An attenuated, yellow corridor on the ground level draws curiosity. At the end the corridor is one of the most remarkable and skillful poetic compositions of architectural space, light and water to be found.

It was Barragan who abstracted the brilliant, saturated Mexican color schemes from folk art, and then applied it in sumptuous fields to his works of serious, reductive modern architecture. Barragan also sidestepped common structural or geometric regulating measures such as repeating bays or controlling grids, releasing his work from that kind of determinism and freeing his compositions to be proportioned by his artful eye.

The ostensible, no, that's not quite fair. The functional purpose of the pool is for swimming. We are seeing the family swimming pool. The pool's red column is helpful, but it is not structurally necessary. More important, the column obstructs our vision, preventing us from seeing everything at once, providing the scene with a powerful layer of intrigue. Subtle shifts in the wall and ceiling planes create edges defining an inner volume, controlling light and stopping color planes. A hidden monitor above controls daylight to slant in. This slot of light reflects on the pool's surface to register up to the opposite wall while refracting down into the water volume. The refracted light defines a second registration of light on the pool's floor. The underwater light also scatters to permeate the entire pool in a gently suffused glow. The pool's wall and floor are painted in a medium tone aqua, which subtly conducts this measure of reflected light.

The intense brilliance of the red column creates a high-contrast visual vibration, so dominating the center of the composition that the rest is made more ambiguous. The red's pink overtone relieves the color of harshness. The green-blue of the pool would appear to be mostly a product of the water's absorption of red (in other words, the pool's color seems natural, though it is carefully contrived). The rest of the house is exceedingly pragmatic, physically grounded, somewhat humble and quite joyful. The chambered water composition is none of these. It functions in high abstraction, manifesting an exotic displacement, or, otherworldliness.

The space is silent and still. The water in the basin interplays with the light from the hidden monitor above in a fixed variety of ways. A slot of light projects down from above, slanting down behind the rectangular, red column. The beam that hits the surface of the pool splits in two. Part of that light reflects up to the wall to strike it with a reflected image of its source. The other part of the light refracts into the water, changing its projection angle, to strike the wall in an underwater position, beneath the projected band of light above.

69 Fuente de los Amantes

The design brief called for a neighborhood watering pool for horses. Barragan's solution involved aqueduct symbolism and a free and open space, abstracted through the highly regarded architectural language he synthesized from international modernism and indigenous Mexican culture.

Horses drink from a wide stone pool, shallow at the edges. The pool is fed off-center by a cantilevered trough from a height of about four meters. The pool under the waterfall is about 60cm deep, I was told. The rose, fuscia and mauve walls are chromatically convincing with the blue sky and the greens of the lawn and pool. The texture of the falling water and its impressive lateral throw result from hidden techniques. The flume textures and aerates the water. The spout drools a little. The circulating water is continuously drained through very small, difficult to see, openings in the rock-seeded shallows at the pool's the front and rear edges, a nice detail in the mid-century style. The green in the water is from algae, but there's not so much as to seem troublesome.

The proportions of the stereometric scene are simple and strong. The boldly napped walls, their saturated colors, the space that projects under the aqueduct, the space-holding rose-toned wall behind, and the visual and sonic actions of the spout and the pool, all combine to create an artful aura of energizing, restorative calm, masterfully provided by a great artist, and touched by some kind of mystery.

The throw is the star, but the long proportions create the star's space. The two sculptures (opposite top) bring something we might not notice unless they were removed. The lateral elevation's simplicity (opposite) is almost disturbing in its ineffable completeness; the throw, and the textured, colored architectural elements are in some kind of magical, Mexican balance. (Below) the pool's perimeter recirculation weeps.

70 Cuandra San Cristobal

The project encompasses a private residence, stables for sixteen horses and grounds. Entrance is gained through a shaded gate, leading to the house and the open spaces for the stables beyond. The water feature is central to the pinwheel parti.

As with Fuente de los Amantes, horses are fed by a wide pool, shallow at its edges, which is supplied by the flume from a metaphorical aqueduct. The basin is white-colored, though in an earlier guise it was painted black. The central pool is surrounded on three sides by a buff-colored, course grained, degenerated granite ground plane. Stone paving flanks the walk alongside the stables.

The spout animates the pool and stirs the otherwise quiet space with its sounds. It's height is about 1.5 meters. The water's attractive throw is created by rock-finished ramp partly hidden within the thin walls of the flume. This clever technique provides the water with momentum and turbulence. A small spout at the end of the flume prevents the water from drooling on the architecture while strengthening the waterfall with an exactingly proportioned, self-referential isolation.

There is a large barn full of organized clutter hidden behind the tall, dark red back wall. It seemed vaguely interesting. Later, I realized it was Baragan's key to the success of the great space, as it relieved the space of countless sundries. An effective trade had been silently negotiated to purify the open space and visible architecture.

The basin is white; its turquoise color is brought from the water's natural refraction of sunlight. The aqueduct-wall is appended by a small channel, which prevents the waterfall from drooling onto the base of the wall, which otherwise would have been a problem. The energy in the impact from the waterfall is sufficient to broadcast gentle wavelets to glide evenly across the full width of the wide pool (opposite and this page).

71 Camino Real

This Ricardo Leggoretto-designed urban resort hotel in Mexico City's posh Polanco district (with Luis Barragan serving as design consultant) is composed of low, grand volumes proportioned by heavily textured walls dramatically painted in saturated colors. The arrival courtyard is dominated by a remarkable central fountain, designed by the sculptor, Isamu Noguchi.

The fountain takes the form of a spherical slice into a white marble floor—a perfect, rimless bowl—partially filled with highly activated, swirling water. The pool's stark geometry and the water's surprising force have garnered enthusiasm since the hotel's 1979 opening.

Camino Real's fountain is driven by a machine pushing a forceful jet of water through an underwater, canon-like, twirling tube, which is anchored on the floor of the bowl, something like a jetting spoon stirring a pot from below. The jet creates a forceful, foaming, unpredictably roving plume on the surface of the pool. Waves rushing away from the plume reflect on the pool's sidewalls and bounce back to meet new and previously generated waves, which are out of sequence with the returning wave front. The wildly overlapping results harken a force of nature.

A perhaps apocryphal anecdote has circulated that the fountain's signature action is accidental. If true, it would hardly be the first time for the accident to be superior to the plan, nor should its appreciation be any diminished, as the fountain is so strong.

A second, indoor fountain occupies an all-blue atrium. This fountain is also clever. The basin is painted dark blue and adorned with a single jet, creating a clear sheet cone of water nearly a meter tall. This glassy form is lit from below to cast huge, flickering light effects on the dark, shaded, four-story walls and ceiling of the space. A glass floor over part of the pool hosts club chairs offering the chance to sit within the volume of the modern fountain.

Mexico City's sunlight on Camino Real's saturated paint (upper left) orchestrates the architecture's radiant, abstract composition, which reflects (or reiterates) in the water. The fountain in the shade (lower left) is less about reflection, and more about white water against the ground of the water's refracted blue tint (the basin is white marble).

The signature, surging froth is frankly like no other fountain's in the world; four images (top right) shows the pool surface's half-meter flexure and the roving froth's continuously changing condition.

Late afternoon golden light on the underwater jet's erruptive, whitewater crest (right, lower center). The perimeter spray system, on at night with underwater lighting (right).

First Falaj

Folded into a small car with three others crossing a Middle-Eastern desert, we finally stopped at a roadside vendor to cool off and stretch our legs. It was a quiet place. There was a fruit stand with a few tables under a striped fabric shade and the moderate breeze passing by was pleasant. We all got bottles of water from a friendly man but while lingering I left the others to investigate the old-looking orchard behind the tents.

Narrow concrete channels had been roughly poured between close rows of what I took to be banana trees. I walked on the ledges of the channels to go deeper into the garden, which I had to myself. The water flowing in the streams was surprisingly lively and it made a pleasant sound, especially when it was directed to turn a corner or split in two directions. There were hand-hewn gates used to control the irrigation, and most of them were open, with the water running all over the place. I found myself hopping about from flume to flume, without thinking, almost dancing.

Soon enough I was feeling sufficiently ridiculous, so I snapped a few photos and made my way back. It wasn't until a couple of years later, after repeated recollections of the interlude that I realized how significant it felt.

I got it into my head how restorative that shady space of trees and water had felt. And that hundreds of years ago irrigation systems like that were never only about technique and agriculture. They were also about the culture that built them and the elegantly crafted feeling they created.

Probably, I imagined, in a less technologically sophisticated time, plantations with artful arrangements of swirling water channels established a sense of human community, joyfully and rightly made in connection with nature, of which this little place only hinted. I recalled Melville, "There is an art in all things."

72 Oman Falaj

Neither old nor famous, this network of traditional irrigation channels conducts sparkling waters to wend and sing beneath the agriculture of shady fruit trees.

We came upon the place while driving across the desert in Oman. We stopped for water and fruit, and discovered the irrigating water feature behind the fruit stand. In spite of its simple, ostensible functionalism, the installation provides a delightful experience for this desert traveler. The farmers sell the fruit to appreciative passersby. The fruit comes directly from the trees behind the fruit stands, which are fed by the circuiting waters. The roughly built system is maintained by the farmers, who attend to its simple needs without great effort. Visitors may wander through the grove and the falajes—local, traditional irrigation channels—which conduct the water to the plantings. The scene is deeply refreshing. The experience certainly offers a criticism of more sophisticated, yet somehow less soulful, water features.

The falaj is a conductive network of troughs of water which lead from a water source, such as a tapped aquifer, to agricultural plantings. Gates are built into the troughs to regulate the drainage of water into the planted lands. The construction of falajes, due to the preciousness of the water they are to hold, is usually of a high quality, fastidious, particularly, in the care for leak-free conditions. Functioning falajes can still be found in the Middle East, where they have been employed for many hundreds of years.

In Spain or the American Southwest, a very similar concept is called an acequia. In places like Valencia or Albuquerque, where water remains a critical and carefully managed resource, acequias are still used exactly as they were when they were first built. In Albuquerque, water rights are a serious matter, some handed down generationally in relation to property ownership. Horse-riding officials in that community still to this day monitor the fields, control the locks and mete out the water in the most conscientious manner.

In the great deserts of the Middle East we can find some of the most poetic iterations of this pragmatic construction, with a soulfulness that belies any capture in photography.

This simple network of falajes was found watering fruit trees in the Omani desert. The rough concrete construction was without any cracks or leaks, slathered in a cement-based waterproofing veneer. Its gates, simply fabricated from scrap wood panels, sufficiently controlled the flows to the various sections. The fruit trees being cared for were healthy, fecund and productive.

The water flowing in the channels made low and medium frequency musical tones. The swirls in the flows were made visible by dark shadow patterns, rippling sky reflections and sunlit sparkles. Various wavelet characters vied for dominance. The struggles at the gates were, in a way, funny. The whole scene was unified in a statement that needed no interpretation.

73 Agra Fort

From the Agra Fort, or the Red Fort, we can see the Taj in the distance. Legend says it was this distant view that the imprisoned Mughal emperor, Shah Jahan was left with after his son, Aurangzeb, seized the thone under the allegations that his father, the Shah, had been bankrupting the country to build the Taj Mahal.

Several exceptional water features are integral to the design of the Agra Fort. These include an elegant runnel, organized axially from a special entrance to terminate into a darkly deep, multifaceted reflection pool with a striking ornamental border expressed as an extrusion into the depths. A much larger rectangular reflection pool is centered in a rooftop courtyard, elaborated with bold perimeter of ornaments, activated by five geysers in a stretched quincunx pattern. A truly lovely (and much published) small, interior pool is made special by a smoothly carved bass-releif that, when wet, is presumably enhanced by the subtle variations in shading wrought by the pool's various depths. The effect would be subtle. There is also a steeply sloped water panel, flushly ornamented by assertive chevron patterning, but I only saw it dry and am skeptical that the water display amounts to much. The chevron pattern is repeated in a shallow pool, elsewhere, to greater success, with finely scaled inlaid devices arranged in a reversing diamond pattern.

For a military fort, one cannot but be struck that its water features are unusually refined and beautiful. These include the runnel and its deep pool (opposite and right), and the ornate fountain presented in an upper level courtyard (right top and middle).

The courtyard pool has not been in operation for some time, and our well-informed guide could answer questions only to a point, leaving us in empty speculation as to its idea. Therefore, we propose: Water is meant to fill the pool, nearly overflowing, and these flooding waters are comfortably drawn away by the decorated, shallow channel aimed to the west. The pool, then, is nice and full. The five tall geyser standards are then almost completely underwater with just their tips projecting above and spraying water into the air, creating a soothing background sound and a significant comforting effect from evaporative cooling. Numerous smaller jets, integrated into the just-underwater ornamental perimeter create a kind of border treatment of wavelet patterns over the stone outine. The many alcoves between the flourishing ornaments are seats. By this reckoning, what we see here is a Mogul-era hot tub for the fifteenth-century participants, or something along those lines.

This marble pool is one of the most exquisitely carved in the public eye. The detail is extraordinary and the carvings in fine condition (opposite and above). Water probably covered the entire volume, held just below the surrounding floor level. The carvings were partly made with the intent to benefit from the varying shading effects that water would bring in relation to its resultant depths. (Deeper water over a white basin imbues a turquoise tint, though it would be subtle with such shallow dimensions.) The rounded nozzle tip would soften how water falls back to the pool. The ripples in the carvings would echo the patterns created by the jet. We see similar patterns in the carved walls. The design is remarkably rich and unified. The aesthetic deliverables of the steep, dry flume (right upper center) defy easy speculation as water's effect over that smooth a surface would seem to lack noteworthy effect. The nearby ornamental pool (right lower center), on the other hand, which appears to be something like a foot bath, would very likely present a shimmering, shallow pool to succesful effect. (Right) the Agra Fort.

74 Shalimar Bagh

This trip was planned, but could not take place due to ongoing political turmoil with sporatic warfare. Still, this is a very significant site with important water components.

The gardens are large and courtly, and in a humanistic manner familiar to Indian culture. Its lengthy pools are shaded by closely bordering canopy trees. Regularly spaced sprays in the pools work with the shade to create lengthy zones of evaporatively-cooled, outdoor space. The scale of the design's cooling fountains is unmatched by any other landscape in the world, I believe.

There is a moment in the afternoon when the sun aligns with the axial pool such that from the summit, looking back to the southwest, all is glitter. Presumably.

The garden plan is a geometrically controlled, richly articulated play of repetitive forms modulating zoned experiences through scale transformations.

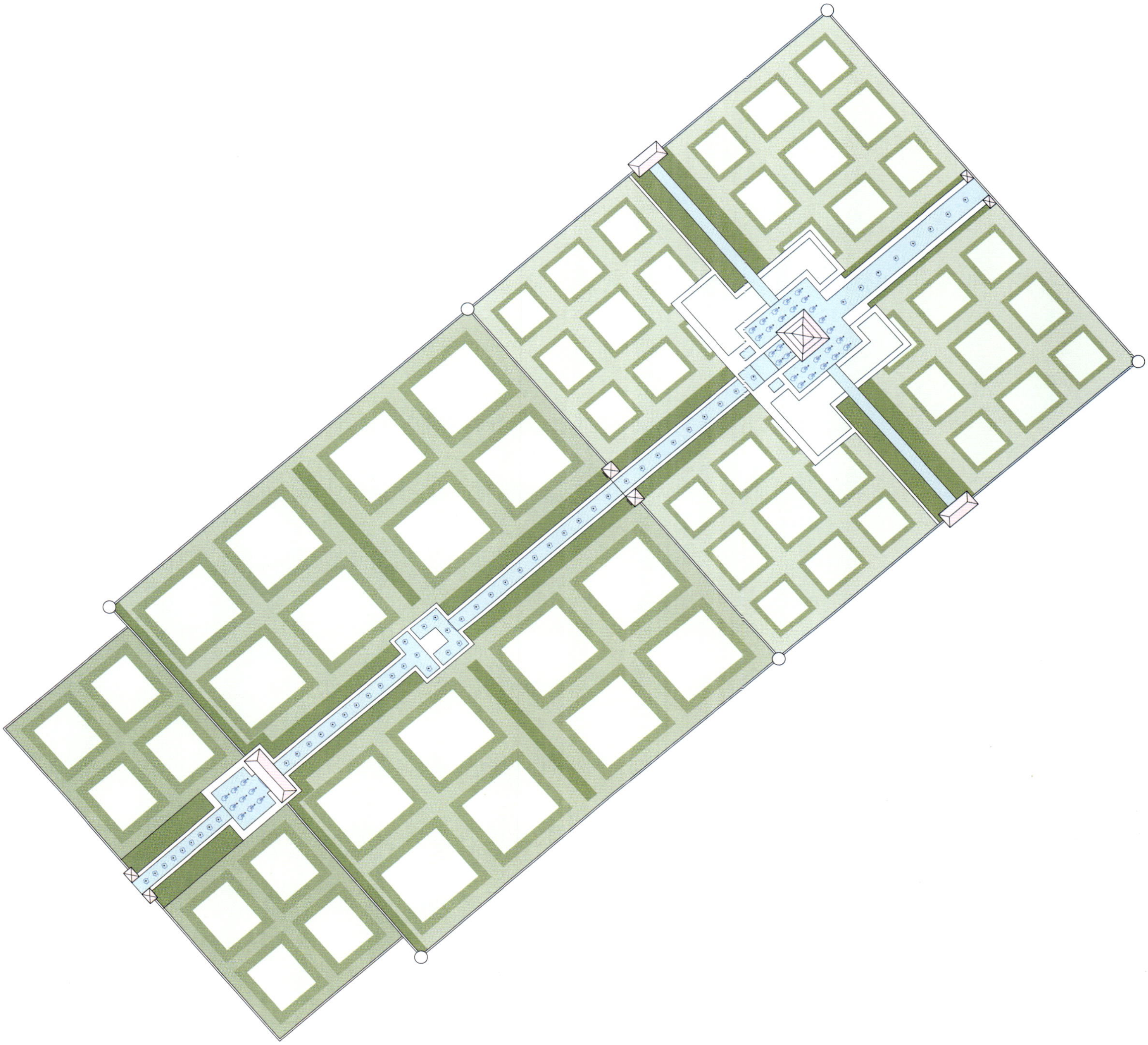

SHALIMAR BAGH, SRINAGAR

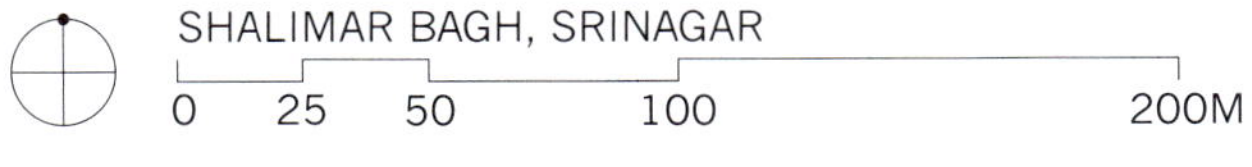

75 The Taj Mahal

Although three hundred and fifty two years old at the time of my visit, the Taj is in remarkably good condition, seeming to glow under Agra's flat, dry sunlight. There is a yielding translucency to the hard, white marble of which it is built, contributing to the architecture's radiance.

The red sandstone structures that surround the Taj should be mentioned more, as they are finelly proportioned, high-minded, and of excellent character. And they complement perfectly the whiteness of the central structure.

In person, one sees clearly that the four minarettes are slightly tilted away from the central form, which we are told is to prevent them from potentially falling into the monument they guard. The way we read photography does not make this obvious.

The axial pool reflects the Taj Mahal with fidelity, in spite of its light-toned basin finish, which runs counter to the contemporary approach using dark finishes to enhance perceived reflectivity. It works here because of the long and low reflective angle, the sharpness of which is automatically highly reflective. If the jets operate, their sprays would texture the pool and blur the image.

The exquisite planning of the Taj Mahal is evident throughout it's experience of composition, scale and proportion. The large site and the reflection pool's emphatic perspective are relieved by a bridge-like belvedere occupying the pool's half-way position, about which one is hardly aware when standing at the classic view position at the approach end of the pool, thanks to the Taj's significant podium. And so, the small pool with its minaret-inspired spindle jet atop the structure is a surprise.

Behind the Taj is the Yamuna River. The Taj is a mausoleum for Mumtaz Mahal, the beloved wife of Shah Jahan. There was a plan to build a silver bridge over the Yamuna leading to an all-black, otherwise identical structure. But the penny pinchers ended it (well, there's more that that story...).

Most of the visitors to the Taj Mahal are Indians, and their obvious proprietary pride enhances everyone's experience.

(Opposite and top right) the classical axial and off-axis views of the Taj Mahal from the Great Gate. The Taj faces exactly south; the sun play over its addressing elevation is idealized. The architecture is perfectly reflected in the famous linear pool, of which we only see the first half. The second half comes into view after the central, raised platform is surpassed (center upper and lower). (Right) view from the Taj Mahal's terrace to the Great Gate, southward, showing both pools and the fine red buildings to both sides.

TAJ MAHAL, AGRA

0 10 25 50 100M

76 Dubai Fountain

The largest musical fountain on Earth, and perhaps always to hold that title, is the performance installation at the Dubai Mall, which aligns with the scale of the adjacent Burj Khalifa, for some time the tallest building in the world.

Rings and lines of gimbaling streams and compressed air-driven pulse geysers combine to create a rune-like graphic if viewed from above, and a collection of volumetrically interconnected, dynamic islands in space, when activated. During the times between its music and water events, the jets fold nicely away beneath the water's surface to leave a large and calm lake, reflecting the wide sky and the surrounding buildings of the Dubai Marina.

Other water features on the property include an excellent arrival area water feature, which represents a noteworthy innovation to the cascade category. Within the Mall, a popularly-photographed interior waterwall is adorned in repeated, miniature, frozen diver sculptures.

Admittedly, these photographs do no justice to the astounding reality of this mammoth fountain, the largest dynamic fountain in the world. There are two reasons. First, that the crowds did not permit many clear shots of the water, but more important was that I really wanted to watch the show and take in its choreographic subtleties. Suddenly near the end, I realized I needed some kind of record, but by then the show was winding down...

(Opposite) the largest fountain in the world, shown at night during a choreographically programmed, music and water concert. (Above right) The Burj Kalife towering over the lake. Fountain mechanicals are visible underwater.

(Center right and right) An innovative cascade borders the Mall's entrance. It's sloped and grooved steps function to generate energy and release it in white-water releases.

Privacy River

It had been several hundred years since the city was considered politically vital. These days its occupants were amiably accustomed to a more passive lifestyle. Things were less beset than before, though perhaps not less complicated. Some patterns, once set, will simply endure, as if expressing some sociological corollary to Newtonian mechanics. The Court had vanished, but much of its behavior lived on.

This psycho-social momentum permeated the city, expressed, for instance, in the quietly fastidious dress, which though commonplace among its residents was viewed as fussy or anachronistic by outsiders. Or more subtly, in the half-beat pause one noticed before the answering of any question, no matter how idle, as if hidden ramifications had first to be carefully considered before risking a response. Although much about the old city echoed its aura of past consequence, its residents enjoyed an avowed relief from the strains of governance.

Charming evidence of the city's heightened attentions was revealed in a way its young people were afforded with needed privacy. The riverbank offered measured public seclusion better than anywhere else, and the water's gentle, white noises didn't hurt. Visiting couples would seat themselves spaced by regular, comfortable distances, which is to say, just far enough apart for quiet conversation to be unintelligible to others nearby, while being easily observed. Even foreigners perceived the enviable orderliness, every six meters or so, along those banks of flowing waters.

77 Otani Hombyo

The ablutions basin at Otani Hombyo, in Kyoto, is hardly the most important element in the site's meticulously articulated plan, but it is integral and presented with great honor and care just to the right of the impressive entrance gate.

The stone basin is fed from a bamboo pipe. All is presented with the most assertive intentionality. The stream's breaking up and impacting the small pool maked a crisp sound which announces the presense of the ablutions station over to the area of the gate and not much further.

(Opposite, center right and right) a Buddhist temple ablutions pavilion is positioned next to the complex's entrance gate. The basin is formed of carved stone with straight planes and a consistent texture. A slender stream of water enters from a freshly cut bamboo pipe, where it's measured flow breaks just above the pool's surface to tap the water in heavy droplets, creating a distinctive calling.

78 Ryoan-ji

The rock garden is the world-famous statement at Ryoan-ji, is said to be one of the finest to be found, but there are water features on the site, too, dotting the grounds sporatically, and they share with the rock garden philosophical underpinnings.

The small, traditional ablutions station is without flaw in its simple, shaded spot. The water chain downspout, made up of wire-linked, little copper tuliip cups probably works to satisfaction, though these kinds of chains are usually more poetic than functional. There is a narrow stream bordered by massive boulders with tiny stones and shallow waters, and another water feature incorporating a large rock, and finally after the displays in miniature is a good sized lake.

The modest water features about the large site serve subtle notices that there was actually water everywhere, working in an invisible natural cycle, keeping the garden green, alive and healthy.

Ryoan-ji's miniature stream (Left), meanders over a nearly flat surface of mossy rock chips between a crowding of large boulders to create just a little sparkle and sound, which is picked out by the beams of light through the tree canopy, above. Thinly trickling flows pour from a bamboo spout over a massive rock, set back from the path (upper middle right). Piled up in the sun, turtles increase the scale of a rock outcropping (lower middle right). Most rain chain water spouts, like these (bottom right and far right) do not do a very good job of conducting water from the roof to a drain system, the purpose of which is to minimize earth line erosion and protect the building's foundation from excessive water build-up in the soil, though their success in poetic expression is undeniable.

79 Koinzan Saiho-ji

Priests began tending the landscape in 731 when the first temple was built. Roughly six hundred years later, after disturbances, the temple and gardens were thoroughly rebuilt by Muso Kokushi, a very highly regarded Zen master, who rededicated the temple. He planned the garden with walks circling and sloping down to a ring-shaped, golden pond, with three named islands. The shape of the pond is intended to convey a meaning in graphic from. The mosses are said to have first appeared after the flood of 1742.

Guests qualify for a garden visit by practicing Kanji with a Sumi brush, after which they find an especially quiet, green oasis. Traces of birds and wind can be heard in the trees, while fish sometimes break the water's surface. While I visited, a light rainfall fell silently into the mossy carpet while tapping silvery pindrop sounds in the green pond.

The shaded pond surface reflecting dark tree canopies offers penetrating views into its aquatic depths, where moist, mossy carpeting continues underwater. The environment might feel too relentlessly upholstered were it not for the pointed interruptions of the barren, broken, gray rocks. Through the strategic absence of any small spring or cascade creating movement and sound, the pond's feeling of timelessness is emphasized.

The plan form of the pool is intended as a Kanji graphic to convey a specific meaning (or perhaps an unspecific meaning, as I received various unrelated interpretations of that content).

80 Katsura Palace

Katsura is, perhaps after the Imperial Palace in Tokyo, Japan's most internationally famous residence and garden. The dialog between the Kyoto building and its landscape are highly considered, explored, developed and refined works of space design. The landscape was based upon Tales of Genji, a favorite of the owner of the property, Prince Hachijo Toshihito, who started the project, and his son, Prince Hachijo Toshitada.

The conceptualization of water at Katsura Palace chiefly involves a natural basin with a still, reflective finish. The pond is alive with fish. The seasons are a reflected parade. The plantings are alive and changing. The rocks are immutable. Clouds pass. Birds visit and sing. The water mirror is contemplation.

The garden's path is a choreographic circuit weaving a dialog through the landscape, with the eye in motion in a way today we could call, cinematographically, as the views unfold in a continuous intentional sequence. By that reckoning, the photos offered here result in misdirection, like publicity stills from a Hollywood film, and similarly fail to convey the theatrical impact of the narrative's continuously eventful and surprising, flowing experience. There are stories within the story. The story has a central theme in the water, which is reinforced by the pathways' flirtations, lacing along its edges and sometimes over the water, with equal measures of drama and restraint.

Two noteworthy bridges offer ways over the water, one spanning in a single span of cambered stone, the other a springing arch in assembled timber with an earthen cradling bearing up a stepped and planted gravel path.

Still photography is an interpretation of the dynamic conceptualization of Katsura's garden. And, no single visit captures the well-known seasonal variations that perpetuate Katsura's beauty and intrigue through the course of a year.

The pond is in the center of the garden. Circulation is around the pond, weaving through numorous settings, views and experiences. Our experience was clock-wise, which may or may not be right, but it felt right. The contemporary eye might find the composition to be busy, but it seemed relaxed to me, and I saw no flaws, problems or complications.

The lake and its calm reflectivity is pervasive, with its articulated perimeter dovetailing with the site's numerous, key feature elements, each of which is in constant dialog with the spatial whole.

The architectural concept of Katsura Palace's main building is today presented as a closed matter (right). In the past, the shoji screens would open onto the calculated scenery to offer the elevated views offering engagement and dominion.

The Poet

It was early and quiet that morning at the lake's edge. A stone bridge in the old Chinese style led out from the shore, drawing me into the pale green, scattered light. Up ahead, a middle-aged man faced away, crouched over, shuffling oddly in rough clothes. As I got closer I could see he was holding a pail and what seemed to be a witch's broom until I realized it was a brush, like an oversized sumi-style, artists' brush, which he was dipping regularly into the pail to re-wet it. He was writing with the brush on the bridge's footpath in water, carefully taking one step backwards with each line exactingly applied. Looking ahead, I could see he had been at it for some time. Evaporation had already erased his most distant poetry.

81 Luzhi

Three of the principle cities of Western China are arranged in a triangle, formed by Shanghai, Suzhou and Hangzhou. Between them are numerous old villages, or water towns, such as Tangli, Zhouzhuang or Luzhi. Jiangsu Province is gifted with an abundance of rivers, lakes, canals and rainfall, yielding a fresh and green environment. Those benefits are pressed away in the larger, denser cities, but utterly apparent in the smaller water towns where an easy-going, old style character is fairly well preserved.

Luzhi, more than two-and-a-half thousand years old, is situated directly east of Suzhou (towards Shanghai), between the Wusong River to the north and Changhu Lake to the south. Stone-built pedestrian ways and canals form Luzhi's arteries, neither of which are particularly loaded with traffic. Shade trees, overflowing plantings and occasional flowers are worked into tiny open spaces throughout the plan. There may be little in the infrastructure that we would call, high architecture, and yet there is a fine scale with a goodly measure of magic pervading the labyrinthine passages.

Numerous stone bridges proliferate across the waterways and play scene to passersby who mingle and (I'm guessing) trade gossip. Although the town is real and is, in fact, connected to contemporary urban activities, the cars and trucks are relegated to roadways appropriate to them, which are layered back from the town's more charming zones. Small-format motorcycles have implicated themselves into the pedestrian streets, but they do no real harm. Old people in hats and heavy shoes seem to be in charge of the town's streets and canals and they keep matters well in hand.

There is little evidence that this planning scheme works in an economic sense, as there is no apparent brisk trade, or even much half-hearted banter. Urban activity characterized by mild-mannered tourists, sleepy restaurants and wedding photography would not appear to be a fetching model for replication, yet, the country is definitively proud of their historic gem. Luzhi, tiny as it is, is quite well known throughout China, and people visit in steady streams.

Luzhi's green waters burrow silently and extensively throughout the town and further, carrying and reflecting, along with the birds, trees, light breezes and fish, their messages of tranquility.

Most of Luzhi's boats seem to be idle (left, bottom) and what water traffic one sees is largely tourtist-dedicated (left, lower-middle).

Stone ramparts, railings, steps and bridges, winding in crannies and elbowing about eventfully create places delightfully relieved of the brazen cheapness of typical modern infrastructure.

Green canopies, low, volumetric plantings and indigenous architecture reflect in the quiet green waters that wend through the town.

WIFI

大块
农家
奥灶
馄饨

82 West Lake, Hangzhou

Hangzhou is a legendarily beautiful city over two thousand years old, with West Lake at its heart. The borders and bridges of West Lake have been built to serve its exploration, which caters equally to residents and a steady tourist population. The character of the lake transforms considerably owing to the acutely changing local conditions of temperature, humidity and sunlight, which alters the lake's presentation through the course of the day, and on through the days of the year. Over three short visits I have seen the lake under an amber sky, a green sky, a pink sky and pale shades of blue. I have seen it tempered by morning mists, thick fog, and sparkling from sharpest, cool sunlight. The gardens and temples, which line the lake's perimeter and populate its small, steep hills, are encrusted with hundreds of years of ornamental devices and rockery. But the festooned bridges, border figures, pavilions and plantings merely serve to underscore the ineffable quality of the West Lake itself, which serenly transmits as it receives.

(Above), Plan of West Lake, with its highly articulated perimeter, down to the smallest scales.

(These pages and the two following), the boats, edge plantings, stone bridges, zig-zag footpath, pavilions, pagodas, gates, framing trees, outcropping rockeries, lighting, signage, and more, are all accessories and celebrants to the larger, West Lake experiential statement, nearly the equivalent to a city-scaled wellspring, or fountain, pregnant with meaning and beauty, the man-made and the natural, working together.

83 Humble Administrator's Garden

Canals, ponds, streams and a lake permeate this naturalistic landscape burgening in paths, bridges, islands, pagodas, pavilions, rockery, ballustrades, grilles, endless varieties of paving designs, sculptures, plantings of all kinds, people, birds, sparkling sunlight, dappled shadows and probably a lot of other important things, all mightily balanced in some very rich style of tranquility.

Confronted by the garden's complexity, and knowing just enough about Chinese culture to be sure to misunderstand it all, this cautious Westerner feels advised to relay as few gross facts and 'insights' as possible. The simplest sketch of history and superficial phenomenological observation would seem the safest path.

The so-called, Humble Administrator's Garden, in Suzhou, was completed in 1526 by Wang Xiancheng, a retired official, whose ambitions for the governorship were thwarted. In retirement, his energies were directed inward to the creation of one of the greatest gardens of China, the largest in Suzhou, a garden city. This historical caricature is weirdly similar to that of the Cardinal Ippolito II d'Este, who built the Villa d'Este after being denied the Papal office. (We must wonder if a contemporary politician should now be pushed out of office to build us a new garden.)

The landscape is arranged into three sections, an Eastern Garden, the Central Garden and a Western Garden, though these territories are subtly separated. Much of the garden today can no longer be dated back to the 1500s as its elements have been reshaped, relocated and replaced, although the basics of the plan remains intact. It would seem that the the garden's ability to evolve contrutes to both its vibrancy and its legitimacy.

The water expressions throughout the Humble Administrator's Garden are tranquil; there are almost no waterfalls, jets or sprays, although very tiny cascades do exist, providing some sounds in small spaces. Fountains in the western sense, with jets, or bowls, etc, have no place in the East, where nature is interpreted differently. Water meanders throughout this garden with great meaning, strategy and effect, and though we see no fountains, as such, we do not miss them too much.

Numerous bridges conduct visitors along paths between and through the islands and perimeter shorelines.

Stone porches, shaded with expressive architectural canopies, trees or in full sun, border the water. The bridges slow the pace. The architecture is complex, but resolved (right, center). The foliage is robust without being overtended. Water is everywhere, alive with plantings and fish.

The garden requires a great deal of maintenance, which appears to be well organized; quietly and purposefully ongoing. Some maintenance staff wear traditional clothing, others are in color-coded uniforms (right).

The garden has numerous shade trees with tall canopies and open leaf structures, allowing for plenty of sun paths to beam through broken shade, balancing cool, comfort with good vision and sparkle.

Charming, small boats like this one (left lower center) are used by the garden's maintenance workers, whose activities seem to be very much a living part of the scenery.

A small, grotto-like opening in garden wall at the end of a brief canal (left) provides action, sound and healthful water flow.

The red framed pavilion (far left, center right) with its varied blue diamond-checkerboard glass panes establishes a rare serenity inside as reflected light from mild wavelets in the pond create shimmers in the textured glass. What is seen in the photograph's Vermeeresque light quality is different in person by those mild reflections.

Rockery is everywhere and expressed in various styles, sometimes as sturdy, pondside retaining embankments interwoven with plantings (bottom right), and always the rock compositions are thoughtfully assembled. Even the shadowed, comparatively simple rock composition in the tiny cascade (opposite bottom) is well modeled.

Visitors might bring extra sketchbooks, as it would seem that no paving, rockery, bridge, flying roofline, stone foundation assembly or nestled plaster railing is repeated or uninteresting. All is alive with variation and invention, recurringly reiterated in the permeating water's reflections.

84 Bank of China

The steeply sloped west side of I.M. Pei's Bank of China Tower, 1990, Central District, Hong Kong, is developed as an abstract, modern interpretation of a Chinese garden, with traditional cloud trees, scholar stones and a network of contemporary water features all organized in a terraced, layout derived from the triangular forms of the building.

Most interesting about the water features is that they are alive with plantings and algae (rather than being treated with chemicals, like most modern fountains), which cast living, green tones alongside the cool white and light gray modernism of the architecture. The water plantings are healthy looking and bestow into the garden a palpable dimension of cultural authenticity.

The landcape composition is a bit remote from the view positions. This is not a garden to walk through; rather, it is for looking at from the outside, presumably briefly to enjoy its energy, then moving on to keep up with a busy day.

The naturalistic waterfall framed between two very large rocks is skillfully delivered with a sunny weir and a rolled, natural surface creating streaked, glassy flows above with vertical rock frictions below transforming the sliding water into a rich, white froth. The waterfall's splash in the pool is, just so. The two flights of triangulated cascades are balanced and energized—a remarkable achievement considering the geometry—but the cut stone formations block most of the views. The shallow pool with its grid of triangular stepping stones, and a touch of the post-modern about it is eye-catching, and though the water action seems not to gather into a graspable event, this part of the scene, which is in the center, beckons attention.

The garden is a gift from the Bank of China to the life of Hong Kong's Central District. It's assertive design, greenery, movements and sounds orchestrate a fine effort towards the balancing of daily life in this, most energetic and quick-tempoed of cities.

The geometrical environements composed over the space generates just as many kinds of eventful water actions. The waterfalls are particularly well done, from the narrow falls (center, right), to the wider, lower type (upper, right). Throughout it all is the green cast, telltale that these waters are alive, like the floating lilies (bottom, right), that these waters are alive, and the space we observe is a sophisticated water garden.

85 Rain Oculus

Rain Oculus is a one-of-a-kind artwork by Ned Kahn. It presents a momentous and unique water action, conceived in two parts with above grade and below grade view orientations. The upper level's spinning, expanding and shrinking, disk of water is mesmerizing and physically impressive, while the lower level's view of the motions, seen through the plastic bowl from below, becomes especially entertaining when the bowl opens to stream down in a twirling spout to the canal in the basement.

At the plaza level one is looking down to see the event from the edge of a transparent railing, so from across the rather large plaza we might have no idea that the fountain is there to be seen. The looking down aspect of the concept may diminish its power a little in that we are so used to looking up to the highly regarded. But the rolling swells of the great mass of water, which at its largest scale, charges so easily and nonchallantly through the many projecting lateral nozzles is extraordinarily impressive.

Singapore has built one of the world's great fountain collections, and the relatively new Rain Oculus takes a position of some honor, there.

Water is delivered from evenly spaced polished steel elbows bolted in a circle to the inside face of a concave plastic dish, about one-third of the distance down from the dish's rim. The dish appears to be roughly fifty feet in diameter. A small hole at the base of the dish is fitted with a valve to open or close, and it is closed most of the time. Water charging laterally from the elbows creates a spinning water body that is not centered in the dish. Rather, the water body traces a counterclockwise pathway around the dish. So, the water twirls in two ways at once; it spins like a vortex, and it traces an orbit around the dish. Notice in the photo to the left as the water mass is momentarily far left of center, and in the photos to the right, where the spinning volume is momentarily right of center. The water's orbit is more captivating than its spin.

The third photo from the top on the right also shows the water volume much diminished as it is being drained away through the then-opened valve at the bottom. Looking through the plastic dish, you can see the spray to the space below, where a canal-like pool receives the spray.

There are other intriguing details. The downward spray changes direction in relation to the position of the orbiting mass above. Also, when the rotating mass is at its largest, it rolls over the charging elbows; interestingly the mass' formal integrity is undisturbed by the steel interruptions, even though they are sizable. The heavy motion just rolls over the impediments, unperturbed. The water's turquoise tint is innate to water's indexing in daylight; the plastic dish is colorless.

Detailing is a little rough, as the installation is built more like a work of engineering than as architecture. The plastic panels of the dish seem to be working perfectly at this viewing (the installation was then three years old), with consistent panel-to-panel curvatures, and no leaks or crazing.

Down Under

Australia, home to a late-mid-century architect who specialized in the design and construction of modern fountains. Word about him was sparce, though he had a solid career. It was rumored that he was working on an important book, but it was not completed before he moved on.

Extra measures of energy and comittment are required for particularly long trips. Fortunately with respect to adventures, reward is often in proportion to the difficulty. I made the 10,000 kilometer trip in our late fall; Australia's early Spring, so the weather was accommodating. Every day was clear and bright. When I met my American colleague, his newly minted local accent was jarring but endearing. He showed me some of the sights, and the better fountains, as we walked through the city. It was getting warm when we took a foot bridge part way across the Yarra River, and we decended to the level of an outdoor cafe, firmly suspended just above the waterline. It was populated mostly by young people in sunglasses, drinking beers. We sat in the sun and traded fountain stories, down under.

86 El Alamein War Memorial

None of the many duplicates of Sydney's 1961 El Alamein War Memorial achieve the original's visual power or the quality of its incorporation into public space—even though many of the copies, such as those in Omaha and New York City, were created by the same architects, Robert Woodward and Phill Taranto. At El Alamein, the installation is closely sheltered by nearby buiildings to the west, which provide a shaded backdrop to its sparkling display, which is further improved by the broken shade of a large sycamore tree. The patches of shade course through the densely spaced droplets in legible swaths. The pool is thereby painted in dynamic light and shadow. In the morning, shimmering beams from the pool's shallow waves reflect up into the tree canopy.

The reception pool is subdivided into three hexagonal terraces, staggering in plan and section. The overflows are subdivided by well-proportioned horizontal dentals, with the primary orientation facing south (we are in the Southern Hemisphere), therefore rendering their glassy water spouts a bit more shaded than ideal. Where the sun does hit them, they shine crisply and the shadows from the projecting dentils create a dark-toned backdrop to profile the sunlit streams.

The pool is framed in red Indian sandstone, color-matching the plaza's red brick paving. The dentals and risers are warm-toned bronze with a turquoise patina. The pool basin is finished in white glass mosaic, which is brighter in person than reads in photographs.

The sounds from the sprays and spouts confront the close traffic noise admirably generate a contemplative zone appropriate for this World War II memorial.

The design arises from the address of an upright water presentation of stature that minimizes the visual conflict of its armature while doing an excellent job managing splash. The metal form is also reasonably attractive when the water is turned off, such as during high winds or maintenance periods. The dandilion identity is secondary to the water design concept and likely accidental, which detracts a little from its needed intentionality and memorial solemnity.

The dense sprays engage sunlight as well as any fountain, and better than most. The sycamores provide streaks of shade and sunlight, bringing the water feature more alive and dimensional, and making more overt the spatial structure of the concept.

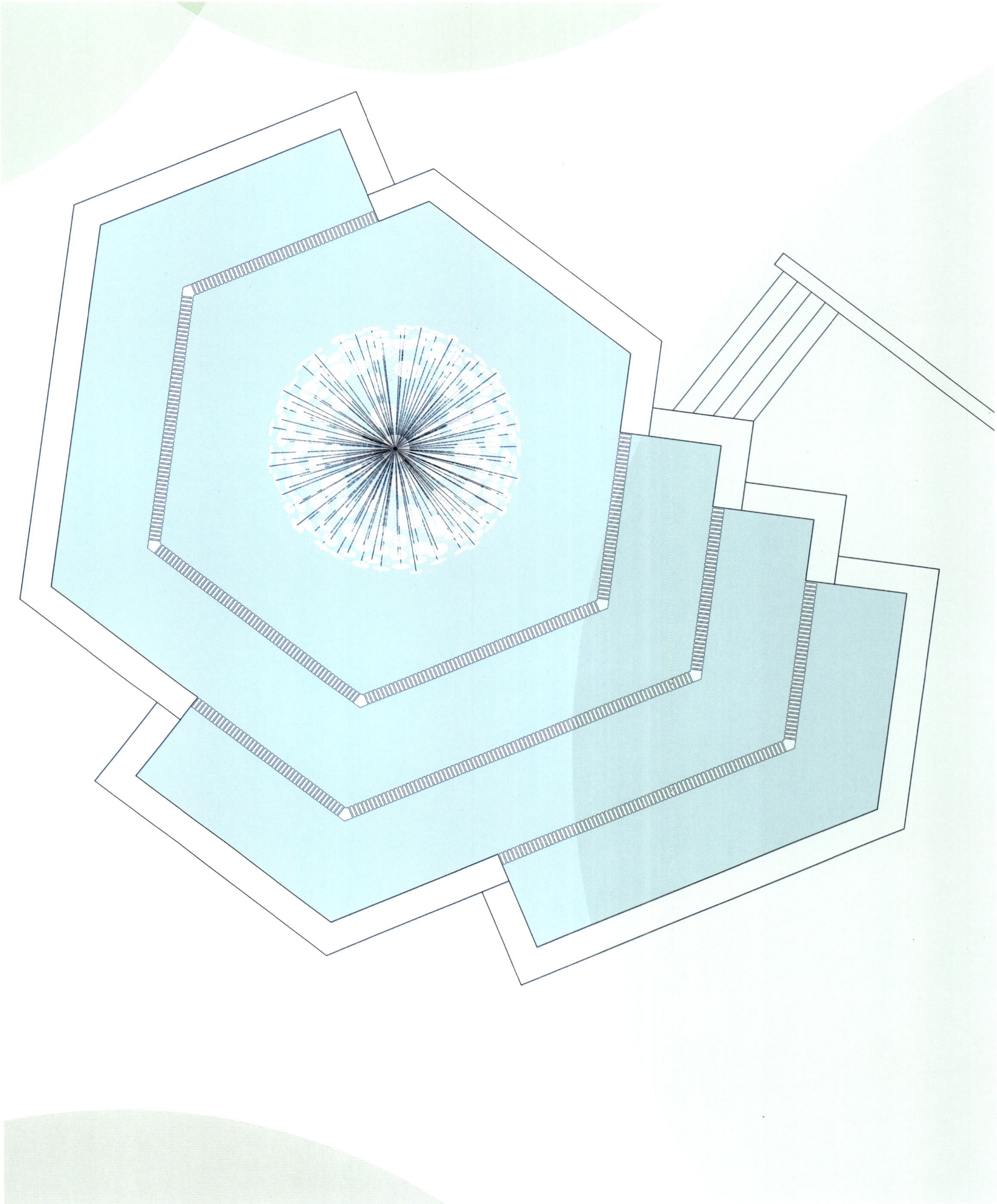

EL ALAMEIN WAR MEMORIAL, SYDNEY

0 1 5M

87 Coles Fountain

The simplicity of the design belies the enormous challenges that had to be surmounted in its all custom-fabricated creation, serving as both architectural structure and waterworks piping. The 1980s-style space frame visual language makes the fountain look a bit dated, but it is beautifully scaled and flawlessly crafted. The design's ceiling-mounted nozzles point down to create chandelier-like vases of water before shattering into rain as it falls. The field of falling water wraps around a slightly raised peninsula-like pathway for entering its scene.

The setting for the Coles Fountain is Parliament Gardens, a modest patch of open space on the eastside outskirts of downtown Melbourne, and just north of the Yarra River. The water feature was designed and built Robert Woodward, the prolific and brilliant Australian architect of fountains. Sir Norman C. Coles, businessman and philanthropist, participated in the fountain's inaugeration on November 27, 1981.

The water pavilion is composed of finely scaled, blackened stainless steel parts with custom-fabricated fittings and hidden fasteners. The assembly was undoubtedly a challenge to develop; the tubing functions both as structure and piping. The bottom nodes stiffen the frames and carry most of the lateral loads while passing water to nozzles stemming down.

Stems oriented downward are mounted with laminar dome nozzles. These upside down nozzles actually function better than the normal orientation, as the water presentation does not have to contend with an inadvertant and undesired trapping of the metal nozzle within its water dome. In this version, the nozzles are above the domes, so the space within the water form is open to its occupation by space and light. Gravity pulls the water into attenuated tulip shapes, which burst into droplets after about 300mm of fall.

The design successfully resolves the most basic challenge in designs of this type: The water expression is more eventful than its steel armature.

88 New South Wales Parliament

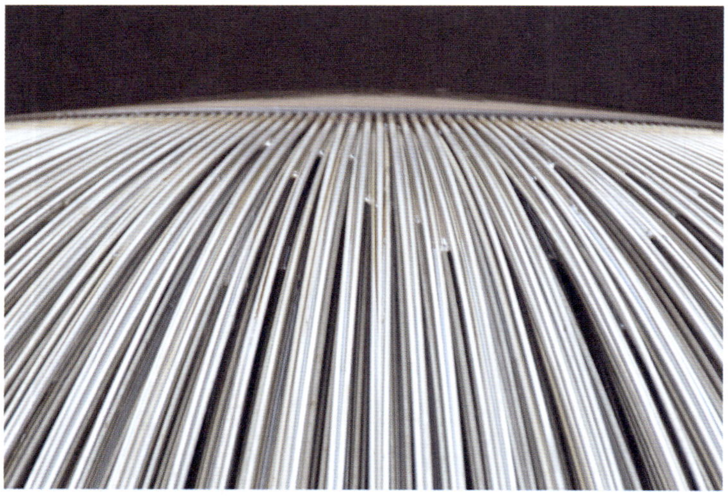

This is a very interesting fountain, another by Robert Woodward, although it must be admitted that the water of the main display is not very visible from the surrounding spaces. The reflection pool conveys the action more than anything else. This 1983 concept balances the presentation such that the reading is more about the sculpture than the water—though the form is largely developed from water action considerations. The approximately 2.25-meter-tall stainless steel element functions as a sculpture very well, and it holds the trying glass-enclosed courtyard in which it is centered with modest but secure authority. The figure is plainly suggestive of primal aboriginal thatched roofs and Bertoia wire sculptures.

Water flows between the strands at the apex, stretching outward in all directions to fall from the tips of the bowed metal strands and rain gently into the pool. The disturbances to the reflection pond is mild, with low waves flowing outward from the sculpture to the perimeter of the 12m x 12m pool, which is infinity-edged all around, therefore obviating all reflected wave action.

The installation employs stainless steel rods in a manner benefitting from water's surface tension. Water wells up through the stem to channel between the bundled rods, to then be released as the rods radiate away from each other and surface tension reaches its limit when it either falls to the pool or is conducted on the rods to weep from the tips in fine streams.

The lighting is selectively considered. The up-lights highlight the lensing effects of the water between the rods, only. Because the light fixtures are above the pool surface, the splash on the pool is not illuminated and water-animated caustic light (which would arise from a common, underwater position) does not illuminate the sculpture.

The glass walls of the courtyard isolate the water feature from the ground floor spaces that view it, preventing its restrained sounds from contributing to rooms' experiences.

89 Tidal Cascade

The fountain is located in Darling Harbour, Sydney, where a beautiful maritime inlet is wrapped in a necklace of open spaces more or less aimed at the public. The city's convention center landed at the southwest edge of the harbour, establishing an expansive open space extending to the water's edge with fine views to the city.

The 1988, Tidal Cascade, is the open space's sole ornament, and it handily performs the job of holding and proportioning the space around its immediate proximity. Within this realm, the fountain is as persuasive as it is surprising. The design is masterful, the physical execution is superltive, and the artistry of its water action, the like of which exists nowhere else. The mind is left a bit dazzled, wondering how this fountain was conceived.

Designed by the architect and fountain designer, Robert Woodward, the work was completed in 1988, to instant local fanfare. The installation takes the form of a pinwheel, roughly twenty meters in diameter, with ten water paths and two pedestrian paths twirling down to a simple, open, twelve-sided base. The total drop is in the neighborhood of two meters. The paths are about a meter wide, ramping down a three or four percent slope. The lateral step down to each adjacent path is roughly twenty centimeters. These dimensions are all pertinent, as they unify with the water performance, which requires exactitude to be functional.

And the fountain's display is a revelation. Its performance plays out an idea that is fully revealed by a small sample of its form, which then progresses, continuing throughout the scope of the wheeling form from top to bottom. The water does not flow evenly. The water boils and marches in evenly spaced, diamond-patterned, goose-egg-shaped wavelets. Their motion is more like a Slinky's stepping than smooth gliding.

The stone dome at the base seems purely decorative, but it is large enough and just comfortable enough to lean against for the enjoyment of a moment or two of introspection—that most common fountain offering provided at a most uncommon fountain.

Still photography cannot convey this installation's intriguing water action. The flows spin down separate, curving channels. The water struggles over the sawtoothed basin profile. Each overflowing ridge creates a surge or pulse, that looks something like a wind-blown wavelet, which carries a rhythm as it steps down the successive ridges. And the many wavelets move densely and altogether. The curving path is not natural; at each level wave pulses bounce against the encrouching (outboard) side walls to generate sideways reflected waves.

The downward marching waves and the sideways reflected waves create fluttering diamond-patterns which are evenly distributed over the surfaces of the multi-tracked, downward spiral march. The effect is quite charismatic. The name of the artwork, Tidal Cascade, is inexplicable to me, having nothing to do with tides and little to do with a conventional cascade.

Simple Reward

The train from Salzburg arrived in Munich midday, where a rental car had been pre-arranged. I had a coffee in the station, then with minimal complication I was on the Autobahn, cruising at a brisk clip up into the Bavarian mountains. My destination was a castle with fountains.

The preliminary research was done, but you never really know until you get there and see things for yourself. As can happen, this visit far exceeded expectations and I was able to make several fresh observations.

I was struck by the look on young Neptune's face as he stormed out of his grotto, thoroughly prepared to set things straight. Waters trumpeted his determination and power. Also impressive was the authoritative unity of the castle and its landscape, the cavern grotto's magical scenic character, the stragetic grouping of golden fountainworks, and the pleasing simplicity of the axially symmetric plan grandly straddling the valley.

A good safari will bag several hundred photos, through which one can sift later for the most instructive. There can be surprises in studying the photos; things which are missed while shooting the scene. With practice, the camera's technical demands don't get too much in the way of the experience, and one finds the energy to switch lenses many times through the course of a visit. On this leg of the trip I'd shot 588 pictures.

Afterwards, I walked over to the small, apparently unpopular hotel on the property, checked in and ordered a light supper to be served on the outside deck. The evening chill was more than an hour off. There was a fine view into the healthy forest. The traditional German meal was casually excellent, and the drink tasted fresh and bright as I leafed through the guidebook I'd picked up in the gift shop.

90 In Absentia

Originally this work was larger, but it was reduced in scope for pragmatic reasons. Marvels were regrettably removed. Not charming examples here and there, but vast tracts of casework, oceans of beauty, edited away.

Removed from this book's pages are the world's natural fountains, such as the Blue Grotto of Capri and the marble pools on the slopes of western Turkey's Pamukkale. The book includes Hanzhou's West Lake, but the treatment focuses on its border and bridge development, hinting only at the awe of the lake, itself. Lago Maggiore is missing. The Wisconsin Dells are missing. The Nile, the Amazon, the Danube, and the Mississippi are all missing. The Tiber, the Seine and the Thames are missing. The Congo is missing, as is the braided Rio Grande.

Iguazu Falls is missing. Niagra is missing. Angel Falls is missing. Old Faithful is missing, with all her geyser ken.

Clouds, which are made exclusively of water, and can be visually astounding, were removed, with all the attendant marvelous and special examples, particularly the cumulonimbus, the lenticular, the cirrostratus, and the altocumulus.

Blue glaciers and the various types of natural ice formations are missing. The snows of the Alpine passes are missing. The big droplet rains of a Louisiana Summer are missing, as are the sudden cloudbursts of Singapore or Portland's thin, misty showers. Rainbows—chromatic sunlight refractions generated through millions of tiny droplets of water—are missing. The trout streams of Spain are missing. Mont-Saint-Michel's tidal flood plane is missing. Mexican cenotes are missing. The waves of Hawaii are missing.

Great unbuilt fountains are missing. Fine fountains that the course of human events has worn away are missing, including nearly thirty at Hadrian's Villa. The Hanging Gardens of Babylon, if that place ever existied, is missing. Palaces of the Moors, with their poetry-laden gardens and winsome fountains, destroyed from war or neglect, are mostly missing—though we certainly visit the Alhambra. The waterways of ancient Egyptian villages, partially excavated, are missing, as are the channels of Machu Piccu. The acequia of New Mexico and Valencia, functional and beautiful, are missing.

Bridges and boats, which are of and all about water, and which populate so much of human history and are clearly worthy of aesthetic recognition from water's perspective, are missing.

The fountains of Iran, in such places as Isfahan, Kashan, and Shiraz, enchanting as they are, are missing. St. Petersburg Palace is missing. Shalimar Bagh, located in a disputed borderland, where there is currently conflict, is missing. The fountains of South America are missing. If there are good fountains in North Korea, you wouldn't know it from this book.

The Blue Grotto, Capri.

Swimming pools are missing, even the very best of them. They occupy a different formal classification.

Very well-known fountains that appear to be insufficiently distictive are missing, such as the small fountains on the north and south lawns of the White House. These also fall into the category of fountains that are likely worth examining, but are unavailble for viewing, which also includes the glorious Spanish Galleon Fountain in the private gardens of the Vatican, which is also regrettably missing.

Legions of contemporary fountains are missing, even though we now live in a Golden Age of fountain building, and many of today's water features are innovative and delightful. But this work is a panoramic overview, so only a fair proportion of today's fountains are included, balancing with those of previous eras.

What could not be included or was outright removed from this review far outweighs what is finally provided. What was removed was a mountain of gold. The situation is not trivial, but hopefully condonable.

Acequia, Albuquerque.

91 Predeceding Studies

It is informative to read the more seriously researched books, articles, and blogs. Even the modest-format guidebooks sold only in site gift shops are good to read, particularly as they seem to be the sole sources for a fair amount of useful information. The comments below regarding the more available texts are meant to be helpful to whomever is interested in following up on the topic. There are respected, decades-old (or older) books that I haven't seen for being long out of print and difficult to find, so I cannot cover those.

Water and Architecture, 1957, Charles W. Moore's PhD thesis performed at Princeton University. The original work was never commercially released but it can still be had through UMI Dissertation Services. It remains the best and most complete word written on the subject. Moore explores the topic from various cultural perspectives, culminating in the persuasive epiphany that all of the waters of the world are physically and meaningfully intermingling, and that they bring their visual and intellectual potency to lift and enhance every environment into which they are beautifully incorporated. Numerious references from around the world, built and unbuilt, are employed to support his thesis. His ideas are fully developed from seemingly every major angle possible. Moore goes further to test his concepts through hypothetical design exercises, which, like his redesign of Mies van der Rhoe's reflection pools at Seagram Plaza, threaten to undo all his brilliant research and lovely writing, though these designs, too, are underpinned by interesting and sometimes prescient ideas.

Water and Architecture, 1994, by Charles W. Moore and photographer Jane Lidz, Moore reworks his text, which is reduced and placed alongside Ms. Lidz's many colorful, icon-style photographs to deliver an accessible compendium. Although professionally published and much more visually inviting, it is less comprehensive and less powerful than the earlier work of the same title.

Fountains Splash and Spectacle, 1998, edited by Marilyn Symmes. Fountains through history are organized and examined by way of thematic topics relating to purpose. Very thoroughly researched, popular fountains are referenced from historic to contemporary times. The thematic categories which organize the book are her invention and serve to make sense of a large subject with numerous eccentric examples.

Crown Fountain, Chicago.

Roman Fountains: 2000 Fountains in Rome. A Complete Collection, 2000. Marvin Pulvers delivers the goods with the definitive, exhaustive itemization of, presumably, every single one of the known fountains in Rome, attended to with at least a paragraph and a sma l photo of each for a grand total of 2,016 fountains. A quite large and heavy book. As of this writing, a few more fountains have been built in Rome, so the book needs updating.

The Waters of Rome: Aqueducts, Fountains, and the Birth of the Baroque City, 2011, by Katherine Rinne, A thoroughly researched, very fine academic work written by a dedicated professional. It is characterized by historical information, numerous engravings, maps and photographs. The subject is treated holistically—almost anatomically, covering rivers, floods, mechanical engineering, drain systems, urban design, aqueducts, public fountains, laundry fountains(!), history, finance, politics, Catholocism, and everything connecting them to each other and to Rome. Of her many ideas worth mentioning is the envisioning of Rome's aqueducts as trunks of trees, stemmed with branching pipes, and the delightful fountains, like the tree's born fruit.

The Fountains of Rome, 1966, H. V. Morton. After Katherine Rinne's and Mavin Pulver's books on Rome's waters, Morton's book might seem flighty, but it is a good if tightly framed overview of Rome's principal public fountains. A delightful colored map is included with the book (fairly common among travel books of the first half of the twentieth century). Morton identifies important fountains missed by some, such as the superb Galleon fountain in the Vatican's gardens (not available for public viewing). Uniquely, the book sports several nighttime photographs.

Water in Landscape Architecture, 1978, by Craig S. Campbell. A good overview seemingly written for design professionals. Water feature effects, engineeing techniques, planning principles and professional lore are covered in the book, which is copiously illustrated with hand-drawn sketches and black-and-white photography. Among a motley collection, a number of important fountains are referenced, such as Naum Gabo's phenomenal and generally underappreciated Revolving Torsion fountain in London, which makes it to the book's back cover.

The Poetics of Gardens, 1988, Charles W. Moore, William J. Mitchell, William Turnbull, Jr. An overview of gardens and meaning, written when the two authors were well established in their careers and the work benefits from that mature perspective. The book is mentioned here because its descriptions of water's role in its carefully curated list of gardens is articulate.

Street Corner, Florence.

Bernini, the Sculptor of the Roman Baroque, 1955, Rudolph Wittkower. The definitive work on Bernini; 320 pages of readable text and some very fine black-and-white plates, with many other support photos. The book includes a brief chapter on fountains and monuments, describing Bernini's contributions to the category as an elevation of the relationship between dynamic sculpture in participation with robust water action.

Fountains of Florentine Sculptors and Their Followers From Donatello to Bernini, 1933, by Bertha Harris Wiles. A scholarly, enthusiastic review with a direct writing style covering a wealth of historical detail supported by 220 photographs. A narrow portrait of a specific place and time covering the transformation of fountains from pre-Renaissance, mostly utilitarian forms, into what she calls "pleasure fountains." Well researched, including an intriguing Appendix on lost fountains, which are identified from fairly obscure texts.

The Alhambra, 1978, Oleg Grabar. Written by the illustrious art historian, this book provides (what we can comfortably assume to be) very accurate detail supported by his superb cultural perspective. The work is penetrating, balanced and concise, if uncolorful. The water features are generally treated as part of a larger scene in association with history, architectural composition, poetry, landscape. Individually, they are examined as artworks in direct respect to sculptural statement.

Official Guide: The Alhambra and the Generalife, (undated), various editors and authors. Substantial guidebook, exemplary work, complete with a detailed appendix.

Alhambra, 2000, text by Michael Jacobs, photographs by Francisco Fernandez. Its icon-style photography does not overwhelm the text, though the text is more interpretive than journalistic. Presents drawings and paintings not found elsewhere, including a watercolored aerial illustration keynoted with a good list of forty-nine important attractions (many more might have been noted).

Hellbrunn - Palace, Park and Trick Fountains, 2004, Wilfried Schaber. A good overview with text, photographs, drawings and maps, including a removable fold-out map. Lamentably limited in detail, considering that this is the site of the greatest number of astounding water-powered automata on earth, but apparently

Opera House, Vancouver.

the best currently available text on the subject. We await a more substantial text on this important place.

Linderhoff Palace, Undated *(early 21st century)*, Edited by Elmar D. Schmid and Gerhard Hojer with a contribution by Manfred Stephan. Small-format guidebook. General descriptions, photos, some good drawings printed in a too-small-format. Good artistic credit list and good bibliography—rare for a guidebook. The work is undetailed, but offers a suggestive description of King Ludwig II, his works and his productive friendship with Wagner.

The Use of Water in Landscape Architecture, 1971, by Susan and Geoffrey Jellicoe. A thorough and splendid compendium of the subject, framed, as the title promises, from the perspective of lanscape architecture. This takes us to projects *Fountain Safari* necessarily omits, such as Falling Waters, the Chateau de Chantilly and Stourhead. Numerous black and white photographs and drawings through the book's 137 pages cover fine examples from around the world, with an extra measure from the United Kingdom, the authors' home country.

The Fountains of San Francisco, 1989, by Bernard Katz. A small format booklet of 139 pages, with representative photos, maps and substantial text. We quickly learn a little about a large number of public fountains in San Francisco which are worthy of consideration. The text includes much anecdotal information unpublished elsewhere.

Villa d'Este', Undated (early 21st century), by Isabella Barisi, Marcello Fagiolo and Maria Luisa Madonna. The definitive contemporary overview of the Villa d'Este. Fagiolo and Madonna's historical portrait is succinct and riveting. Barisi's coverage of the garden's design strategies and the labor involved in their construction makes clear how very difficult a project the garden was to physically accomplish. Smaller treatments on the water organ and the site's hydraulic method by Leonardo Lombardi contribute to the book's value.

Guide to Villa d'Este, 2004, Isabella Barisi. Guidebook. Excellent small-format summary of the palace, artworks, gardens and fountains. Succinct explanations, satisfactory photographs and good drawings.

Die Villa Lante in Bagnaia, 2001, Fritz Barth. A beautiful study of 432 pages with 77 pages of superb photography, including water action close-ups, some in color. Numerous illustrations. At the time of this writing, only available in its original, German text.

Italian Gardens, A Cultural History, 2006, Helena Attlee. An attractive tribute to Italian garden designs from the Renaissance to the twentieth century. Aimed at a popular audience, well-researched, numerous photographs and good, historic drawings.

Park Guell, Barcelona.

The text brings the locations to life. The water features are secondary to the garden subject, and they are not critically examined, but several excellent examples are identified.

Vizcaya, An American Villa and Its Makers, 2007, by Witold Rybczynski and Laurie Olin, with photography by Steven Brooke. The book covers one of the few, great, private American fountain collections in a most rambling manner, made helpful (regarding water design) chiefly by its good maps and key photography. Olin's garden visit description is informative and definitive.

The Alhambra Reealed, 2017, by Michael B. Barry. A very clearly written historical portrait of hundreds of years of complexity, and a closely observed exploration of the buildings and grounds. Descriptions of items past is particularly interesting, including the observation that the plantings in the Court of the Myrtles used to be in recessed planter beds so that they did not interfere with spatial perspective. The format is small, which is regrettable given its good photography and diagrams.

Guide, Real Sitio de La Granjua de San Ildefonso and Riofrio, 2019, by José Luis Sancho and Juan Ramón Aparicio. This guidebook is brief but informative at 97 pages. A single chapter on the gardens, which could benefit from a full book's examinations. The book includes a two-page, color plan of the gardens, which is simplified but articulate. Valuably, a schedule for the working fountains is given, helpful for a place where they are both important and rarely operated.

The Reggia of Caserta, 2018, by Giuseppe Pesce and Rosario Rizzo. Visitor guidebook, small format, 95 pages. Diagrammatic plans of the landscape and the palace are provided. Some history provided, a tour of magnificent interiors, some explanations of the Royal Park. Good detail regarding the landscape is provided, listing participants and dates. Bibliography provided, references in Spanish and Italian.

Park Gűell, A Garden City Planned as a Utopian Work of Art, 2018, by Richard Regas and Daniel R. Caruncho. Visitor guidebook, small format, 142 pages, in the contemporary style—crowded with overlapping imagery and text, but well sequenced. There are many books such as this dedicated to this popular subject; this is one of the better ones. The chapter given to the entrance stairway is informative. An aerial diagram of the park shows details that a visitor would likely miss. Close-ups of ceramic mosaics. Surprisingly good analyitical drawings of the park's architectural components.

Torre Diana, Mexico City.

Vaux le Vicomte, France.

92 A Brief History of Western Fountains

UTILE

COMMEMORATIVE

ALLEGORICAL

Through research and field work, a picture of the evolution—or at least the historic sequence—of western culture water feature design begins to take form. Examining simultaneous developments of the various arts; architecture, painting, sculpture, etc., we see that each category experiences a unique progression, though they are mostly driven by shared cultural forces. For instance, in Italian architecture we can identify Mannerist or Baroque expressions as important categories, but in fountains of the same eras, though we might apply those names to certain designs, we do this to no significant effect. During those periods, fountain design was more specifically concerned with other matters.

The so-called, styles or what I call here, 'chapters' of aesthetic paradigm are not all-inclusive within any time period. There will always be works created in styles out of their milleau, or others unrelated to any style. For example, the architect, Edwin Lutyens created buildings in a 19th-century Neoclassical style well into the Modern era. Or, the painter, Friedrensreich Hundertwasser (Friedrich Stowasser), whose work rings with authenticity while defying the catagorizations of his time. (Admittedly, this statement is open to some argument.) But even with cross-currents and unique creations, we can sense and define outlines of various era's works, and describe a general progression from one to the next. The chapterizations described are simple and clear. An unfolding exploration from one chapter to the next is retrospectively discernable. There is no inevitability of any following direction, as alternative paths might have been taken (or were, to lesser extents), yet the sequence holds together as a narrative. The progression covers six eras, identified as: Utile, Commemorative, Allegorical, Abstract, Entertainment, and Environmental.

Seeing good representations of each category in person, one begins to sense how very different the examples within each chapter are from those of other chapters, how much they share within each chapter, and how authorative each chapter managed to be within their times. We do not explore the forces behind any chapter's establishment. Rather, we simply examine the nature of each while considering something about them and their place in the progression. We also risk a classification of our own era.

UTILE works, the earliest forms of water features, would seem to be mostly about irrigation, but this is a simplification and, I think, an error. There is an undeniable poetical power in utile water features, and this soulfulness is emphatic when seen in person. Their basins, canals, falajes, gates, etc. are useful and efficient, and they can be quite moving in context. The circular relationship between people, water and plantings is plain to see and their summations about life are profound. They have no elaborate displays in the sense of later works; they may not attempt beauty in the classical sense (they predate Classicism). The installations are built in a practical manner, with a fine aesthetic hand. This poetic touch permeates the work, which we apprehend.

COMMEMORATIVE fountains arose in villages and towns, for the most part, and were expressive regarding their messaging. In Viterbo and other places, their compositional strategy is repeated, or archetypal. (Fountains like these are still built today.) There is a fount or wellspring, often a post or posts issuing water from spouts, which is connected with sculptural expression, graphical devices, and/or epigrams. Like the Utile chapter, the fountain delivers fresh water for use, in this case as drinking water, for people and sometimes for animals.

ALLEGORICAL fountains formed during eras with larger populations and more developed governance bodies. The controlling forces were served by the storytelling capacities of fountains with carefully carved sculptures. The fountains became elaborate, showy and demonstrative, employing religious or mythological figures to communicate societal values, sometimes as propoganda. The innate symbolic life of fountains contributed

ABSTRACT

ENTERTAINMENT

ENVIRONMENTAL

to the message of vitue. Water was used to convey truthfulness or rightness.

ABSTRACT fountains developed as society advanced in personal liberty while artists explored more pure, self-motivated forms of artistic expression. A wide-ranging variety of sculptural experimentation took place during this phase. The work was often framed to address individual audience members rather than broad populations. Many very fine abstract water features were built, and are still built. Some artists became well-known for their fountains, such as Isamu Noguchi or Jaume Plensa (Here we make a fine point, as Plensa would be more identified as a practitioner of Contemporary or Conceptual art, but for our purposes, I believe we can classify his work within the Abstract category.)

ENTERTAINMENT fountains, or show fountains developed as technology allowed and as more leisure time became available to larger populations. Show fountains brought communities together to enjoy programmed entertainment, usually incorporating music, either live or pre-recorded, and they established festive, celebratory experiences. In Barcelona, Las Vegas, Prague, and many other places, large fountains shows go so far as to incorporate changing-color lighting in tempo with music. Some fountains incorporate projected cinema into the water. At Longwood Gardens, special fountain shows are made even more spectacular with the incorporation of synchronized fireworks. Earlly forms include 'trick fountains' or automata, such as at Hellbrunn Palace.

ENVIRONMENTAL water features emobdy something of the aesthetic tone of the contemporary era. They integrate intensionally into their urban and architectural contexts with meaning of integration being primary in their idea, weaving together space, ecology, community, etc, of the immediate, consequential moment.

It must be noted that during each chapter the styles of fountains of previous eras continue to be built as epochs are not sharply divided and situations will vary. Often, the best works from any era perform in the ways of other categories, as well, but in these cases those other ideas are not their primary motivation. Trevi Fountain, obviously, is brilliant environmentally, but it was not created primarily for that purpose. Its primary purpose was to celebrate the power of the office that repaired the high value aqueduct, without which the fountain would not have been possible or worthy.

One might claim, with some experience in seeing all the categories, that the earlier, simpler constructions manifested a particularly valuable poetic depth or physical connectedness, suggesting some trade-off has taken place with the increasing sophistication or complexity of subsequent evolutionary development.

Thoughtful consideration of the parade of eras will lead to speculation about future chapters' qualities, as we are hardly seeing an end game. A reinvigoration of lost poetic depth might be a component of the next paradigm's central concept.

93 The Huxtable Assertion

Ada Louise Huxtable, architecture critic of the *New York Times* from 1963 to 1982, in something of a proclamation wrote in an article published 1970 that, "On Tuesday, Portland will start water flowing in the fountains of what may be one of the most important urban spaces since the Renaissance. The word 'fountains' requires a little clarification. 'Waterfalls' would be a more accurate description."

This statement, often quoted, or at least the first part of it, is general in nature, about the space and the fountain. But what if it meant something specific? What if, in fact, she had a particular place in mind? We can take her comment at face value and interpret it to draw a direct comparison between the most celebrated fountain in the world—Trevi, a rather conspicuous product of Renaissance design, and what we now call, the Ira Keller Fountain.

Their differences are obvious enough. Trevi, built almost 300 years ago, employs neoclassical architectural motifs, naturalistic set-piece scenery and Renaissance sculpture in a composition of a super-scaled allegory. The Ira Keller Fountain, on the other hand, built in the 1970s, presents a rusticated interpretation of Nature wrought not by sculptors, but by normal construction contractors.

The siimilarities between the two are more intriguing than their differences. They are both about the same size, they both face the sun (Trevi tilted a bit to the east, Keller tilted almost the same amount to the west), they both provide places for people to sit in front, socialize with others and gaze at the waters, and they both invite the more adventurous visitors to delve further with intimate experiences on their northeast sides. They were also both built to glorify their host cities.

On the flip side, the comparison is unfair. Trevi is world famous; Keller is a bit of a hidden gem. Trevi generates huge crowds every day. Keller's visitor levels are much sparcer, even though Keller is certainly one of the greatest fountains in America. That's partly because although Trevi and Keller have a grea deal in common, and both are appealing, Rome and Portland are profoundly different, and their is a dualism between fountains and their cities, part of which leads to available traffic. It is also true that the great fountain in Rome simply offers a bit more.

When Ms. Huxtable made her statement, she was applauding the city's (and the country's) important, new urban success, not as a successful park, square, or real estate real estate development, but as a humanistically valuable brand of urban glory.

(Above, upper and lower), Trevi's allegorical formal vocabulary is starkely differing from Keller's abstract, sculptural nature references, yet they are both offering messages, both are frontal, engage a central axis, are firmly rooted in their materiality, share a monumental frame, etc.

(Opposite, upper left and right), the Plans of Trevi and Keller are in the same scale.

(Opposite, left and right photos), note the panels over the pool at Keller, where immersive experiences are encouraged by trading away the color and sparkles of a reflection pool, such as Trevi's. Both projects offer intensive experiences on the right hand side, with Trevi providing a space with a rocky surround and a fountain within the fountain, while Keller gives us a waterfall and the space to go behind it, though a semi-hidden, L-shpaed chamber. (The blur behind the falls is a person.)

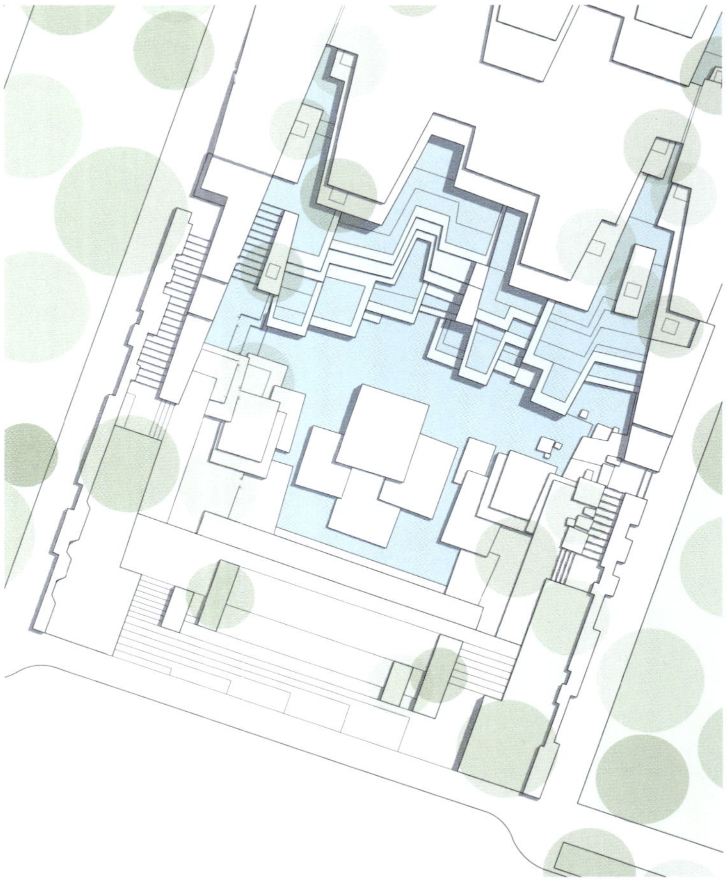

94 Fountain Collections

There are cities known for their fountains, and there are particular properties with substantial fountain collections, all concentrated in one place. Being aware of these collections is helpful to learning because of the convenience of seeing several good examples all in one place, but also because those fountains, during their development, were improved by their authors learning from nearby examples, such as took place in Rome, where the artists were in regular study of the other artworks around them.

Europe's larger fountain collections (that I know) include: Rome, Boboli Gardens, Villa Andobrandini, Caserta, Hadrian's Villa, the Villa d'Este, Viterbo, the Villa Lante, Aix-En Provence, Paris, Luxembourg Gardens, Park Citroen, Buttes Chaumont, Vaux Le Vicomte, Versailles, The Alhambra & the Generalife, The Royal Palace of La Granja, Hellbrunn Palace, Linderhof Palace, Sanssouci, Berlin, Wilhelmshohe, Prague, Peterhof Palace, Tivoli Gardens, Alnwick Castle, and London.

Asia's larger fountain collections require we stretch the definition a little, since in this part of the world, traditional water features are mainly naturalistic in character and may not look like fountains to the Western eye. Those I know include: Suzhou, The Humble Administrator's Garden, Shanghai, The Lingering Garden, Yuyuan Garden, Singapore, the Taj Mahal, the Agra Fort, the Indian Presidential Gardens, Shalimar Bagh, Achabal, Chashma Shaki Garden, Wah Gardens, Sydney and Melbourne.

North America's larger fountain collections of which I am aware include: New York City, Washington DC, Longwood Gardens, Vizcaya, Kansas City, Dallas, Portland, Disneyland, and Mexico City.

There are good, historic fountains in Iran, South America, and other places, to be sure, but I can only comment on those I've seen first hand.

Vizcaya, Miami.

95 In Praise of Engineering

I knew an engineer who deeply loved his profession. He claimed his favorite film was Mayazaki's, *The Wind Rises*, a fictionalization of the life and work of the Japanese aircraft engineer, Jiro Horikoshi. He was impressed by the film's statement, "Engineers make dreams into reality." He took this to be the perfect summary about engineering and life.

For reasons of place, culture, meaning and skill, fountains over the world vary widely, with each offering unique engineering problems. Even today, there is no modular equipment package that will perfectly fit the circumstances of a particular situation. So, engineers analyze each design for structural integrity, flow rate, lifting energy, friction loss, filtration, lighting, power, controls, and many other matters. Engineers know that any single item poorly resolved will negatively effect the entire fountain's performance, and possibly prevent it from functioning at all.

Fountains are much more complex than they look. They are members of that category of project requiring a great deal of serious professional diligence just to achieve basic functionality. Attempts to produce a special, truly excellent job—like many of the examples presented here—requires astounding committments in concentration and time. In reflection, we cannot be grateful enough for our fountains.

Notwithstanding their extraordinary contributions, throughout history engineers have been largely in the shadows. We know Gian Lorenzo Bernini designed the Fountain of the Four Rivers, but we do not know who performed its hydraulic studies. I rather doubt it was Bernini, although he likely reviewed the calculations. Few engineers, even brilliant ones, seek the limelight. Wernher von Braun was perhaps the most famous engineer of the 1960s, but even he wasn't exactly charismatic.

Most engineers are quite happy knowing when they achieved something very difficult—even if they are the only ones who understand how challenging the effort was. Engineers are generally satisfied relying solely upon their own opinions about things. But engineers are not recluses. They often know of each other, working in the various design teams over the course of years, working with or hearing about other engineers. There is a mechanical engineer who works for Disney who is something of a legend; she is unusally experienced and quick with ideas. Not all engineers are developing next-generation, autonomous, self-landing re-entry vehicles, but fountain engineers are doing difficult work that lights up cities and makes their audiences—who can be kings or kids—tremendously happy. Without great engineers doing a terrific job none of the wondrous fountain dreams would ever be made into reality.

l'Observatoire, Paris.

96 Placing

In Chapter Three it was identified that a fountain's first reason for being is to mark and celebrate a highly regarded place. No comments were made about how this was done, though several examples were noted. As it turns out, the compositional strategy for each is different from all the others, and needed to be.

Creativity in placement is not simply part of a judged response to the unique contions of place. The fountain, itself, requests the creativity due to its essential nature. Fountains are symbols of life, and their symbolism extends naturally to encompass renewal, regeneration, cycles, time, birth, creation—and creativity. A fountain that does not express creativity is not fully symbolizing life. And placement is the first vital act.

At the Villa d'Este, the Wall of a Hundred Fountains is presented on a single side of a lengthy pathway with a wall and a gate to the east and the Romanza assembly to the west. Beyond the western edge is a panarama of the valley with the real Rome in the distance. Through the gate to the east is the intimate coutyard holding the Oval Fountain. All three compositions are uniquely and impeccably sited. At Tivoli Gardens, the pathways are reminiscent of medieval streets with arcane meanders. Here, fountains present like rewards along the journey as spaces suddenly open up with their waters sparkling in the light. Hellbrunn Palace's setting is a pleasure garden with countless charming fountains and astounding automata. Hellbrunn's pathways to the west merge with the landscape to improvisationally emphasize surprise and excitement. The spaces to the east are larger, orderly, predictable, and calming. The two territories are complementary. Luxembourg Garden's Medici Fountain is hidden under a canopy of dense sycamore trees and wrapped in perimeter garlands of topiary. The plantings work to scale the fountain's experience, and the discretion of the installation, with its eccentric, veiled location, contributes significantly to its powers. At La Granja, the positions of the fountains are ultimately more important than their individual designs. In the Piazza Navona, today at least, the three widely spaced fountains serve to activate their proximities within the lengthy space. Versailles' orderly composition of gardens is made into a creative adventure by the innovative variety of garden/fountain installations, while at Shalimar Bagh, the landscape's disciplined orderliness establishes an idealized realm.

In all cases, the nature of the placement of the water features in space are central to their creative expression and success in space.

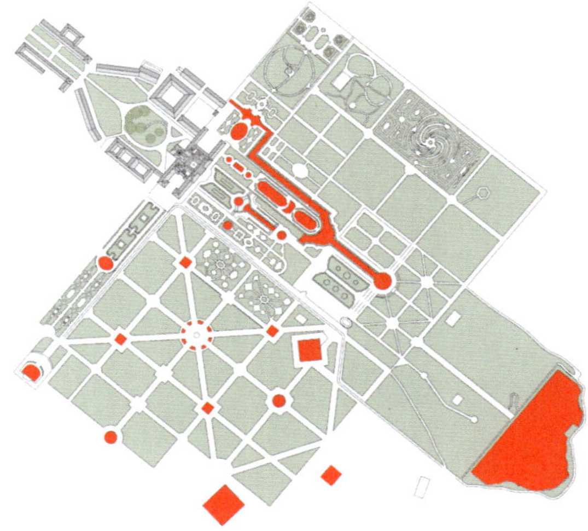

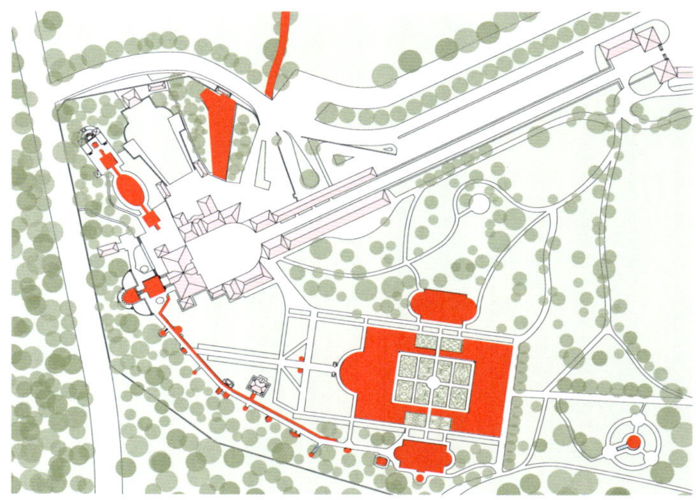

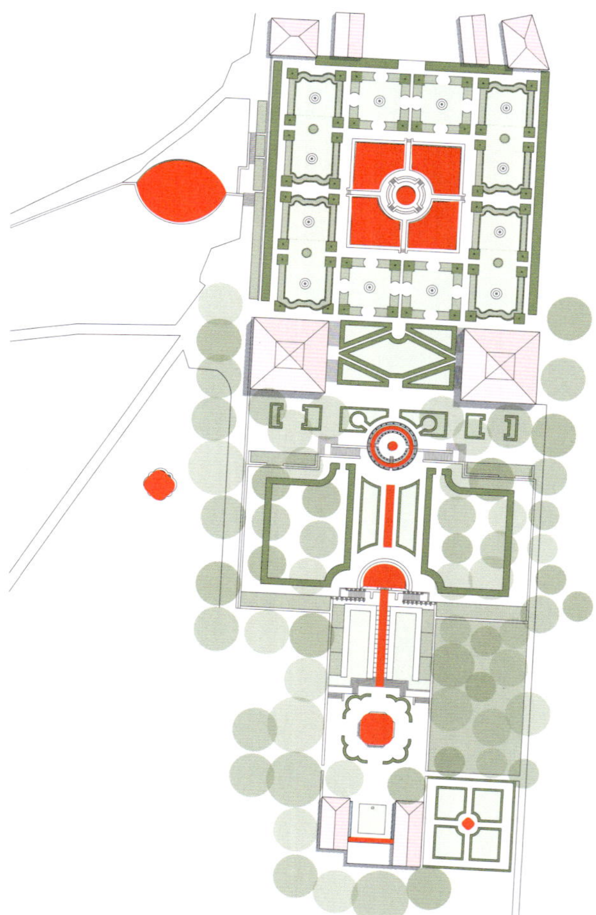

(This page, Center) Hellbrunn Palace, (Top) La Graja, (Right) Villa Lante. (Opposite, upper left) The Alhambra, (Upper right) Tivoli Gardens, (Center left) Villa d'Este, (Center right) Shalimar Bagh, (Lower left) Luxembourg Gardens, (Lower right) Piazza Navona.

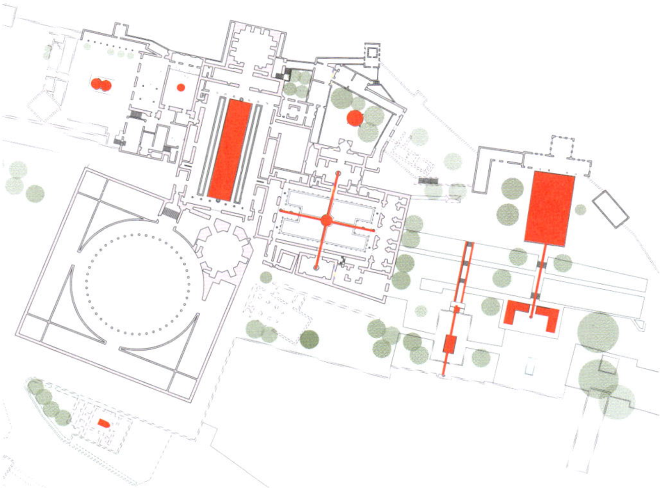
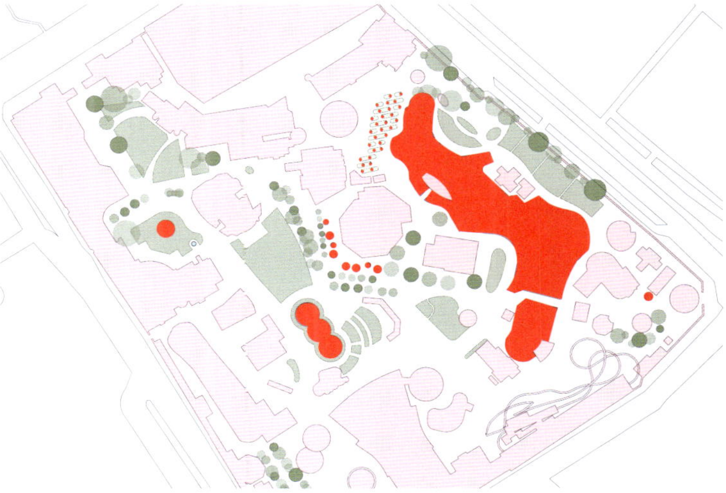
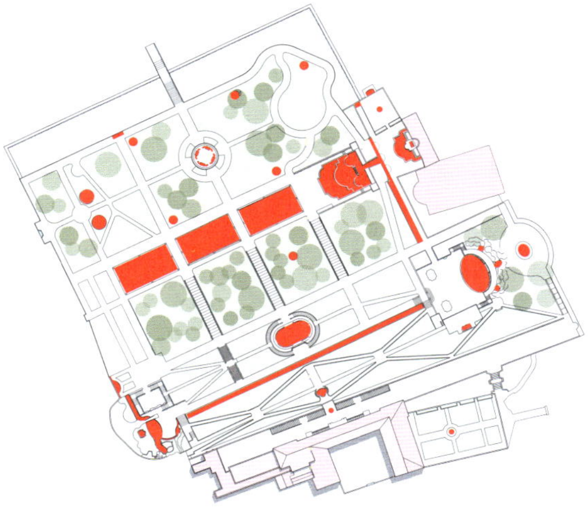
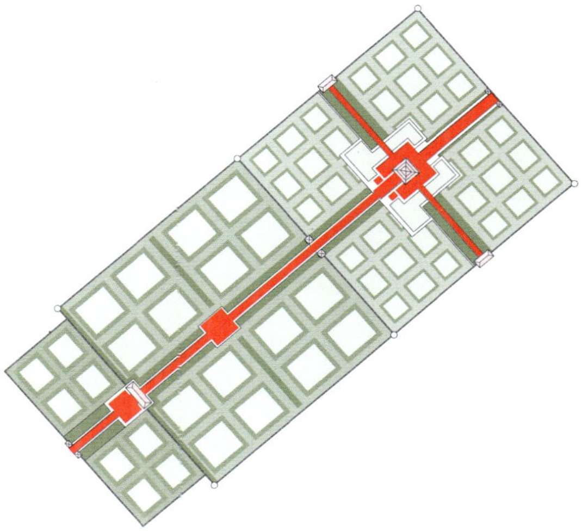
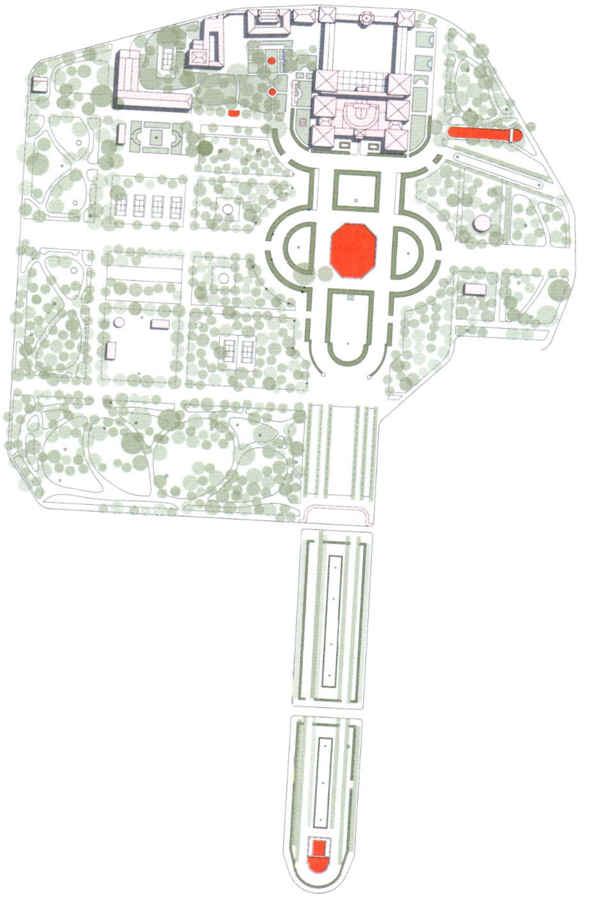
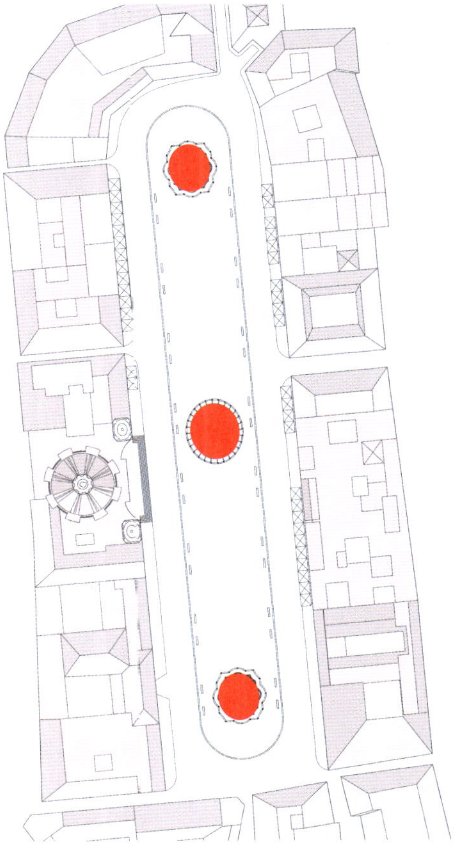

97 Before and After

If we visit sites repeatedly over time we find they look different, sometimes better, sometimes very much not, sometimes changed in unexpected ways. There are any number of explanations. Fountains are complex constructions and they are built to especially high tolerances (which means they can be finicky), and most of them operate outdoors in the elements, so they are prone to all sorts of intrusions and vagaries, such that they are in, more or less, a constant state of flux.

Visible character changes can be due to material decay, the accretion of grime, changes in maintenance policy, or even simply the encroachment of adventurous plants. Hidden components such as pipes, cisterns, pumps, filters, etc. need maintenance and have mechanical lifespans, which will effect the quality of the displays and will shorten their lifespans if not installed correctly or maintained properly. Regular mainteance is very important, as is the availability of funds for that upkeep, which often shifts in the tides of fortune. The changing appearance of fountains can also depend upon changing tastes about the way things ought to look. For the Ira Keller Fountain's recent refurbishment, the concrete's aura of age was preserved, while at a similar project for the Peavey Plaza Fountain, the finishes were made new-looking; in both cases the decisions were apprporiate.

An intriguing example of the reinterpretation of a work as it is aging is seen in Bernini's mosaic amphora at the Villa d'Este, which seems to offer more in its romantic clothing of vibrant greenery than in its restored version, which could be considered comparatively wanting though presumably closer to Bernini's intention.

The Latona Fountain, at Versailles, on the other hand, hardly justified its very important location in its before state, veneered in scum and barely operational, whereas after its remarkable restoration it had entirely recovered its original glory.

Bernini's amphora, the Bicchierone, (top, left), Villa d'Este, before and after restoration.

Versaille's prominent Latona Fountain, (these pages) with stained stone, covered in slime, with faulty jets, and corroded gilt statuary. We could not even detect that the floors of the design's steps were cleverly finished in dark stone, while the faces were in red marble and the weirs in white, selections which venerate the water presentation. Afterwards, the sunlight in the water and gold are unsurpased by any fountain.

(Following pages) at the Villa d'Este and the Alhambra: the Neptune Fountain and the Oval Fountain, clean and flowing well vs. low flows, encroached in algae and plantings. The Court of the Lions, with a new-looking lion fountain (the original is 700 years old) and a marble floor replacing its previous, gravel paving. Luxuriant water plants now encouraged to flourish in the reflection pool at the Yusuf III Palace.

98 Climate Change Influences

The Metropolitan Museum of Art, NYC

Many of history's most famous fountains, such as those in Grenada or Rome, were built in spite of, or even partly because of, limited water availability. And the skill of maximizing the water's poetic effect while minimizing its consumption was refined over the course many designs in Andalusian Spain, the estate gardens of Italy and Mogul India. Lately, we've entered a heightened era of conscienciousness, and the issues of environmental sustainability and resiliancy place an indelible mark on contemporary water feature design, which is reorienting the art.

Early policy in environmental planning led to the construction of fewer fountains. Parks were built in the US in which potential fountains were strategically omited. But these places proved less less alluring. Subsequent approaches called for water features requiring less water, energy or treatment chemicals, and built with smaller carbon footprints.

In many cases, early sustainable water features looked something like fountains of old. Then, comparison studies revealed that reflection pools lost less water to evaporation than lawns or traditional planting beds, signalling an opportunity for arid landscapes. Sustainability investigations influenced water design thinking, and a new generation of fountains began to be conceived.

The rectangular reflection pools at Sunnylands, near Palm Springs, establish a luxurious—almost sybaritic water presentation. The apparently motionless pools, designed by OJB, present enchantingly in that desert garden while losing very little water to evaporation.

At the Metropolitan Museum of Art, a very different sensitive context, the entrance plaza fountains' jets are slenderer than they would have previously been, and they work together such that a lively, composite dynamism is formed, by virtue of which, at any given time, rows of jets may be only modestly performing without dampening in the least the excitement of the displays.

We can look forward to upcoming fountains to employ sun, wind, water plantings, shade systems, make-up harvesting, and responsive or performative displays, all of which will be organized to put forward new and creative visual statements while consuming significantly less resources. The preciousness of water is emphasized and appreciated in such strategies, though some of the frivolity or zest may be traded. This new generation of designs will arise from a completely new conceptual paradigm, though their success will be measured, to be sure, by the timeless values of place response, water character, and meaning.

Sunnylands, Rancho Mirage

99 In Closing

Seeing in person so many of the world's finest fountains, and along the way discovering, exploring and celebrating cities, architecture and landscapes, is profoundly rewarding. A wider overview begins to take shape. Shared attributes are preceived and a deeper understanding into the various ways fountains function as aesthetic artifacts becomes apparent. Hunting for quality, any kind of quality, contributes to the quality of one's life. Hunting great fountains presents us with the kinds of experiences where participation and interpretation enhance the experience of being alive. It isn't helpful to summarize all the findings of these safaris, but a few salient qualities merit noting.

Its spatial concept arises as the first attribute of a fountain's quality, having to do with the installation's contextual situation and its response. Water action is next. The great water expressions are independant of sculptural or architectural framing. The craft is not in the fashioning of the stone or bronze; the craft is in the water and the veracity of its expression, and all of the finest fountains present wonderfully developed water character. The idea of the fountain is also important, relating to its purpose and the value of its contribution to a space.

The highest observation I made regarded something intangible. There was a repeating tone of feeling I encountered at the Alhambra, at the Villa d'Este, at Trevi, at Vaux le Vicomte, at Trafalgar Square, at the Taj Mahal, and some other very powerful places. I sensed this quality pertained to a particular hamony of proportion, a well-organized compositional calmness, an aura of clear poetical purpose. Above all, the quality involved an abiding maturity, which engaged every aspect of its manifestation. This quality embraced the immediate moment just as it engaged the timeless. The water in those places, with that magical quality, becomes a tether, with one end in the beautifully physical and the other, elsewhere.

Sunlight, the only aesthetically higher material than water, asserts itself inevitably into a dance of the two. Their entanglings serve in the enhancement of both. The living water is made visible in living light, with light made more dynamic by water's effects, while water is transformed by light's exploration as the sun arcs across the sky.

It may seem esoteric, but water expression transforms with scale. Expression cannot simply expand or contract in size without changing character (light can do this, but water cannot). The great fountains present water actions nicely suited to their scales.

Every fountain, truly, is different from the others, and some are deeply wonderful. All have their secrets. Nearly all are pleasurable. With seeing, they speak to us. Fountains are undemanding, but like any art form, they offer a continuing request that we see them.

Trevi Fountain, Rome.

85
WALLETS GLOVES

100 The Text

Every attempt is made to keep the text simple and direct. Weight is given more to observation and reportage than interpretation. Poetic elaborations are mostly restrained.

This book employs three different textural styles, for the most part used categorically. Under the titles of each fountain heading is a brief outline of the subject. This is intentionally lean, as such information is available elsewhere and need not be repeated here. Some anecdotes are shared to help bring the subject alive.

The photographs, which form the main evidence of the editorial thrust, are captioned. The captions point out much of the specific observations upon which the idea of this book is founded, and carry much of the load of the phenomenological, conceptual and aesthetic arguments. The captions are more critical than the chapter outlines.

The opening and closing chapters focus on the ingredients of the subject, rather than the particulars of certain places. These are also written in a tersely unvarnished manner for reasons of clarity, but a few of them go into their subjects with greater depth, such as the chapter about "Seeing," or are based in poetry, and must carry a poetic tone, such as, "Why," which is written in a reverential referential style, specifically connoting an insider allusion.

The photography-overlaid interludes speak in a different voice, and are intentionally few and romantic. These relate to the sympathies of the subject, and are provided to add a necessary, alternative poetical dimension to the experience of the book entire.

Although there are many chapters, they are all brief. Like Melville's, *Moby Dick*, the chapters fit together into a larger narrative, but they are also written to function individually, as stand-alone articles. In that sense, it is perfectly reasonable to pick up the book and begin or stop anywhere and expect to enjoy a more or less complete experience.

101 The Photographs

The images are guided by an editorial viewpoint, focusing and commenting on subjects with specific ideas and purposes in mind. The shots are all framed to contribute to the telling of specific narratives. There are "establishing shots," as phtographers say, to be sure, but not many. Most of the images attempt to focus upon a specific observation or intepretive moment which in almost all cases pertains to water action, narrowly and to the exclusion of the numerous other admittedly important dimensions of any given fountain or its interrelated space or artworks. There are exceptions to this, too, especially at those places where the water was partly or fully turned off, and what we had to observe (aside from our water action imaginings) was the setting or revealed details, which are also important and useful.

No complicated techniques were employed in this project's photos; no multiple exposures, no time-lapse images, no exotic films or their simulations. The photos are intentionally simple and unglamorous, though some care is taken in framing the shots and achieving light and color balance. Post-production work was performed for re-framing, perspective correction and other such adjustments normal to the endeavor and always for the purpose of improving descriptive quality. No photograph is honest, but the attempt here is to simply and directly convey poetic truth.

Necessarily, during any faraway travel, some days have better sunlight, tourist population levels, bureaucratic interference, etc., than other days, which effects the quality of the imagery and sometimes to a very strong and distorting degree, but which can't be helped. It is also regrettably common that fountains are under repair, in bad shape, improperly operated, or simply not turned on during a faraway visit. These are tragedies to the long-distance traveller, but inevitable. When possible, I have returned to sites to get better images, though constraints of time and means can preclude extra visits. Some places, like the Royal Palace at La Granja, operate the water features so rarely that one has to give up and be satisfied with their dry versions.

None of the photographs in this book are as engaging or informative as looking at the real thing in person, although on the flipside, the installations are often so overwhelmingly impressive that some kinds of specific observations or realizations happen later—when quietly reviewing the captuired images.

102 The Drawings

The purpose of the drawings is to help convey important ideas or conditions about the designs in a general way. The plans are all oriented with north pointing up on the sheet. Graphic scales are provided, which vary from drawing to drawing. All dimensions are in metric.

The drawings were performed in a busy design studio over the course of almost twenty years, during those hours when project needs were less demanding. The drawings were created by may different people. Attempts for consistency and accuracy have been made, and some of the drawings have been redrawn several times or in different ways for better communication. None of the drawings are masterpieces, but some are quite engaging, like the plans of Vizcaya, Hadrian's Villa—of course, or the town of Viterbo.

A certain abstractness was necessary in the drawings' execution for several reasons. Exactitude is beside the point in the conveyance of the fountains' ideas, although we attempted to be as accurate as we could. There are some factual errors in the drawings, though we have done our best. The work of creating the drawings was in all cases performed at a long distance from their subjects, which was hampering. In most cases, the person performing the drawing had never seen the fountain in person, regrettably..

Some drawings are more abstract than others. Perhaps the least detailed is the plan for Trevi, whose rocky folds proved every bit as challenging to portray as the fountain is important. The drawing of Barracaccia—the boat fountain at the base of the Spanish Steps—on the other hand, I believe to be fairly good in the depiction of its counter-intuitive curves and hand-carved, worn surfaces.

The drawings were made by Fluidity's talented design professionals, except one, which was done by the studio manager who substituted academic training with dedication. Everyone working on the drawings did their best, and the work was reviewed, redlined and approved by me. Where they are incorrect, the fault is mine.

The Medici Fountain, Luxembourg Gardens, Paris.

103 Index

Acknowledgments

The author is grateful to his family and his longtime colleagues for the encouragement this work required.

Many at Fluidity helped along the way, including Tom Yankelitis, Valorie Born, Karen Adhikari, Dolly Wisco, Leo Prezioso, Chinmoy Panigrahy and Shannon Hoff. The drawings were researched and executed by Fluidity staff and interns, including Nick Arcuri, Jenille Amerman, Alice An, Dawn Aveline, Andrew Boquiren, Cristina Calistru, Alexandra Denisoff, Abel De La Toree, Ann Giacometti, Janelle Herrara, Milan Kothari, Wen Li, Zhihuang Li, Georine Pierre, Chris Roy, Joshua Sommers-Dehaney, Alyce Torrez, Lena Watanabe, and Min Zhang. Graphics consultant, Jessica Castro, provided initial and follow-up layout work.

Special professional support arrived from Don Breaux, Walter Ernst, Charles W. Moore, Lou Naidorf, Geraldine Forbes, Stan Berteaud, Mark Fuller, Alan Robinson, Claire Kahn, Carolyn Nott, Kim Lange, Debbie Jaloma, Brandon Haw, Jon Jerde, Brian Honda, David Moreno, Curtis Scharfenaker, Jeri Oka, Joe Kaplan, Robin Perkins and Clifford Selbert. Steve Koch and Debra Smith read early drafts and offered influential commentary. Special thanks are reserved for Gordon Goff and his fine coworkers at ORO Editions for experience and thoughts.

Fountain Safari was typeset in TT Commons. All photography is by the author, with the exceptions of the night photo of Pat O'Brien's courtyard, by Michelle Minyard, selected images of the Princess Diana Fountain, by Cristina Calistru, those of Longwood Gardens' Main Fountain Garden, by the professional photographer, Daniel Traub, and the photo of the author (opposite page), by anonymous.

About the Author

James Garland is an architect with a career specialization in water design. He received his Master of Architecture from UCLA after a Bachelor of Architecture from the University of Louisiana. He interned with Charles W. Moore at Urban Innovations Group, worked at WET Design with Mark Fuller, Alan Robinson, and Claire Kahn, and worked on urban design projects with Jon Jerde before founding Fluidity Design Consultants in 2002. Fluidity is based in Los Angeles. Jim has often lectured before various academic and professional groups. In 1998, two of Jim's sketchbooks were exhibited at the Smithsonian Institute's National Design Museum, and in 2020 he was awarded an honorary PhD and a Lifetime Achievement award by the University of Louisiana. He is a member of the American Institute of Architects and an affiliate member of the American Society of Landscape Architects. Jim has two sons.